'Am I Less British?'

FRINGE

Series Editors
Alena Ledeneva and Peter Zusi, School of Slavonic and
East European Studies, UCL

The FRINGE series explores the roles that complexity, ambivalence and immeasurability play in social and cultural phenomena. A cross-disciplinary initiative bringing together researchers from the humanities, social sciences and area studies, the series examines how seemingly opposed notions such as centrality and marginality, clarity and ambiguity, can shift and converge when embedded in everyday practices.

Alena Ledeneva is Professor of Politics and Society at the School of Slavonic and East European Studies of UCL.

Peter Zusi is Associate Professor of Czech and Comparative Literature at the School of Slavonic and East European Studies of UCL.

'Am I Less British?'

*Racism, belonging and the children of
refugees and immigrants in north London*

Doğuş Şimşek

First published in 2024 by
UCL Press
University College London
Gower Street
London WC1E 6BT

Available to download free: www.uclpress.co.uk

Text © Author, 2024
Images © Author and copyright holders named in captions, 2024

The author has asserted her rights under the Copyright, Designs and Patents Act 1988 to be identified as the author of this work.

A CIP catalogue record for this book is available from The British Library.

Any third-party material in this book is not covered by the book's Creative Commons licence. Details of the copyright ownership and permitted use of third-party material is given in the image (or extract) credit lines. If you would like to reuse any third-party material not covered by the book's Creative Commons licence, you will need to obtain permission directly from the copyright owner.

This book is published under a Creative Commons Attribution-Non-Commercial 4.0 International licence (CC BY-NC 4.0), https://creativecommons.org/licenses/by-nc/4.0/. This licence allows you to share and adapt the work for non-commercial use providing attribution is made to the author and publisher (but not in any way that suggests that they endorse you or your use of the work) and any changes are indicated. Attribution should include the following information:

Şimşek, D., 2024. *'Am I Less British?': Racism, belonging and the children of refugees and immigrants in north London*. London: UCL Press. https://doi.org/10.14324/111.9781787351776

Further details about Creative Commons licences are available at https://creativecommons.org/licenses/

ISBN: 978-1-78735-179-0 (Hbk.)
ISBN: 978-1-78735-178-3 (Pbk.)
ISBN: 978-1-78735-177-6 (PDF)
ISBN: 978-1-78735-180-6 (epub)
DOI: https://doi.org/10.14324/111.9781787351776

To all children of refugees and immigrants

Contents

List of figures ix
Series editors' preface xi
Acknowledgements xiii

1. Introduction 1

2. Between Britain's hostile environment and Turkey's authoritarian regime 29

3. 'My north London accent indicates my working-class background': north London, class, ethnicity and community 53

4. 'I enjoy the diversity of London but also feel excluded': London, conviviality and racism 85

5. 'Turkey is not my home. I've never lived there': discovering parents' country of origin 113

6. 'Am I less British because I am a descendant of an immigrant?': citizenship and belonging 135

7. Conclusion 169

Bibliography 177
Index 189

List of figures

1.1	Harringay-Green Lanes.	17
1.2	Logo of Day-Mer.	20
2.1	A 'Vote Leave' poster in Salford.	33
2.2	Window of a Turkish patisserie shop.	45
2.3	Day-Mer's Culture and Art Festival poster.	49
4.1	Fusion dish recipes in the window of a Turkish restaurant.	89
4.2	Window of a kebab shop.	94
4.3	Future Hackney project, Ridley Road Stories Exhibition in Mare Street.	104
4.4	Making *gözleme* [stuffed flatbread] at a Turkish restaurant in Harringay.	107
6.1	Turkish tea and *künefe* [sweet cheese pastry].	142
6.2	Street art representing John Lennon and Alex de Souza (football player for Fenerbahçe) in Green Lanes.	148

Series editors' preface

The UCL Press FRINGE series presents work related to the themes of the UCL FRINGE Centre for the Study of Social and Cultural Complexity.

The FRINGE series is a platform for cross-disciplinary analysis and the development of 'area studies without borders'. 'FRINGE' is an acronym standing for Fluidity, Resistance, Invisibility, Neutrality, Grey zones, and Elusiveness – categories fundamental to the themes that the Centres support. The oxymoron in the notion of a 'FRINGE CENTRE' expresses our interest in (1) the tensions between 'area studies' and more traditional academic disciplines; and (2) social, political, and cultural trajectories from 'centres to fringes' and inversely from 'fringes to centres'.

The volume *'Am I Less British': Racism, belonging and the children of refugees and immigrants in north London* explores the complex and layered ethnographic context that children of the significant Turkish and Kurdish communities in north London inhabit. This social group inhabit grey zones of different kinds: between nations, identities, generations, and indeed between being invisible and all too visible. Şimşek does not simply provide a case study of a specific ethnic group, however, she uses her material to draw out more general questions regarding identity, nation and race. In important ways all of these categories are shown to be fluid and context-driven, rather than stable and essential, in the lived experience of the subjects Şimşek addresses.

In this empirically driven account of how categories that aim to create clear labels – nationality, ethnic identity, race – in fact shift and engage in complex interactions and overlappings, the volume pursues the FRINGE agenda of bottom-up sociological investigation. Understanding the 'messiness' of lived experiences not as the imperfect or distorted embodiment of theoretical principles, but as the ground from which theoretical principles should first be drawn, is central to Critical Area Studies and the values of the UCL FRINGE Centre.

Alena Ledeneva and Peter Zusi
School of Slavonic and East European Studies, UCL

Acknowledgements

This book is the product of a long research journey. During this journey, I met inspiring young people whose stories reflect the changing nature of the conditional relationship between states and individuals, what racism does to people and the impacts of everyday bordering on their everyday lives across the borders of nation-states, which made me think about my experiences in moving between different countries. I am grateful to and want to thank all the young people who agreed to be interviewed for this book, and openly shared their experiences, which are often traumatic. Without their time and willingness to tell me their stories in depth, this book could not have been written. Special thanks go to my cousins Naz Şimşek and Alura Şimşek, whose experiences across the borders of nation-states led me to write this book. I am grateful to Çağdaş Canbolat and Elina Canbolat for helping me reach the young people. It would have been impossible to hear the inspiring stories of young people without their help.

I would like to express my gratitude to Fringe series editors Alana Ledenava and Peter Zusi for their editorial enthusiasm and support since the beginning of the publication process of this book. I would like to thank UCL Press, and particularly Chris Penfold, the Commissioning Editor, who made the publication process smooth, and the reviewers for their insightful comments. Special thanks to John Solomos and Milena Chimienti for their continued support during my academic career, which always gives me strength and encouragement. Their writings have always been an inspiration to me.

I am extremely grateful to Maurice Biriotti for his encouragement and support, which I value enormously, and which made the idea of writing this book real. I am grateful to Eric Gordy, Donat Bayer and Helena Fallstrom for commenting on the proposal. For reading and editing sections of the book while they were in progress, thank you to Fionn O'Sullivan, June O'Sullivan, Christopher Laudan, and Karen Thomas. Thank you Erdoğan Usta and Burcu Toğral for reading the draft manuscript and discussing my ideas with me. For helping me take the images in Harringay, thank you Hazel Tulgar Coleman.

I am grateful to Ayşe Çağlar and colleagues at the Institut für die Wissenschaften vom Menschen (IWM) for allowing me time to write the earlier sections of this book during my fellowship. Many thanks to Vron Ware for her insightful input and support. Thank you Macide Şimşek and Yalçın Şimşek for your encouragement and support. Thank you Fionn O'Sullivan, for always being there for me.

1
Introduction

During my fieldwork in 2019 in Hackney, a neighbourhood in the northeast of London, I sat in a cafe with a few young people whose parents are Kurdish and Turkish. A few days earlier Shamima Begum's citizenship had been revoked, and we started talking about how they would feel if they were stripped of their British citizenship. Erkan[1] said 'I would feel lost'; he was interrupted by Kenan, who added 'they cannot strip our British citizenship. We were born in this country.' Erkan asked Kenan, 'Do you know Shamima Begum's case?' Kenan shook his head; Erkan answered his question: 'Shamima Begum is a British-Bangladeshi whose British passport has been taken away by the British government because she joined ISIS. She was sent to Bangladesh, where she has never lived, and cannot return to the UK.' He followed up: 'Imagine if this happens to us. I have never lived in Turkey and would not want to live there. I do not even speak proper Turkish. I am British. Here is my home and there is no other place to call home.' Mehmet interrupted: 'You are lucky because you are Turkish and Turkey is not a dangerous place for you. Returning to Turkey in my case is not safe as there are lots of racist attacks taking place in Turkey against Kurds.' Erkan added: 'Yes, but I do not feel comfortable in Turkey. I do not want to live there. I am British. I was born in this country. I belong here.' Kenan said 'Do not worry, guys! They will not send us back to Turkey. They want to get rid of black and brown people, not us. We are white compared to them.'

Their conversation[2] highlights racialised hierarchies of Britishness, what constitutes a sense of belonging, and in which ways whiteness plays a role in how they position themselves with other racialised groups. It also confirms their views about what constitutes a sense of belonging, which varies depending on their experiences in one another's hierarchical positions that are defined by their parents' country of origin, ethnicity, religion and class. By looking into how the children of refugees and immigrants position themselves within a range of places where they face racism and discrimination, how they make sense of their identities and belonging within the contemporary political context in Britain and Turkey, and what it means to be a citizen of Britain and/or Turkey, this book, by drawing on ethnographic research conducted in north London, aims to provide a conceptual tool highlighting a need to focus on these young people's experiences of racism and discrimination within the political spectrum of Britain and Turkey.

While I was completing this book Rishi Sunak became the first ever British Asian Prime Minister in Britain. Since then, racist memes about his Britishness have been shared on social media and comments such as 'he is Asian, not even British',[3] have been made, questioning his Britishness. His Britishness is not only questioned by English people but also by minorities. Before he became Prime Minister, in one of his speeches he said: 'People say "you have a great tan". I say "I stay in the sun a lot"' – to position himself in close proximity to whiteness. Although Rishi Sunak revealed that he had experienced racism when he was a child and a young person, he also said in one of his speeches: 'I don't think this would happen today because our country has made incredible progress in tackling racism.'[4] When addressing questions posed by reporters he said: 'I absolutely don't believe that Britain is a racist country. And I'd hope that as our nation's first British Asian Prime Minister when I say that it carries some weight.'[5]

In line with this assumption, the Conservative government's policy and discourse around immigration and citizenship reproduce 'a racialised notion of what it means to be British, and who deserves to be British'[6] that often ignore racialised minorities' experiences of racism. Seemingly, the children of refugees and immigrants, and people of colour, are not considered British. Who is British and who is not British is not related to being born in Britain or holding British citizenship; rather, it indicates the structure of a racialised hierarchy of Britishness. Britishness for the children of refugees and immigrants has always been questioned and, in many cases, it is questioned by the minorities within their communities.

The idea of writing this book first occurred to me when witnessing my cousins' experiences, particularly the challenges they faced with growing up in a transnational social space and engaging with both the country of settlement and their parents' country of origin. Mixing Turkish with English when they speak with their parents and 'performing' their identities depending on their location has become a daily routine for them. During our conversations about Turkey, and Britain, their sense of cultural and national belonging(ness) and identities, they highlighted that they have a heightened awareness of how a place can impact a person through their experiences in both countries and realised that other children of immigrants would also perform their identities depending on their location; they became intrigued by the diverse and multiculturalist cities of the world. The challenges, they stated, are mostly associated with language, traditions and cultural practices, especially when they visit Turkey, rather than experiencing racism based on class or migratory background. Race and class are not significant in their experiences of living in a transnational social space and especially in 'Brexit Britain'. However, this might not be the case for other children of immigrants whose parents are from Turkey. This case made me explore the experiences of the children of refugees and immigrants in the country of settlement and their parents' country of origin, their sense of belonging and their feelings, as well as their relation to the identities surrounding them.

Am I Less British? is a study of hierarchies of belonging, racism and transnational experiences of the children of refugees and immigrants in London, whose parents migrated from Turkey. The book rethinks the questions of identity and belonging beyond the category of culture as a form of resistance to racism and exclusion in a transnational context. It combines the lenses of migratory background with a more explicit emphasis on racialised, classed and gendered dynamics of belonging within the political spectrum of Britain and Turkey, and the complexities of their intersection when exploring the young people's relationships with London, north London and Turkey. In light of this, the book focuses on four main approaches – the role of the social and political circumstances of Britain and Turkey; transnational experiences; places in which the young people interact; and racialised, classed and gendered dynamics of belonging in how young people understand their sense of belonging and identities.

By delving into the role of the social and political circumstances of the children of refugees and immigrants in a transnational context to explore their sense of belonging, this book offers insights into the experiences of young people from Turkey in north London. It aims to explore how the children of refugees and immigrants position themselves within a range of locations (London, north London and Turkey) where they face racial and class hierarchy, racism and sexism; how they think about their sense of belonging within the contemporary political context in Britain and Turkey.

The children of refugees and immigrants' relationship with their respective nationalities, cities and identities raises the question of whether they are seen as British, regardless of how they feel about their Britishness, especially in Britain's 'hostile environment', which was established with the set of immigration policies introduced with the Immigration Act 2014 and intensified with the 2016 Immigration Act to exclude 'illegal immigrants from all public services and encourage them "go home"'.[7] Due to the British government's 'hostile environment' approach to immigration policies, some members of the Windrush generation – those who arrived in Britain from Caribbean countries between 1948 and 1973 – were wrongly detained and deported by the Home Office in 2018. People who have only lived in Britain were being deported even after the Windrush scandal. In his book *Deporting Black Briton*, through engaging the individual stories of the deported people who migrated to Britain in the early 2000s and were all deported following a criminal conviction, Luke de Noronha argues that the 'hostile environment' demonstrated 'the settled status of black Britons remained revocable and raised several questions about race, citizenship and belonging in "Brexit Britain"'.[8] In this light, racism has increased for the children of refugees and immigrants, especially after the European Union Brexit referendum in 2016, which is also confirmed by Shamima Begum's case and the Nationality and Borders Bill.

Therefore, the fact that someone holds British citizenship does not mean that they are unconditionally settled in Britain and belong to Britain. What it means to be a citizen of Britain has been changed, and every single British child of a British parent born overseas finds themselves in the structure of racialised hierarchies of Britishness. The new 'hostile environment' has been introduced with the approval of the British government's Nationality and Borders Bill in 2021.[9] These citizenship-stripping policies not only create second-class citizens but also corrode, especially, many Muslim, Asian and black people's sense of belonging within Britain. The power to remove British citizenship based on what is 'conducive to the public good' will immensely affect people of colour and determine that citizenship is defined by whiteness.

Although I have provided examples of the 'hostile environment' and the erosion of citizenship in recent years, it is crucial to state that these dynamics were pre-existent and they have their roots in the British Empire. Nadine El-Enany shows that the immigration system in Britain was constructed to control the entry of former colonial people after the collapse of the British Empire.[10] This political rhetoric on immigration and citizenship continues even more harshly in recent years in attacking racialised minorities.

Am I Less British? shows what it means to be British in 'Brexit Britain' through the narratives of British Kurdish and British Turkish in north

London and how they experience 'new hierarchies of belonging'[11] in London. They imagine their future is more blurred than before, as stated by Dilan, a British Kurdish youth: 'I feel and experience a clear division between myself and a European British or English young people even though I was born in Britain and do not speak English with a foreign accent as my parents [do].' This highlights that there is not only a clear distinction between migration and citizenship status, but also between citizens. I discuss the racialised hierarchies of Britishness further in Chapter 6. How the children of refugees and immigrants make sense of their Britishness should be explored not only by focusing on their experiences in Britain. Their sense of belonging and belongingness should also be situated in a transnational context, because their social relations, emotions and identities are situated across the borders of nation-states.

From this perspective, *Am I Less British?* also examines transnational links between the children of refugees and immigrants, particularly focusing on their experiences in Turkey and their thoughts about Turkey. The dynamics of the Turkish context, and the political climate in Turkey, especially the exclusion of Kurdish identity and racial discourses, are looked into. I argue that the children of Turkish immigrants deidentify themselves from national identities, such as Turkish and British, due to their experiences of racism and exclusion transnationally. As a result, they find themselves in a constant process of negotiating their identity. However, the children of Kurdish refugees identify more with their Kurdishness as a response to racism in a transnational context, both in Turkey and Britain. So their identity-making process is not only influenced by the environment in which they live in Britain, but also by the political atmosphere in their parents' country of origin. I touch on racism in a transnational context to gain a better understanding of the ways experiencing racism in both settlements influences their sense of belonging in relation to how they feel about Britishness, Kurdishness and Turkishness. Most of the young people are also Turkish citizens and have transnational links with the country; therefore, the migratory trajectories of their parents, their experiences when they visit Turkey, the socio-political changes taking place in Turkey, and how these changes are affecting the ways the participants make sense of their Kurdish and Turkish identities are as important as their attachments to Britain (more on this in Chapters 2 and 5).

Another important point the book makes is that the processes of racialisation in a transnational context plays a central role in how young people define themselves and how they account for the everyday dynamics of their relationships across the borders of nation-states. I pay particular attention to the processes of racialisation, the experiences of racism and the hierarchies of whiteness that are visible in the everyday experiences of the children of refugees and immigrants in London. Racialisation informs how they constructed and challenged a sense of belonging (see Chapters 4, 5 and 6). The whiteness that is associated with white supremacy, and racial domination is a shifting category that is constantly reproduced and articulated within the political and social lexicon and should be framed historically,[12] and a difference becomes a racial one when markers of identity are invested with political meanings that can be mobilised in conflict. The ways young people refer to their sense of belonging and how they are seen by others are very much related to the hierarchies of whiteness that depends on the places, societies and power dynamics in both countries. I am interested in exploring how the racial categories of those who fall into white and non-white differ, how these categories change over time, whether this change depends on class, gender, the places where they interact, and how the hierarchies of whiteness play a role when they interact with young people from different ethnic and racial backgrounds. In her book *Who Cares about Britishness?*, Vron Ware demonstrates that there are various kinds of Britishness internalised by people whose experiences differ depending on communities and places they intersect within multicultural Britain.[13] As Ware shows, while Britishness means nothing for some people, it represents important things, especially, for people with a migratory background, which is very much related to belongingness.[14] The narratives of the children of refugees and immigrants on how they relate to Britishness and whiteness is explored further in Chapter 6. The transnational experiences of young people present a deeper understanding of the complexity of their lives in changing political and social circumstances across the borders of nation-states. In this book, I shall also examine how encountering racism and discrimination in both societies affects the sense of belonging among young people.

As argued by Victoria Melangedd Redclift and Fatima Begum Rajina, transnational activities among Bangladesh-origin Muslims in Britain increased as an escape from the hostility they experienced.[15] Transnational context is important when exploring how the children of refugees and immigrants relate to Britishness, Turkishness and Kurdishness, especially when reflecting on their experiences of racism. However, the transnational context is not always an escape for the young people who are alienated from their parents' country of origin as a result of the racism, exclusion and sexism they experience. Overall, the book demonstrates that the intersections of local, national and transnational approaches, the political context through which the lives of young people are framed, their experiences of racism, and the role of class, ethnicity and gender are a *sine qua non* in exploring their relation to Britishness, Kurdishness and Turkishness. It shows how the intersection of racial hierarchies, class, ethnicity and gender plays a crucial role in their identification, not only in the British, Turkish, Kurdish and transnational contexts but also in the local context.

This introductory chapter sets out the theoretical framework of the book and engage with the relevant literature on racism and belonging in a transnational context to which the analysis of my ethnographic material responds. It aims to challenge the existing theories based on methodological nationalism that does not account for the lived experience of the children of refugees and immigrants. In the next part, I explore the concept of transnationalism.

Why does transnationalism not offer sufficient understanding beyond nationalism?

The transnational perspective was developed in the 1990s as a replacement or addition to the concept of diaspora. In the 1990s, a new shape of migration, the transformation of the nation-state in a global age and the level of diasporic exchanges focusing more on the individual, challenged the notion of diaspora and led to the concept of transnationalism entering the field of migration. The transnational perspective in migration studies has emerged as a new theoretical framework and analytical tool that accounts for the changing nature of contemporary migration, which is now received as more fluid rather than being fixed to nationally defined borders. It entails the movements of people, groups or entities across borders, with the implication they are doing so because of the developments in globalisation. Border-crossing activities as transnational practices are not limited to traditional or physical border-crossing activities and are now easier in the global context as a result of new technological developments.[16]

The main focus of the transnational perspective is on border-crossing activities, which attempts to avoid 'methodological nationalism' that refers to 'nationalist thinking and the conceptualisation of migration in post-war social sciences'.[17] Andreas Wimmer and Nina Glick-Schiller argue that the nation-state-building processes have shaped the ways migration has been perceived and suggest an analysis of migratory movements from a transnational context that represents a shift of perspective beyond methodological nationalism and is classified as a challenge to the nation-state.[18] Transnationalism has emerged as a new theoretical framework and analytical tool that accounts for the changing nature of contemporary migration, which is now received as more fluid rather than being fixed to nationally defined borders. The concept of transnationalism has become one of the fundamental ways of understanding the practices of migrants across the borders of nation-states.[19] In the literature, transnationalism is most of the time defined as a 'process by which migrants, through their daily activities, forge and sustain multi-stranded social, economic and political relations that link together their societies of origin and settlement, and through which they create social fields that cross-national boundaries'.[20]

However, transnationalism has been criticised because it does not answer certain questions such as, what sort of migrant community it refers to, what is its historical limit and what kinds of migrant practices it includes.[21] Despite transnationalism becoming a modish concept in the recent decade, some scholars have provided radical critiques of the concept.[22] For example, Alisdair Rogers argues that 'not all migrants are transmigrants and not all cross-border moves are transnational. The various policies and programmes described as a mobility order set the conditions under which individuals, families, and communities make their decisions.'[23] Peter Kivisto also criticises the efficiency of transnationalism by not offering a convincing argument about which sort of migrants it includes,[24] and Janine Dahinden questions the concept because it focuses on migrants and ignores non-migrants who might also be involved in transnational activities.[25] In Janine Dahinden's account, if globalisation has had a huge impact on people's lives in terms of constructing social networks across borders, it should be said that almost everybody nowadays, to some degree, is transnational, but their level of transnational activities distinguish varying social positioning in a globalised world.[26] Social networks play a crucial role in her understanding of transnationalism, as they also do for Bruno Riccio, who argues that transnationalism is about constant networking within transnational spaces and encompasses differing practices.[27] On the other hand, Paolo Boccagni highlights the interplay of the 'here' and 'there', which impacts both the host and home societies, rather than limiting the transnational perspective solely to the relationship of migrants with their home societies.[28]

The effects of transnational links on both sending and receiving countries have been studied in relation to economic, political and sociocultural aspects in the multidisciplinary literature. The studies focus on cross-border entrepreneurialism and remittances,[29] dual citizenship and voting practices[30] and everyday practices.[31] How it is possible to talk about the meaningful effects of the transnational perspective on both sending and receiving societies without challenging 'national accounts of the history of nations in the Global North';[32] transnationalism does not offer a sufficient analysis of migrants' experiences beyond the nation-states. As stated by Ipek Demir, the concept of transnationalism does not take into account how colonial legacies and racial hierarchies are relevant to our time when positioning itself as an alternative to nationalism.[33] From another point of view, Janine Dahinden argues that membership and identification refer to ethnic categories and nation-states; the nation needs to be taken into account when researching transnationalism because it influences the level of transnational practices among migrants.[34] In her later work, Dahinden states that it is important to focus on both 'a de-nationalized epistemology while simultaneously analysing the potential force of nation-state categories'.[35] The categories of nation-state and ethnicity still shape the identities of many transnational migrants because not all migrants identify with multicultural cultures.[36]

There are several reasons why transnationalism does not offer sufficient understanding beyond nationalism. Firstly, the transnational perspective treats minorities who migrated a long time ago and were granted citizenship as 'migrants' and analyses their links with the receiving society by measuring their levels of 'integration' and on what basis they contribute to the receiving society.[37] Secondly, its territorial understanding of 'home' and 'homeland' assumes that all 'transnational migrants' have a 'home country' that they feel they belong to besides a settlement country, which intensifies a state-centred approach. How can home and homeland be conceptualised in a transnational context if there is no 'homeland' state? Does the concept of transnationalism explain the links of 'transnational migrants' to a place that is imagined? These questions should be taken into account when defining transnationalism and exploring the experiences of transnational communities. 'We [Kurds] do not have any country, territory', said Rozerin. She continued: 'We do not have anywhere to call home.' The perception of the 'homeland' is only an idea or a part of the political project for stateless communities. As argued by Nancy L. Green and Roger Waldinger, 'the "home" to which the migrants prove attached is as likely – if not more so – to involve the village, region, or even ethnic minority of origin, as opposed to the sending state or the imagined nation to whom that state is presumed to belong.'[38] Thirdly, transnationalism does not take into consideration colonialism when questioning nation-centred thinking.[39] The legacies of colonialism are affecting the lives of many children of refugees and immigrants today who are not migrants but are treated and referred to as migrants even though they hold British passports, because the term migrant carries racial implications for anyone who is not white British. Racism has a huge impact on the ways immigrants have been defined. In order to challenge the nation-state-centric perspective, transnationalism must take into account the impact of colonial legacies and racism on the cross-border experiences of many children of refugees and immigrants.

The world is a political and social structure that is the product of a 'dual revolution' – a 'dual revolution' whose two elements mutually feed each other and offer mutual causality. On the one hand, the Industrial Revolution created capitalism as a universal norm and, on the other hand, the Enlightenment shaped political and social consciousness and determined its norms, which are deeply intertwined with racist and colonial thinking and practices. Nationalism as an integral part of both the Industrial Revolution and the Enlightenment that concentrates on the obvious negative effects of nations and neglects to examine the underlying causes is a form of habitus that results in the loss of this dual revolution.[40] This situation is not much different in terms of transnationalism. I argue that transnationalism does not offer sufficient understanding beyond nationalism, and dismisses considering racism as an impact of colonial legacies on the cross-border experiences of many children of refugees and immigrants, which are reflected in the socio-political context of both the receiving and sending societies. The concept of transnationalism falls short in fully comprehending the experiences of children of refugees and immigrants and overlooks the impact of racism. It disregards the socio-political contexts of Britain and Turkey that exacerbate cross-border experiences.

In this book, I use terms such as 'transnational activities' and 'transnational experience' instead of transnationalism when exploring the experiences of the children of refugees and immigrants across the borders of nation-states as transnationalism carries connotations of nationalism. Migrants' and minorities' experiences of racism have not received enough attention in the literature on transnational migration. Therefore, I pay close attention to how the children of refugees and immigrants whose parents migrated to Britain from Turkey are affected by racism in both settlements.

Below, I explore racism in a transnational context to gain a better understanding of which ways experiencing racism in both settlement countries and the country of origin influence the sense of belonging among the children of refugees and immigrants and how they identify with Britishness, Kurdishness and Turkishness.

Racism in a transnational context

Racism is a political phenomenon, it is global and transnational and should be understood in the historical context that is inspired by the structural system of power and domination.[41] However, it is rarely discussed in its transnational dimensions. Paul Gilroy offers a transnational perspective in understanding the shared experiences of racism and resistance among black American travellers.[42] How racism transforms itself and is altered through social networks across national borders, and what experiencing racism across national borders can do to people, are important questions to ask. Exploring racism within its transnational perspective becomes crucial not only to illustrate it as a worldwide problem but also to highlight its historical context. As argued by Martin Bulmer and John Solomos, without a clear understanding of the historical context it is not possible to understand how racial ideas have emerged out of and become an integral part of societies.[43] Similarly, Eduardo Bonilla-Silva highlights that racism is inspired by the structured system of power and domination that has a historical basis.[44] In the case of Turkey, for instance, the Kurdish identity has been racialised through power dynamics in cultural, social and economic terms ever since the establishment of the Turkish Republic in 1923.[45] This legacy of an overlap between race and power, which has marginalised the Kurds in Turkey, has also oppressed many migrants and refugees in Turkey.[46] The process of racialisation shows how racism is based on lived experience and grows in line with the processes of exclusion, as referred to by Frantz Fanon.[47] Racism, in this book, is defined as a structured system of power and domination grounded in enduring historical narratives.[48] I am interested in exploring how racism as a lived experience in a transnational context is influencing how young people whose parents migrated from Turkey make sense of their identities and belonging within the contemporary political context in Britain and Turkey.

The transnational perspective on migration not only highlights the fact that the sending societies are important to the lives of migrants; it also focuses on the positive impacts of interactions established between the receiving and sending societies on migrants' lives in both societies.[49] When exploring the relationship between the sending and receiving societies in understanding migrants' experiences, the transnational perspective often analyses the experiences of migrants from one angle, which is the positive impact of engaging with the sending society on their lives in the receiving society.[50] For example, Annemarie Klingenberg *et al.*, focusing on the experiences of South Africans who migrated to Australia, argue that the transnational experiences of migrants provide distinct benefits for their lives in the receiving society.[51] Conversely, other studies use the term 'reactive transnationalism' to show that migrants' experiences of discrimination in a country of settlement make them identify more with a country of origin as a reaction.[52] These studies draw on Alejandro Portes and Rubén G. Rumbaut's notion of 'reactive ethnicity', suggesting that reaction occurs when racialised minorities experience discrimination and compensate by bolstering ethnic identities.[53] Exploring the cases of 'reactive ethnicity' studies show that, as a result of discrimination, ethnic group solidarity and group consciousness become more visible.[54] Adopting 'reactive ethnicity' in the context of transnational migration, it is argued that migrants identify with their countries of origin, and engage more in transnational activities as a reaction to the experience of discrimination.[55]

However, these studies look into the relationship between discrimination and transnational engagement, neglecting racism as one of the main experiences among migrants and their children in the countries of origin. In examining the linkage between transnationalism and racism through drawing in-depth interviews with first, second, third and fourth-generation Bangladesh-origin Muslims in London, Luton and Birmingham, Redclift and Rajina introduce the concept of 'protective transnationalism' as a specification of 'reactive transnationalism'[56] and argue that protective transnationalism was invoked only about land and property.[57] They show that transnational practices in the case of Bangladeshi-origin Muslims in London function as a form of protection, especially when immigrants experience racism in the country of settlement.[58] Alice Bloch and Shirin Hirsch, from a comparative and inter-generational approach, explore transnational activities among the UK-born 'second generation' from three refugee backgrounds – Tamils from Sri Lanka, Kurds from Turkey and Vietnamese – and argue that 'experiencing racism during visits to the heritage country reinforced the specificity of the refugee context that led to their parents' migration'.[59] There is little research on how experiencing racism in both the receiving and the sending societies influences the children of refugees and immigrants' transnational ties and sense of belonging. Transnational ties can change over time depending on the political and socio-economic conjuncture of both countries.

'Second generation' within the transnational perspective

The children of refugees and immigrants are often referred to as 'second generation' and their transnational activities are called 'second-generation transnationalism' in the literature. The term 'second generation' includes lots of connotations in its definition. It is used to define the group of people who were born or grew up in the country of the settlement who are seen as not belonging to the country in which they were born and are often recognised as foreigners. In most cases, they are referred to as 'second-generation migrants', even though they are citizens of their country of birth.[60] I do not use the term 'second generation' when referring to the children of refugees and immigrants, as both categories of 'second generation' and 'second-generation migrants' are associated with exclusion and emphasise colonial and assimilationist perspectives towards them.[61]

Most of the research on transnationalism has been based on the experience of the first generation, such as visits to their country of origin, the idea of returning to the homeland, constructing strong ties with family and friends in the country, sending remittances, investing in the country, and being politically active in both country of settlement and origin. The focus on the first generation is justified by some scholars as the 'second generation' may have less connection with their parents' country of origin than their parents and, therefore, they should be less transnational than their parents.[62] In other words, it is assumed, especially in the case of the 'second generation', that 'assimilation appears to have implications for understanding transnationalism'.[63] According to this view, cultural assimilation offers the ability to speak English, which in turn helps migrants construct close ties with the receiving society and have a better standard of living. The experiences of the first and 'second generation' might be differentiated regarding the length of their stay in their parents' country of origin and the settlement country, as well as the level of their interaction with the settlement society. Young people who were born or raised in the settlement society may engage with this society more than their parents because they go to school, make friends there and may adapt to the ways of life of the settlement country more easily than their parents. At the same time, they know and learn about their parents' country of origin from them, community organisations, transnational media, and through their visits to their parents' country of origin. Generally, young people negotiate social and cultural positioning within both societies. Susan Eckstein states that 'the second generation, in particular, has ties to the broader receiving society through language, education, friendships, work, marriage, and children that their parents may not have'.[64] Several studies on 'second-generation' transnationalism explore the link between transnational relations and integration.[65] For Peggy Levitt and Mary C. Waters, 'second-generation' transnationalism exists and will continue, as 'transnationalism and integration should not be seen as opposites'.[66] They argue that 'there are multiple ways in which immigrants and their children can combine transnationalism and assimilative strategies, leading to diverse outcomes, both in the United States and in immigrants' countries of origin'.[67] According to these authors, young people are more likely to engage in the receiving society than their parents through education, language and friendship. As they have grown up in the receiving society, they have built their social networks and social environment in the receiving society under the lifestyle and rules of this society. At the same time, however, they are aware of the socio-cultural life in their parents' country of origin through their families, transnational media and visits to the country.

Language is one of the most important factors in young people's level of participation in transnational networks. Also, not being fluent in their mother tongue affects the ability of young people to participate in transnational networks.[68] According to Susan Eckstein, this situation makes young people more reliant on their family or community, making it less likely for them to act independently.[69] Similarly, Tracey Reynolds argues that, for the Caribbean 'second generation', transnational ties are strengthened by the family, holidays, and improved telecommunication systems.[70] Rebecca Golbert also supports that Ukrainian Jewish youth have adapted to the linguistic, cultural and socio-economic life of another country that assists them to be transnationally active.[71] Focusing on the experiences of 'second-generation' Italians in Switzerland and Italy, Susanne Wessendorf argues that transnational relations of many members of the 'second generation' and integration into co-ethnic peer groups help construct a strong sense of belonging and attachment to where they live.[72] Focusing on the transnational experiences of Palestinian and Lebanese 'second generation' in Australia, Heba Batainah shows that their transnational involvement involves the religious and cultural practices of the migrant community.[73] In the case of 'second-generation' youth from refugee backgrounds living in Britain, Alice Bloch and Shirin Hirsch explore that, similar to the 'second generations' from non-refugee backgrounds, they have fewer social transnational connections and little economic engagement; however, their political consciousness is higher.[74] Laurence Ossipow, Anne-Laure Counilh and Milena Chimienti's research on the experiences of children of refugees and immigrants in Switzerland suggests that the children of refugees are identified as foreigners even though they hold Swiss passports and have socio-economic success, whereas the children of immigrants manage to socialise with the Swiss population.[75]

Most of the studies concerning the children of immigrants from Turkey have been conducted in Germany,[76] neglecting the situation in Britain. Likewise, most of the research on transnational links of migrants from Turkey has focused on a limited number of issues, such as socio-economic exchanges, the formation of Turkish cultural identity, difficulties in education, and adaptation to different cultural spaces. The research conducted by Ayhan Kaya focuses on the cultural practices and identity positioning of young people whose parents are from Turkey and shows that these young people in Germany have multiple identifications, such as German, Turkish and global.[77] Ayşe Çağlar argues that the children of immigrants whose parents are from Turkey are connected to Berlin – an urban space – rather than a nation and/or ethnic communities.[78]

This book aims to fill some of the gaps in the literature, taking into consideration a population that has been so far under-researched, that is British Kurdish and British Turkish youth living in London, and using a broad approach, exploring the everyday experiences of this population. Besides, rather than focusing on integration and cultural aspects of transnational links, it explores how the children of refugees and immigrants make sense of belonging within the contemporary political context in Britain and Turkey. The role of political circumstances in the sending and receiving countries on young people's sense of belonging and transnational links has not been paid much attention. This book, distinctively, focuses on how the 'hostile environment' policy, including Brexit and the Nationality and Borders Bill, are impacting the lives of the children of refugees and immigrants and their sense of belonging in Britain, and how Turkey's authoritarian regime, including anti-Kurdish sentiment and anti LGBTQ+ policies, are affecting their sense of belonging to their parents' country of origin and how they identify with their Britishness, Kurdishness and Turkishness. I now discuss the ethnographic context and methods used in this study that guides the book.

Fieldwork and research setting

Why this book focuses on the experiences of British-born Kurdish and Turkish youth in London is the main question I have been asked. In the first instance, given that I am a British national from Turkey, knowing both contexts well, makes it easier to understand the experiences of young people within both the context of Britain and Turkey. There are various reasons why the experiences of the Kurdish and Turkish youth are of interest to a wider audience. First, the complexity in the way the children of refugees and immigrants in north London identify themselves is expressed through the experiences of these young people in local, national and transnational spaces where they interact and has not been paid much attention to in the field. Importantly, I want to raise the voices of the young people from Kurdish and Turkish backgrounds living in north London. I hold the belief that their experiences speak volumes about the experiences of numerous other young people of non-European origin in Britain, particularly in London. Second, the challenges Kurdish and Turkish youth have been facing growing up in a transnational social space, and how British Kurdish and British Turkish youth relate to transnational context differently depending on their ethnicity and gender, offers a unique case in exploring the transnational experiences of the children of refugees and immigrants. Third, the impact of political climate in Turkey, especially the racialisation of Kurdish identity on how British Kurdish youth identify themselves and relate to Turkey differently compared to British Turkish youth suggests divergent understanding of transnational experiences of the children of refugees and immigrants.

London, a postcolonial city,[79] has been chosen not only because of its 'multicultural' and 'super-diverse' characteristics but also its complexity. Les Back describes London as a 'metropolitan paradox' in his book *New Ethnicities and Urban Culture* which refers to a new possibility of what multicultural London could be and the portrayal of racism that is shifted over time.[80] Focusing on how young people experience living in London, and particularly north London where the fieldwork took place, I explore the complexity of everyday life in an urban setting, and refer to Paul Gilroy's writings on conviviality through the narratives of young people. North London, the district north of the River Thames, is where the majority of Kurdish and Turkish migrants settled, particularly around Green Lanes, which starts in Newington Green and extends to Winchmore Hill. A significant number of British Kurds and British Turks live in northeast London, in areas such as Hackney, Dalston, Stoke Newington, Harringay and Tottenham. Kurdish and Turkish first generation have established their businesses, community organisations and language schools in north London. North London not only represents a neighbourhood where the majority of Kurdish and Turkish migrants settle, it also indicates their class identity, reconstruction of gender, cultural exchanges and solidarity (see Chapter 3). London, on the other hand, while offering a rich perspective for these young people in understanding other cultures surrounding them, is also a city where everyday multicultural practices display ethnic and racial differences within convivial formations and is a reminder of being an outsider and the experiences of racism for these young people (see Chapter 4). The interpretations that young people ascribe to places such as north

London, London, and Turkey in a transnational context are in a state of constant flux. More generally, their relationships with their respective nationalities, cities, local contexts and identities raise the question of whether they are seen as British or as white-British, regardless of how they feel about their Britishness.

My field site was mainly around Harringay, Green Lanes, Tottenham Hale, Seven Sisters and Hackney. Green Lanes, especially Harringay, is an interesting area. It is predominantly a Kurdish and Turkish area, which has a community spirit. According to the 2011 census, 65.3 per cent of the Harringay population is made up of non-white-British ethnic groups. This is higher than both London (55.1 per cent) and England and Wales (19.5 per cent), and it is the capital's most linguistically diverse area, with over 16 languages spoken.[81] It can be described as a diverse neighbourhood hub.

In the London borough of Harringay, between Turnpike Lane station and Green Lanes, there are many businesses, including restaurants, cafes, off-licences, hairdressers, flower shops and law firms run by British Kurds and British Turks. While some name the area as 'Little Istanbul', others refer to it as a rural part of Turkey.[82] I was already familiar with the area before starting to conduct fieldwork for this research. I attended social events organised by local community organisations and participated in cultural events organised by the Day-Mer (Turkish and Kurdish Community Centre) Youth Committee. At Day-Mer young people from

Figure 1.1 Harringay-Green Lanes. Photo by author.

different backgrounds, including Caribbean, Kurdish and Turkish, perform traditional dances and other social activities. I have been acquainted with the social milieu of the participants, thereby creating proximity between me and them. Having lived in north London and been a member of the community created a particular engagement with the positionality of the young people I interviewed. However, my background did not mean that I could fully comprehend the experiences of these young people. Accordingly, I aimed not to relegate myself to a specific, marginal position in the course of the research. Rather, I sought to consider myself both an insider and an outsider. In a way, I had a unique viewpoint as an insider and an outsider. The participants could relate to me because of their closeness in terms of origin, but at the same time, they felt removed from me because I was Turkish-born and they were British-born – except for one participant who was born in Germany and sought asylum in Britain when she was two years old. Due to my Turkish background, I had many opportunities to explore and analyse certain issues related to Turkey and migrants' life in London from an insider's perspective. During the fieldwork, as a researcher who is from Turkey, I did not experience any difficulty when conducting interviews with young people whose ethnicity is Kurdish, as I was not an 'outsider' to them. Nonetheless, politics might play a part here as one of the Kurdish participants said during the interview that she could not openly state her views about the Kurdish question in Turkey if she was going to be interviewed by a Turkish nationalist researcher. The participants openly shared their experiences of living in London, and also north London, and their relation to Britishness, Kurdishness and Turkishness. I had more advantages compared to outsider researchers as I was able to bridge the gap of socio-cultural misinterpretation. Furthermore, knowing both the Turkish and British contexts gave me an advantage in observing the transnational activities in the lives of young people whose parents are Kurdish and Turkish. This may have been more difficult to analyse for someone from outside the community. However, occupying the role of an insider researcher provides an opportunity for practical negotiation of the research process, such as accessing the Kurdish and Turkish communities and conducting interviews.

I conducted the fieldwork between 2019 and 2022; however, most interviews were conducted between 2019 and 2021, with some additional interviews in 2022. In finding participants, I used my social networks and reached them through community organisations in local areas where the young people live. All interviews were conducted around north London where the majority of Kurds and Turks live. Forty young people, aged between 18 and 23, took part in the interviews. Some identified as male or female, while others identified as LGBTQ+. They were bilingual, educated in London and came from middle-class or working-class backgrounds, with parents of Kurdish and Turkish origin. Even though the research participants reflect the heterogeneity of the Kurdish and Turkish societies in terms of class, gender, belief and political views, all of them stated they do not support the current governments in Turkey and in Britain and their politics. I also conducted interviews with 14 first-generation British Kurds and British Turks, including the directors of community organisations, who migrated to Britain in the 1980s and 1990s, to explore their motivations for migration, socio-political spaces they established in north London and their thoughts about Brexit. All research participants except one are anonymised. Pseudonyms were used when referring to research participants. Written and oral consent were obtained from participants using an information sheet before starting the interview process. The collected data was anonymised by removing both direct and indirect personal identifiers.

The common features of these young people who were raised in London are speaking Turkish and English (only a few of them stated that they speak very little Kurdish), and having transnational links, especially through regular visits to Turkey. Focusing on both Kurdish and Turkish young people in north London assisted me in analysing how their social relationships might be shaped by institutional factors on different levels, depending on the background of their family and socio-cultural factors. More importantly, it contributed to exploring the power dynamics, racism in a transnational context, the positionality of young people among themselves and with other racialised groups, and their relationships with Turkey.

My approach to the field research was drawn to provide insights into the lives of young people; I observed their interactions with one another in the neighbourhood, community organisations and cafes where they usually hang out. In Green Lanes, Harringay the young people know most of the Turkish and Kurdish people in the neighbourhood. They looked like an extended family. I also observed that they switched between Turkish and English languages depending on to whom they were speaking. For example, in community organisations, young people spoke Turkish with the first generation of the community, but they mostly spoke English among each other. I visited community organisations that run specific activities, such as dance, theatre, and Kurdish and Turkish language courses for young people.

Among the community organisations that were established by the first-generation Kurds and Turks, Day-Mer is the one that continuously organises activities for young people; I came to know the majority of the young people whose narratives I share in this book through Day-Mer, where I attended youth events and spent some time in the communal area. The founders of Day-Mer were politically active in Turkey and migrated to Britain as political asylum seekers. Since settling in Britain, they have been just as politically active as they were in Turkey, and have set up parallel structures in London. So this was the idea behind establishing Day-Mer, set up in 1989 to work with Turkish and Kurdish people living in London. Its main objectives are to help solve the problems of Turkish and Kurdish people related to housing, employment, settlement status, to promote their cultural, economic, social and democratic rights, and to strengthen solidarity between themselves as well as local people. They also provide recreational activities; for instance, there is a free annual festival organised by Day-Mer, which promotes the integration of different communities and ethnic groups.

Many of the young people whom I met in Day-Mer stated that, through the organisation, they met young people from the Kurdish and Turkish communities. The young people who regularly participate in Day-Mer's events have also constructed transnational links with Turkey in the same way the first-generation Turkish and Kurdish immigrants have, and are familiar with the social and political atmosphere in Turkey and have an interest in Turkish politics.

I also met young people in other community organisations, such as Gik-Der, Komkar (Kurdish Advice Centre) and IAKM (England Alevi

Figure 1.2 Logo of Day-Mer. Photo by author.

Cultural Centre and Cemevi). Gik-Der and Komkar, which were founded by migrants fleeing political and racial persecution in Turkey in the 1990s, provide support and advice to the community in terms of housing, employment, immigration and citizenship, and run activities such as Kurdish language courses and traditional dances.[83] IAKM, which is a faith-based organisation for Alevis,[84] and the largest community organisation in size and number in service of the Turkish and Kurdish community, offers educational, cultural, social and sports activities to everyone regardless of age, religion, ethnicity or nationality.[85] The directors of the community organisations stated that these organisations provide a safety net for young people, guarding against delinquency in London, and if they attend the socio-cultural activities of community organisations they are more likely to stay away from the streets, where they are threatened by drugs, gangs and criminality. Turkish and Kurdish community organisations foster a sense of cultural identity among young people by encouraging them to learn the language and culture. They create a social space in which young people can participate, as well as provide various social and cultural activities, which contribute to reducing youth crime.

So, community organisations play an important social, cultural and, to a lesser extent, political role for the young people living in north London, and improve their well-being by creating a sense of belonging to the community. These community organisations are important places that connect young people with their parents' country of origin. Most importantly, these organisations inform young people about the political climate in Turkey, and the dynamics of the Turkish context, including the Kurdish issue, racial discourse and migration from Turkey to Britain. However, the children of refugees and immigrants question the political positioning of these organisations and are selective in the organisations they prefer to attend. I explore these community organisations further in Chapter 3.

Empirically, this book presents a rich ethnography of the lives of young people and shows how they relate to Britishness, Kurdishness and Turkishness, as well as how they position themselves with other racialised groups. I facilitated young people in discussing their transnational experiences, relationships forged across national borders, and experiences of racism, rather than imposing artificial identity categories. This was achieved by asking them how they feel about identities surrounding them rather than making them choose from a list of identity categories established by nation-states and policymakers. My approach to the field research was designed to get a deeper understanding of how young people negotiate and translate social relations within a range of spaces where they face racism.

Overview of the book

The chapters of this book are organised to explore how young people negotiate identities within intersecting socio-political spaces in a transnational context, which draws on rich material about transnational experiences, identity, and belonging among British Kurdish and British Turkish youth in north London. In this chapter, I have set out the theoretical framework of the book and engaged with the relevant literature on racism and belonging in a transnational context to which the analysis of my ethnographic material responds, and have explored the transnational perspective in analysing the sense of belonging of the children of refugees and immigrants and their experiences of racism across the borders of nation-states. I have argued that transnationalism does not offer sufficient understanding beyond nationalism because it treats minorities as migrants. It has a territorial understanding of home and dismisses experiencing racism as having an impact on the cross-border mobilities of many children of refugees and immigrants. For it to challenge nation-state-centric thinking, transnationalism should consider racism as an impact of colonial legacies on the cross-border experiences of many children of refugees and immigrants. Throughout the book, in exploring the experiences of racism among the children of refugees and immigrants in both sending and receiving societies, I use terms such as 'transnational link', 'transnational experience' and 'transnational social space' instead of transnationalism, because transnationalism carries connotations of nationalism. The literature on transnational migration has not paid enough attention to the experiences of racism among migrants and minorities.

Drawing on interviews with the first generation of British Kurds and British Turks, Chapter 2, 'Between Britain's hostile environment and Turkey's authoritarian regime', provides insight into the historical detour of migration from Turkey to Britain to better understand the transnational socio-political participation of the Kurdish and Turkish communities who migrated in different periods and had different reasons for migration.[86] This historical detour is essential for understanding the transnational political participation and cross-border activism of the first generation, which plays a crucial role in the processes of identity-making among the children of refugees and immigrants. This chapter also sets out the dynamics of the British and Turkish political context, including Brexit and the rise of authoritarian politics in Turkey, which affects the experiences of the young people interviewed.

In Chapters 3–6 I present the ethnographic data that explores the narratives of the children of refugees and immigrants in north London whose parents migrated to Britain from Turkey that inform their transnational experiences and how their experiences are racialised, classed and gendered within the socio-political transnational context in which they live. These empirical chapters are organised to introduce the places that are significant in the construction of their identities and senses of belonging across the borders of nation-states and their thoughts about identities, belonging and citizenship that are framed by their transnational experiences. The rationale behind the organisation of the chapters is to introduce the transnational experiences of young people, which are constructed by the socio-political context of places they interact with, which affect the ways they think about identities and the question of belonging and how they are seen by others.

Chapter 3, '"My north London accent indicates my working-class background": north London, class, ethnicity and community', focuses on the north London context, where Kurdish and Turkish communities settled. To have a better understanding of how Kurdish and Turkish communities create their own social spaces and, in particular, how these social spaces influence the lives of young people, this chapter shows what north London signifies for young people whose parents migrated from Turkey and discusses young people's identity-making processes through their relationship with the Kurdish and Turkish communities. In exploring north London in-depth as a transnational social space that offers transnational elements, I also examine the role of community organisations as a crucial transnational resource, which brings the socio-cultural and political aspects of Kurdishness and Turkishness to the identity-making processes of young people. I analyse the impact that the urban environment inhabited by Kurdish and Turkish communities has on how young people identify themselves. This analysis focuses on their perceptions, views on living in north London, and their relationship with this area, rather than emphasising the particular cultural elements in an urban space. In this chapter, I also discuss how young people transform traditional discourses of the neighbourhood into their everyday life, how they respond to and negotiate these discourses on their terms, and how they articulate classed and gendered dynamics of belonging. I put forth the argument that, on the one hand, north London, as a socio-cultural space for Kurdish and Turkish communities, provides a sense of safety, security and community for the children of refugees and immigrants. However, on the other hand, their affiliation with this space also categorises them as *Other*, particularly when they enter homogeneous white spaces. The notion that 'diversity is cool' dismisses the experiences of racism among young people.

In Chapter 4, '"I enjoy the diversity of London but also feel excluded": London, conviviality and racism', I discuss how young people experience London and make a home in this city. Bringing together Paul Gilroy, Les Back and Shamser Sinha's works on conviviality,[87] I argue that young people's experiences in London show the realities of racism that shape everyday life within multicultural conviviality. It shows that the broader social and political contexts influence the ways young people view themselves within the hierarchies of belonging.[88] How young people experience the city varies depending on their everyday life patterns. In order to understand how young people can transform the city, and how their interaction with London influences their identity-making processes, the chapter draws on young people's experiences of living in London. In exploring how London became the locale for expressions of conviviality and racism for young people, I delve into the concept of multiculturalism, Britain's multicultural discourse and how young people confront the multicultural discourse in their everyday lives. I examine how British Kurdish and British Turkish young people view London and make a home in London, how they respond to the multicultural discourse they encounter in the social context of London, and negotiate and interpret their experiences of racism. London, itself, represents a constant reminder of being *Other* for the children of refugees and immigrants who experience racism and exclusion. This chapter also portrays the importance of solidarity and empathy in convivial moments that are forged from their common experiences of racism.

Chapter 5, '"Turkey is not my home. I've never lived there": discovering parents' country of origin', examines the meaning of belonging and home through transnational engagement. In this chapter, I focus on whether Turkey becomes a place of emotional security and stability for the reproduction of self and collective identity in the narratives of British Kurdish and British Turkish youth in London. In exploring this question, I delve into young people's experiences of their parents' country of origin when they visit. The experience of visiting Turkey is a focal point for discussing their relationships with Kurdish and Turkish societies. I explore how British Kurdish and British Turkish youth reflect on Turkey, belonging and mobility, and what types of transnational links they construct through their narratives. I argue that their relationship with Turkey is fragile and influenced by the political transformations in the country that creates a lack of belonging. In this chapter, I inquire into how young people adapt to various political, social and cultural resources transnationally, and the complexities of young people's negotiation and interpretation of their experiences during their visits to Turkey. I also seek to understand how the dualism of inclusion/ exclusion is experienced within Turkey's socio-cultural and political context, especially in the case of Kurdish youth because of long-standing violence against Kurds in Turkey.

Chapter 6, '"Am I less British because I am a descendant of an immigrant?": citizenship and belonging', departs from the young people's experiences of the spaces they interact with and explores the more exceptional and explicitly self-conscious practice of performing identity. In this chapter, I investigate whether socio-political context plays a role in young people's negotiation of identities. Using empirical evidence, I demonstrate how young people perceive their positions in society; whether racial hierarchies, class, ethnicity and gender are important in one's identification; how young people's transnational background is reflected in their perceptions of their identities; how the socio-political context of Britain and Turkey and experiencing racism and exclusion influence their Kurdishness, Britishness and Turkishness; and how the young people feel about being British, Kurdish or Turkish. In doing so, I explore young people's sense of belonging within the contemporary political context in Britain and Turkey and discuss whether their engagement with the socio-political context of the countries they relate to has an impact on the ways they identify themselves. I argue that the children of Turkish immigrants deidentify themselves from national identities, such as Turkish and British, due to their experiences of racism and exclusion transnationally; and the children of Kurdish refugees identify more with their Kurdishness as a response to racism in a transnational context, both in Turkey and Britain. Concentrating on the political context of both countries in exploring how young people position themselves in both the receiving and sending societies allows for a wider lens that considers not only how these young people cultivate a sense of identity and belonging, but also the often overlooked reasons why.

In the final chapter of the book, Chapter 7, 'Conclusion', I summarise the insights provided by the analysis of this research. This chapter allows me to bring to the fore the narratives of Kurdish and Turkish youth in London, enabling readers to comprehend what these young people's experiences tell the wider discipline.

Notes

1. All names are pseudonyms.
2. Before I started conducting interviews with them, I had their consent to take notes during the conversation for my research.
3. See Solomons 2022.
4. See Forest 2022.
5. 'Absolutely don't believe Britain a racist country: Rishi Sunak', *The Hindu*. 20 December 2022. https://www.thehindu.com/news/international/absolutely-dont-believe-britain-a-racist-country-rishi-sunak/article66284992.ece.
6. See Saini *et al.* 2023: 9.
7. See De Noronha 2020: 12.
8. See De Noronha 2020: 4.
9. Information relating to the Nationality and Borders Bill, introduced in the House of Commons on 6 July 2021. https://www.gov.uk/government/collections/the-nationality-and-borders-bill.
10. See El-Enany 2020.
11. See Back and Sinha 2012.
12. See Ware and Back 1994.
13. See Ware 2007.
14. See Ware 2007.
15. See Redclift and Rajina 2021.
16. See Levitt 2002; Glick Schiller 2003; Klingenberg *et al.* 2021.
17. See Wimmer and Glick Schiller 2002.
18. See Wimmer and Glick Schiller 2002: 301.
19. See Pries 1999; Faist 2000; Vertovec 2001; Glick Schiller 2003.
20. See Basch *et al.* 1994: 6.
21. See Guarnizo and Smith 1998; Mahler 1998; Portes 2001; Al-Ali and Koser 2002; Levitt and Jaworsky 2007; Dahinden 2009; Vertovec 2009; Faist 2010.
22. See Al-Ali and Koser 2002; Soysal 2000, 2015.
23. See Rogers 2004: 174.
24. See Kivisto 2001.
25. See Dahinden 2009.
26. See Dahinden 2009: 1383.
27. See Riccio 2001.
28. See Boccagni 2012.
29. See di Giovanni *et al.* 2015; Sommer 2020; Elo *et al.* 2022.
30. See Spiro 2019; Vink *et al.* 2019; Finn 2020; Klingenberg *et al.* 2021.
31. See Favell and Recchi 2019; Innes 2019; Savage *et al.* 2019; Erdal 2020; Kwon 2022.
32. See Demir 2022: 29.
33. See Demir 2022.
34. See Dahinden 2009.
35. See Dahinden 2017: 1482.
36. See Dahinden 2009.
37. See Portes 1996; Vertovec 1999; Levitt, 2001; Smith, 2002.
38. See Green and Waldinger 2016: 2.
39. See Demir 2022.
40. See Hobsbawn 1990; Woolf 1996; Lawrence 2005; Özkırımlı 2020.
41. See Gilroy 1993; Bonilla-Silva 2001; Lentin 2008; Bulmer and Solomos 2018.
42. See Gilroy 1993.
43. See Bulmer and Solomos 2018: 1004.
44. See Bonilla-Silva 2001.
45. See Saraçoğlu 2010; Ergin 2014.
46. See Şimşek 2021.
47. See Fanon 1986.
48. See Bonilla-Silva 2001.
49. See Boccagni 2012.

50. See Basch *et al.* 1994; Portes *et al.* 1999; Vertovec 2009; Goldring and Landolt 2012; Klingenberg *et al.* 2021.
51. See Klingenberg *et al.* 2021.
52. See Itzigsohn and Saucedo 2002, 2005; Snel *et al.* 2016; Beauchemin and Safi 2020.
53. See Portes and Rumbaut 2001.
54. See Portes and Rumbaut 2001; Snel *et al.* 2016; Herda 2018.
55. See Itzigsohn and Saucedo 2002, 2005; Snel *et al.* 2016; Yıldız and Hill 2017; Beauchemin and Safi 2020.
56. See Redclift and Rajina 2021: 206.
57. See Redclift and Rajina 2021: 209.
58. See Redclift and Rajina 2021.
59. See Bloch and Hirsch 2018: 16.
60. See Berggren *et al.* 2019; Midtbøen and Nadim 2019; Falcke *et al.* 2020; Mavrommatis 2021; Varshaver *et al.* 2022; White and Goodwin 2021.
61. See Chimienti *et al.* 2019.
62. See Vickerman 2002; Levitt 2009; Lee 2011, 2016; Fokkema *et al.*, 2013.
63. See O'Flaherty *et al.* 2007: 840.
64. See Eckstein 2002: 232.
65. See Levitt and Waters 2002; Crul *et al.* 2012; Dekker and Siegel 2013.
66. See Levitt and Waters 2002: 223.
67. See Levitt and Waters 2002: 231.
68. See Correa 2002.
69. See Eckstein 2002.
70. See Reynolds 2006.
71. See Golbert 2001.
72. See Wessendorf 2010.
73. See Batainah 2008.
74. See Bloch and Hirsch 2018.
75. See Ossipow *et al.* 2019: 14.
76. See Çağlar 2001; Kaya 2001.
77. See Kaya 2001.
78. See Çağlar 2001.
79. This refers to London being a previously colonial society, and having done time as an imperial metropole, because of the large postcolonial populations it attracted following the end of the empire, and also migrants from these ex-colonies (King 2009).
80. See Back 1996.
81. Harringay Council 2021.
82. See Husband 2002.
83. GikDer: http://gikder.org.uk/introduction/; KomKar (Kurdish Advice Centre): http://www.kurdishadvicecentre.org.uk/. Accessed 2 June 2021.
84. Alevi is a branch of Shi'a Islam based in Anatolia that is strongly differentiated from Sunni and fundamentalist Islam and comprises Turkey's largest religious minority community.
85. IAKM (the England Alevi Culture Centre and Cemevi): https://www.iakmcemevi.org/hakkimizda/. Accessed 2 June 2021.
86. See Çicekli 1998; Küçükcan 1999.
87. See Gilroy 2004; Back and Sinha 2012, 2016.
88. See Back and Sinha 2012.

2
Between Britain's hostile environment and Turkey's authoritarian regime

Hanif Kureishi opens his novel *The Buddha of Suburbia* with the following statement:

> My name is Karim Amir, and I am an Englishman born and, bred, almost. I am often considered to be a funny kind of Englishman, a new breed as it were, having emerged from two old histories. But I don't care – Englishman I am (though not proud of it), from the South London suburbs and going somewhere.[1]

Kureishi's 'almost', a feeling of being an incomplete self, is constantly reminded to the second, third and even fourth generations who have been asked the questions such as, 'Where are you actually from?', 'Are you considering living in your country in the future?', during their everyday interactions with white British people regardless of whether they were born, grew up, and the fact that they have only lived in Britain. This is a constant reminder that they will always be a migrant in a multicultural Britain, as discussed by Paul Gilroy in his book *After Empire: Melancholia or Convivial Culture*: 'we need to conjure up a future in which black and brown Europeans stop being seen as migrants'.[2] Looking into a close relationship between racism and nationalism, Paul Gilroy refers to debate around immigration, crime and religion within populist politics.[3] Similarly, Étienne Balibar sees racism in the heart of politics from the birth of nationalism.[4] The rise of nationalism in many countries has resurged fears around immigration, which then in turn exacerbates racism. Nationalism has served as a cornerstone of the 'modern world', shaping modern political thought through the assumption that every individual is born a member of a nation and that every nation has the right to establish its own state in its lands, with this right being actively encouraged. This approach, which locates individuals within the nation to which they belong, elevates the nation to a position of primacy in politics, and transforms into the driving force behind the inclusive formation of concepts such as 'national identity' and 'citizenship'. It also creates exclusion, with concepts such as non-nationality, foreignness and difference. Undoubtedly, it is inevitable that the mass migration movements that are being experienced throughout the world are seen as a 'problem' in terms of these inclusion/exclusion practices built on a nationalist ideology. It cannot be stated that discourses, such as multiculturalism, globalisation or transnationalism, which have been widely debated at various times over the past 60 years, will have a significant impact on these issues. As a matter of fact, racism, anti-immigrant sentiments, xenophobia, hate speech against LGBTQ+ individuals, sexism, anti-Semitism and Islamophobia, which are seen in almost every geography, are an indication that these issues, far from disappearing, are deepening.

In Britain, instances of hate crimes against immigrants, European Union nationals, refugees, asylum seekers, second, third and fourth generations and Muslims have surged since the 2016 Brexit referendum. Due to the British government's 'hostile environment' policy, Commonwealth citizens who had settled in Britain prior to 1973 and were entitled to unrestricted entry and residency, as well as access to public services, were wrongfully deported and denied access to healthcare, welfare benefits and housing. This is referred to as the 'Windrush scandal'.

The 'hostile environment' is an example of 'the expansion of everyday, everywhere bordering'.[5] In his book, *Deporting Black Britons*, Luke de Noronha demonstrates how the deportations of Jamaicans who arrived in Britain as children highlight the production and reproduction of racial hierarchies through borders as a consequence of the 'hostile environment' and the conflict between legal and lived forms of belonging. Through the narratives of four black Britons who were deported to Jamaica,[6] he illustrates the effects of racism on people's lives.[7]

The word genocide is frightening, and none of us can ascribe genocide in the 'modern' societies in which we live. However, the line between hate speech, covered with thousand-fold allusions, or hate crimes, which are witnessed in daily life but not given much importance, and genocide is not as thick as it seems. Herbert C. Kellman stated that that willingness to prevent monstrous violence dissolves if any or all of the following three conditions are present – the legal authorisation of violence by authorised authorities, the routinisation of violence, and the dehumanisation of victims of violence through ideological descriptions and humiliations.⁸ It is possible to say that these three conditions are brewing in the heart of modern societies, especially in the context of anti-immigrant sentiments and xenophobia. In his essay, *England Your England*, George Orwell wrote:

> As I write, highly civilized human beings are flying overhead, trying to kill me [...] They do not feel any enmity against me as an individual, nor I against them. They are 'only doing their duty', as the saying goes. Most of them, I have no doubt, are kind-hearted law-abiding men who would never dream of committing murder in private life. On the other hand, if one of them succeeds in blowing me to pieces with a well-placed bomb, he will never sleep any the worse for it. He is serving his country, which has the power to absolve him from evil.⁹

Orwell referred to the fact that serving their country saves them from being criminals. Similarly, Prince Harry's remarks about the people he killed while serving in Afghanistan – 'I didn't see them as human beings'[10] – are a typical example of the 'dehumanisation' ideology underlined by Kellman. The dehumanising of immigrants and specific immigrant communities through racialisation and humiliation is a dangerous cause of anti-immigrant and xenophobic practices in today's societies, ranging from hate speech to hate crime or the legal exclusion of black Britons, as demonstrated in de Noronha's book. This creates an ideal breeding ground for these practices to flourish.

In Turkey, authoritarianism has risen due to regime transitions under the Justice and Development Party (Adalet ve Kalkınma Partisi, hereafter AKP) government. Since 2010, Turkey has evolved from a 'tutelary democracy' to a 'competitive authoritarianism'.[11] After the Gezi uprising[12] in 2013 and the June 2015 election, extreme nationalism and state violence have increased as a response to rising democratic demands that challenge the government's authoritarian policies, aiming to suppress opposition political groups and civil society. Another important turning point in the process of regime change in Turkey took place after the attempted military coup of July 2016. Following the 2017 constitutional referendum, Turkey's political regime changed from a parliamentary system to a presidential one, when Recep Tayyip Erdoğan's presidential rule started in July 2018.[13] AKP's Islamist outlook has evolved strongly in domestic and foreign policy and caused rising conservatism in society. The Kurdish civilian population, activists, Alevis, women, LGBTQ+ individuals and intellectuals have become the main targets of the AKP's state ideology. AKP's discourse, adopting Islamism, populism, neoliberalism, authoritarianism and nationalism, polarises society and divides between 'AKP supporters [us]' and 'the others [them]'. The political situation has become more volatile since the AKP came to power. Focusing on the socio-political context of Britain and Turkey helps me understand how experiencing racism and discrimination in both countries has an impact on the children of refugees and immigrants, more specifically how the political situations in these countries affect their sense of belonging and relation to Britishness, Kurdishness and Turkishness.

In this chapter, I aim to delve into the political context of Britain and Turkey, including the ramifications of Brexit and authoritarian politics in Turkey on the transnational experiences of young people who were interviewed, to have a better understanding of the impact of racism on the experiences of children of refugees and immigrants in both settings. I also introduce the historical detour of migration from Turkey to Britain. To have a better understanding of the role of political circumstances in the sending and receiving countries on the young people's sense of belonging, the following sessions discuss the contemporary political context in Britain and Turkey.

Britain's 'hostile environment' immigration policies and Brexit

The origins of the 'hostile environment' are connected to Enoch Powell's[14] 'Rivers of Blood' speech in 1968, in which 'the immigration of non-whites from the former colonies came to be seen by Powell as a threat to British cultural homogeneity'.[15] The 'hostile environment' immigration policy was first introduced by Home Secretary Theresa May in 2012. She said that, 'the aim is to create, here in Britain, a really hostile environment for illegal immigrants'.[16] The 'hostile environment' immigration policy does not only target the 'illegal immigrants'; it has boosted discrimination against racialised minorities who have been living in Britain for their entire lives.[17] To make the lives of 'illegal immigrants' insufferable, the UK government introduced the Immigration Act 2014, which requires all landlords to confirm a tenant's right to remain in Britain before agreeing to rent property to them and temporary migrants entering Britain for more than six months to pay a health surcharge before entry in order to access the NHS. Two years later, the Immigration Act 2016 came into force, to require banks to check the immigration status of anyone when opening accounts. Through these measures, the government has created and recreated borders into the daily lives of migrants.[18] Everyday bordering that has developed as a result of the Immigration Acts 2014 and 2016 in Britain 'create and recreate new social-cultural boundaries'[19] and form the hierarchy of belonging between who 'belongs' and who 'does not belong'. The impact of these policies and anti-immigrant racism on migrants and racialised minorities has been terrifying.

Four years after the implementation of the 'hostile environment' policy, anti-immigrant discourse intensified following the Brexit referendum in Britain 2016. 'Taking back control of our borders' became British

Figure 2.1 A 'Vote Leave' poster in Salford. © Neil Theasby. CC BY-SA 2.0.

government policy, rather than a slogan.[20] It represented a chance to limit entry not only to EU residents but also to non-EU residents, especially Muslims.[21] Brexit is an expression of 'nostalgia for empire'[22] as referred to by Nadine El-Enany. In the wake of the Brexit vote, an increase in nationalism and racism against migrants and racialised minorities was witnessed.[23] Many eastern and southern Europeans, Muslims, dark-skinned refugees and racial minorities have experienced racist attacks in everyday life. As argued by Satnam Virdee and Brendan McGeever, 'Brexit and its aftermath have been overdetermined by racism, including racist violence.'[24]

The Brexit campaign was defined by concerns over immigration, especially the prospect of Turkey's membership of the European Union. In a Vote Leave poster, it was written that 'Turkey [population 76 million at that time] is joining the EU. Vote Leave, take back control.' It was also stated in the discourse of the Vote Leave campaign that 'murderers, terrorists and kidnappers from countries like Turkey could flock to Britain if it remains in the European Union'.[25] Additionally, Michael Gove made Islamophobic comments about the birth and crime rate in Turkey, claiming that immigrants from Turkey (Muslim) posed a threat to national security, as well as to public services.[26] The caricature of Turks (Muslim) has become a racial figure. Migrants from Turkey have become 'undeserved' migrants to whom 'the border is being opened up very selectively'.[27] Many British Turks in Britain have felt that they are no longer heroes who protected the businesses and streets in north London during the London riots in 2011;[28] they are seen as a threat and unwanted migrants.

After the controversial political poster claiming that Turkey was joining the EU and that many Turks would come to Britain, and comments about the Turkish birth rate and Turks being terrorists and criminals, I interviewed British Turkish people in London who migrated to Britain in the 1990s, to understand their thoughts about anti-Turkish slogans in the Brexit referendum. Ahmet[29], a kebab shop owner who migrated to Britain from Turkey in 1997, reacted as follows:

> We, Turkish people, are not like Roma migrants who beg on the street and do not work. We work very hard in this country. We pay the highest taxes. We do not get involved in any crime. We are not terrorists. We are not like other Muslim migrants. I think politicians should be aware of this. [British Kurdish]

Ahmet criticised the Islamophobic comments of the British politicians by making rather xenophobic comments about other migrants, which is an example of how hierarchies are visible in the ways migrants see each other. The distinction between Turks, Roma people, and other Muslims in Britain, as referred to by Ahmet, is that Turks are considered 'good', as they work hard and pay taxes, whereas other migrants are seen as 'bad'. Ahmet reproduces racial hierarchies between different migrant groups and associates the Turkish community with a 'good immigrant' dichotomy. The 'good immigrant' dichotomy is created by othering Roma migrants and other Muslim migrants by Ahmet, who recreates the racialisation and othering discourse of Brexiters. These forms of racial rankings, cultural racism or 'hierarchies of belonging', as suggested by Les Back and Shamser Sinha, are the product of the 'hostile environment', which makes migrants racist towards each other.[30]

Mustafa,[31] who migrated to Britain from Turkey in 1992, also made a distinction between migrants from Turkey and eastern European migrants:

> I do not understand why they do not want Turkish people to come to Britain. We [Turks] see Britain as our country. We work too hard. We are not like other migrants who are taking advantage of the system and living on benefits. We helped the police and protected our streets from rioters in 2011. We are not criminals. Our community organisations organise lots of activities to keep young people away from the streets and reduce crime. Not all Muslims are criminals. We are secular. [British Turkish]

Both Ahmet and Mustafa made a distinction between 'good' and 'bad' migrants, based on who contributes to the economy by establishing a business, working hard and paying taxes, and who benefits from the system. Highlighting the fact that migrants from Turkey protected the streets during the London riots, he referenced that they were successfully 'integrated' into British society and felt that they belonged to Britain, especially when he said 'our streets'. Mustafa tried to describe how the figure of migrants from Turkey has changed over time, from good' migrants in 2011 to 'bad', 'criminal' and 'undeserved' migrants in 2016. The politics of belonging is defined by Nira Yuval-Davis *et al.* as 'specific political projects aimed at constructing belonging to particular collectivity/ies, which are themselves being assembled in these projects, within specified boundaries'.[32] Such politics draw sharp distinctions between insiders and outsiders, construct the narratives of 'good' and 'bad' migrants, undervalue migrants into 'deserving' and 'undeserving'. Who is defined as a 'deserved' or 'undeserved' migrant changes depending on the conditional relationship between a state and the individual.[33] Within the past five years, not only have migrants from Turkey become 'undeserving' migrants, they have also begun to look down on other migrant groups. This phenomenon, as argued by Frantz Fanon, is a result of the dynamics of racism, where the oppressed may internalise the racism they face and end up becoming racist towards others.[34] When referring to being 'secular', Mustafa relates to being more Westernised and 'civilised' than other Muslim migrants. Both Ahmet and Mustafa internalised a racial hierarchy that is constantly reconstructed in Britain. Even though some migrants from Turkey believe that they pose less threat to British society compared to black and Asian people because of having a 'whiter skin' – as stated by Ceren 'the Windrush scandal is happening to black people. I have white skin, so maybe it will not happen to me' – they have realised that they are not safe either, especially during and after Brexit. Two years after the Brexit vote, what is known as the 'Windrush scandal' happened. As a consequence of the 'hostile environment' policy, black Britons known as the 'Windrush generation', who had arrived on the *Windrush* in 1948, and were granted an automatic right to remain in the country under the 1971 Immigration Act, were suddenly classified as 'illegal immigrants' by the Home Office. The Windrush generation had come as citizens and their landing cards – the only proof when they arrived in Britain – were destroyed by the Home Office in 2010. This left them without any documents to prove that they have a residence permit to reside legally in Britain.[35] The consequences of the 'hostile environment' for some of the victims of the Windrush scandal who were wrongly deported, detained and denied access to healthcare, and made jobless and homeless, were tragic and fatal.[36] The mistreatment of the 'Windrush generation' and the passing into law of the Nationality and Borders Act in 2021, which gives the government the power to remove British citizenship without prior notification, have shown that the naturalised status of minority groups in Britain is not secure and can be revoked, as a result of the 'hostile environment' policy. The distinction between 'citizens' and 'migrants' – although still available – has taken a different form and is transposed to 'the citizens who belong' and 'the citizens who do not belong' in the political language of the nation-state. Through these political projects, questions about belonging and identities are raised by the receiving states as well as racialised minorities. I explore how the 'hostile environment' impacts young people's sense of belonging and relation to Britishness in Chapter 6.

The global right-populist wave, of which Brexit is a part, actually includes a new kind of anti-immigrant opposition. It is possible to denote the traces of this on both sides of the Atlantic and on the whole of continental Europe. For example, even though the workers who went to Germany from Turkey say that they had very serious adaptation problems – they often referred to Germany as a 'bitter homeland' and a 'longing for *sıla* [homeland]' – they stated that they did not encounter any racism at first.[37] There are a few important points that are related to the case of Britain. Firstly, the wider German society tended to perceive Turkish migrant workers as a temporary solution to fill the labour gap at that time, and they called them 'guest workers' to point out the temporality aspect of their migration. Both the emphasis on temporality and the perception of instrumentality were visible. These guest workers were viewed as some kind of temporary tool in the eyes of the migrant-receiving state and society.

Secondly, the 'guest workers' may not have been faced with much open racism, but they are subject to clear and intense discrimination and labour exploitation. The living and working conditions of Turkish workers are so bad that they cannot be even compared to German workers' conditions. Günter Wallraff's book *The Lowest of the Low*[38] and documentary work *At the Bottom* show this very strikingly. But it is clear that migrant workers from Turkey are not yet aware that this is a form of exclusion and racism. In other words, the perception of a racial practice by the perpetrator and the victim is also determined by social consciousness. While one person may use racist discourse without even being aware of it, or even having such an intention, another may not even be aware of the discriminatory and racist practices in place where they live.

Thirdly, when these 'guest workers' went beyond 'doing their jobs' and started to be visible in various areas of social life (which is mainly a process that takes place after family reunification), they came across racist rhetoric more often. This situation shows that in a world built on a nationalist basis, two models – assimilation and isolation – are actually proposed for 'tolerating immigration'. In other words, immigrants are asked to assimilate completely and absolutely into the country in which they have settled, or immigrants are required to be invisible, to live a completely isolated life. Similarly, Americans' views about immigrants from Turkey were positive until the events of 9/11.[39] As with many irregular migrants in the United States, Turkish migrants living and working conditions were so bad that they could not be included in social life. This situation changed after the 9/11 attacks. It was remembered that the Turks are Muslims. In the climate of rising Islamophobia (to use the official discourse, 'the war on terror'), racist discourse and attacks began to rise against Turks.

Fourthly, Turks in Germany also say that the racist wave increased rapidly after the reunification of East and West Germany in 1990. Various political and social problems that emerged with the reunification of the two Germanys were inflicted on them. Political uncertainty triggered the fears of the wider German society. It is possible to draw parallels between this state of fear, uncertainty, the resulting hatred, and the psychology of post-9/11 American society and post-Brexit Britain. Hajo G. Boomgaarden and Rens Vliegenthart sums it up as follows:

> Traditionally, economic and immigration-related factors are used to explain support for anti-immigrant parties at the aggregate level [...] Some critics of immigration argue that the presence of immigrants may distort the national identity of the native population. That means that the native population opposes immigration because they fear they may lose their sense of belonging to their own nation, as represented by distinctive traditions, culture, language and politics.[40]

Confronting this new anti-immigrant format with a classical discourse, such as 'immigrants contribute to the country's economy' (as if they have such a contribution obligation), does not work either. As a matter of fact, this new 'hostile' climate is closely related to the loss of trust caused by xenophobic discourse and mainstream policies of the nation-states. As Martin Schain puts it, 'trust in politicians and institutions has been decreasing across Europe, it is not the fault of populist radical-right parties, but rather a symptom of broader societal trends that encourage their support'.[41]

The following part explores the Kurdish question and the rise of authoritarianism in Turkey to better understand the social and political context of Turkey to which the young people refer.

The Kurdish question and the rise of authoritarianism in Turkey

Kurds make up one-fifth of Turkey's population and are the largest ethnic group. Kurds have been experiencing high social and economic inequality and facing exclusion for a long time in Turkey.[42] The struggles faced by the Kurds have become known as the Kurdish question. This is a concept that refers to an ethnic conflict that existed before the establishment of the Turkish Republic, and has been at the centre of politics for more than 100 years, with its genesis in the late nineteenth century during the government of the Ottoman Empire. The conflict between the Kurdistan Workers' Party (Partiya Karkerên Kurdistan, PKK) and the Turkish state reached its peak in 1984, but since then has been ongoing, as the PKK demands greater cultural and political rights with the objective of establishing an independent Kurdish state. Under the AKP's governance, tension has risen between the Turkish authorities and the PKK. In 2009, the AKP government started discussions on granting cultural and linguistic rights to Kurds as part of the *Kürt Açılımı* (Kurdish Opening). However, this policy granted limited cultural rights to the Kurds and did not bring any solutions to end the conflict.[43] The AKP's liberalisation process did not last long. Since the third election of the AKP in 2011, the political and social climate has moved to a more neoliberal, populist and authoritarian style of governance.

The AKP's authoritarian and conservative populist governance led to the Gezi Park protest, one of the largest uprisings and social movements in Turkey's history, which started in the last days of May and continued throughout June 2013. Following the Gezi uprisings, the AKP's neoliberal, Islamist conservative and authoritarian governance under President Erdoğan's leadership increased. A two-year ceasefire between Turkey's government and the PKK collapsed in 2015 following a suicide bombing by suspected, self-proclaimed Islamic State militants – as a result of this attack, approximately 30 Kurds were killed near the Syrian border.[44] A year later, on 15 July 2016, Turkey witnessed a failed coup attempt. The Turkish government blamed the Gulen movement, which is a widespread and influential religious movement that owns foundations, associations, media organisations and schools in Turkey and abroad, for the failed coup attempt.[45] A few days after the coup attempt, the Turkish government declared a state of emergency. According to the Associated Press, Government of the Republic of Turkey, 251 people were killed and more than 2,200 people were injured resisting the coup attempt; 77,000 people were arrested after the coup for alleged links to 'terror' organisations; more than 3,000 people were sentenced to life in prison for involvement in the coup attempt; 35,000 people were convicted for links to the Gulen movement; more than 125,000 public sector workers lost their jobs; and 24,000 people were expelled from the military.[46]

Following the coup attempt, both the Turkish government and the PKK returned to the situation before 2015. The Turkish President increased air strikes on PKK militants in southeastern Turkey and also began conducting military operations in Syria against the YPG (People's Defence Units)[47] and the self-declared Islamic State, while the PKK continued attacks in the southeast of Turkey. Since the failed coup, Kurds in Turkey have felt that the level of racialisation and exclusion against them in Turkish society has rapidly deepened. For example, Murat, who is British Kurdish, mentioned the experience of his cousin in Diyarbakır, a Kurdish-populated city in southeast Turkey, after the failed coup: 'My cousin was displaced in Diyarbakır after the Turkish government started attacking the city. He had to move to Istanbul, where he has experienced racism at work and on the street when speaking Kurdish.' Kurds who have been experiencing racism, exclusion and racialisation since before the establishment of the Republic of Turkey are the most oppressed and marginalised 'indigenous group who questions nation-centric conceptualisations and borders'[48] during the history of the Ottoman Empire and the Republic of Turkey. Ipek Demir conceptualises the Kurdish diaspora as an example of 'transnational indigeneity' rather than understanding them only as 'ethnopolitical' struggles and violence within nation-states, referring to the 'we are here because you were there' sentiment, which highlights the colonial history and suppression they face.[49] Without understanding the colonial history of the Ottoman Empire and the modern history of the Republic of Turkey, it would be hard to explore the process of racialisation and the experiences of racism against Kurds in Turkey and abroad.

As mentioned in the previous chapter, during the 2017 constitutional referendum, Turkey's political regime changed to a presidential one and Erdogan's presidential rule came into being in July 2018. Since then, the era of one-man rule has made the AKP's Islamic outlook to be dominant in domestic and foreign policy, with evidence of rising conservatism that points particularly to women and the LGBTQ+ community as a target. Women resisted the populist conservative authoritarian politics of the AKP government against the abortion ban and achieved its withdrawal. However, due to these policies, Turkey pulled out of the Istanbul Convention, the Council of Europe's treaty on preventing violence against women and domestic violence, despite Turkey's long history of femicide. Women do not feel safe in Turkey: in 2022, 116 women were murdered by their partners, 75 women's murders remain unresolved, 37 women were murdered by family members, and 31 women were murdered by men whom women were trying to divorce or to break up with.[50]

The government justified its decision with claims that the Istanbul Convention was being used to 'normalise homosexuality', and that, as such, it was 'incompatible with Turkey's social and family values'.[51] This was one of the outcomes of the AKP government's hostility towards the LGBTQ+ community over the last decade. The government's pressure on LGBTQ+ individuals has significantly increased in the last few years. For example, the authorities have detained many LGBTQ+ activists and banned LGBTQ+ Pride events. In December 2022, Turkey's President called for a referendum on the constitutional amendment, mainly focusing on outlawing same-sex marriages. Due to the government's anti-LGBTQ+ rhetoric, LGBTQ+ individuals have increasingly been subject to hate crime in Turkish society.

In this section, I have summarised the recent political history of Turkey to have a better understanding of the Turkish context the children of refugees and immigrants are referring to when they talk about Turkey. As explained above, Britain's 'hostile environment' and the post-Brexit landscape, and Turkey's authoritarian and anti-Kurdish landscape, might impact how young people construct transnational activities with their parents' country of origin.

The next part focuses on the historical detour of migration from Turkey to Britain to have a better understanding of how Kurdish and Turkish communities have created transnational social and political links across the borders.

Historical detour of migration from Turkey to Britain

Much of the research on the so-called 'Turkish-speaking' population conducted in Britain has tended to conflate Cypriots, Turks and Kurds.[52] As Pınar Enneli, Tariq Modood and Harriet Bradley acknowledge in their research:

> [T]he term 'Turkish origin' is not right, because it does not cover those who are from Cyprus; nor is 'Turkish-speaking' because, for many Kurds, it is Kurdish, not Turkish, that is their primary language. If we use 'Turks and Kurds', this will omit the Cypriots. We use all three of these terms because no single term itself is satisfactory no other term. We mostly use 'Turkish speaking' for the majority of the people studied as their families do indeed speak some Turkish.[53]

Enneli, Modood and Bradley address the problem of combining Kurds with Turks, but they still define them as 'Turkish speaking', which does not take into account the political, cultural and ethnic differences between Turks and Kurds.[54] I will not use the term 'Turkish speaking' when referring to the ethnic identity of Kurdish youth as I aim to have an accurate description.

Migration from Turkey can be traced back to the late 1960s and early 1970s, mostly due to economic reasons. Migrants from Turkey were employed in the textile and food industries, which were run by Turkish and Greek Cypriots.[55] After this period, the number of migrants from Turkey increased throughout the 1970s.[56] The first migration movement from Turkey to Britain was to work in textile factories established by Turkish Cypriots, as stated by Hüseyin:

> After the 1960s, our population has risen to 80,000. At that time, there were some mainland Turks. In 1966–1967, one of my friends wanted to bring workers to work for his factory. We were bringing Turkish workers from Bursa and Izmir, Turkey. We were helping these workers find accommodation and construct social networks. They did not have the same problem as we had because we were here to help them. [British Turkish]

The main reason for migration in the late 1960s and early 1970s was economic, and first men migrated to Britain to work. After they settled, they brought their families over to join them in Britain. Turks who came to Britain in the early 1970s started to work at the textile factories owned by Turkish Cypriots. However, since the 1970s, especially following the military coup in Turkey on 12 March 1971, migration from Turkey to Britain was mostly political. As a result of this, the first political migration from Turkey to Britain started with young people who established socio-political networks in Britain. Besides the military coup in 1971, there was another political clash in Kahramanmaraş, a region of Turkey. This conflict was between Sunni and Alevi groups. These two groups have different interpretations of Islam and religious identity.[57]

In 1978, Sunni Muslims massacred Alevis in Kahramanmaraş. More than a hundred Alevi people were killed and many villages and houses were destroyed. In the late 1970s and early 1980s, a large number of Alevi from Kahramanmaraş migrated to Britain. It was the starting point of Alevi migration from Turkey to Britain; they constructed transnational networks among Alevi in Turkey, Britain and also in Germany. From the mid-1970s onwards an increasing number of people from Turkey started coming to London on their initiative using their social networks and kin relations. The third military coup in 1980 must also be recognised as a driving force for Turkish migration to Europe, especially to Germany and Britain. It was the second wave of migration from Turkey to Britain. The coup pushed many intellectuals, trade union activists and professionals to migrate to Europe, some seeking political asylum in Britain.[58] People who migrated after the 1980s came from the rural areas of Turkey, and differed from the migrants who came to Britain in the 1970s from the larger cities of Turkey. Those disillusioned with economic and political instability sought alternative places of work and residence. The process of migration has emerged from economic stagnation and political instability. Migration from Turkey was motivated by both economic and political reasons, while the choice of England as the migrants' destination was motivated by their social networks.

Even though there is no accurate record of the number of Turks and Kurds in Britain, it is estimated that the number of migrants from Turkey is around 200,000. The number of Turkish immigrants has changed at different times due to variable political situations.[59] The first arrivals of Turkish migrants worked with Cypriots and lived in the same areas. The reason for living in the same areas might be related to the need to be closer to other members of their communities, their relatives, and workplaces, and not being able to speak English. In choosing locations, knowing someone was important for newly arrived migrants, and so the number of Turkish migrants increased within certain locations, as stated by Ahmet:

> Lots of Turkish people live in London. My shop is in the Turkish area. I can't work in the centre of London, because I can't speak English. It will be difficult for me to communicate with people whose mother tongue is not Turkish. I have to work in the Turkish area with Turkish people. I don't have any other choice. [British Turkish]

Migration from Turkey rose again at the end of the 1980s because of the conflict between the PKK and the Turkish government, in east and southeast Turkey. As a result of this conflict, many Kurds were displaced from their villages and forced to seek refuge in Europe. While a significant number of people from eastern and southeastern Turkey came as students and with business visas, many others sought political asylum in Britain. The migratory status of Kurds differed from that of many Turkish migrants, as some of the latter migrated to Britain voluntarily, while the Kurds were forced to migrate as refugees. As in the case of Turks, Kurdish men arrived first in Britain and, after finding work, they brought their families to join them. After bringing their families to Britain, it became easier to construct social networks and socio-cultural spaces. Kurds suffer the highest levels of disadvantage compared to Turks because they were displaced.[60]

The number of Kurds from Turkey in Britain is usually estimated between 100,000 and 180,000, and the majority of them live in London.[61] The fact that Kurds are routinely registered as Turks by local authorities[62] leads to an undervaluation of their real number in Britain. Therefore, many organisations use the term 'Turkish-speaking community' when considering this population. However, Kurdish organisations do not accept this terminology, as explained by Ali:

> Kurds are a diasporic community. Many Kurds are living in London, and they are different from Turks and Turkish Cypriots. Our language [Kurdish] is also different from the Turkish language. We just have a Turkish passport. Turkish nationality tries to cover everyone, but Kurds are different from Turks. For this reason, we regret the terminology of the 'Turkish-speaking community' which excludes Kurds. [British Kurdish]

Ali's view about the term 'Turkish-speaking migrants' rightly addresses the reflection of the assimilation policy of the Turkish state even in the use of the terminology. As mentioned above, Kurdish migrants are political refugees in Britain because they left Turkey as a result of the ethnic conflict between the PKK and the Turkish state. The 'Turkish-speaking community' in London is heterogeneous and includes three different groups – Kurdish, Turkish and Turkish Cypriots – who are differentiated in their migration histories, motivations, languages, cultures, socio-economic status, religion, beliefs, political ideology and rural/urban division. Among these groups, Kurdish refugees take a strong stance on political activism and fight for Kurdish independence and rights. They have strong political awareness and levels of political activism.[63]

As a result of the increased amount of Kurdish and Alevi migration in the 1990s, settlement choices were affected by the political and ethnoreligious features of community members. In the last ten years, while Kurdish and Alevi migrants have settled in Harringay, Dalston and Stoke Newington, Turks have settled in Newington Green, which is the beginning of Green Lanes. After the settlement of significant numbers of Kurdish and Turkish migrants in Harringay, these migrants also established their businesses there.[64] In everyday life within the same locations, the Kurds and Turks interact with each other by establishing businesses or working together. As a consequence, marriages do take place between the communities, though the tendency is still to keep to one's own grouping. This is especially true of the Kurdish community.[65]

Figure 2.2 Window of a Turkish patisserie shop. Photo by author.

The mobility in social and economic situations, the increased number of migrants, and the diversity of jobs within the communities assisted Turkish migrants and Kurdish refugees in creating their own social space without the need for Turkish Cypriots. While each group constructed its own social space with regards to its political, cultural and social standpoint, at the same time their social spaces continue to interlink through economic and social exchanges at community organisations, etc. The ethnic and ideological divisions among Kurdish and Turkish communities are also reflected in their settlement patterns. For example, while Harringay and Stoke Newington are known as Kurdish, Kurdish-Alevi neighbourhoods, Newington Green becomes the settlement choice of nationalist Turks. Kurdish and Turkish communities constructed their own community organisations based on the political ideologies of their communities. These organisations represent both a similarity and an element of separation between the groups. I asked a journalist who migrated from Turkey to Britain in the 1990s about the scope of community organisations established by the first generation and their role in building transnational social and political links with Turkey He said the following:

> There are different organisations established by Turks and Kurds. These organisations work for the rights of their communities. For this reason, there is tension between the two groups. Whatever happens in Turkey between Turks and Kurds is reflected here and

in Europe. The tension is between the state sympathiser Turkish organisations and leftist Kurdish organisations. Turkish organisations which support the state do not even try to talk to Kurdish organisations. When there is no negotiation, there is tension. There is always tension between Turks and Kurds. [British Turkish]

The tension between Kurds and Turks is mainly because of the nationalists on both sides, according to Zehra:

At some point, Turkish women discriminate against Kurdish women, but it was not because of ethnic differences. It was related to ignorance about Kurdish people among Turkish women. They were saying that 'we came here earlier than Kurds, but they took over our jobs, houses'. The tension between these two communities is not too serious, but nationalist Turks and Kurds sometimes create problems. [British Kurdish]

The clash between different political standpoints and ethnicities in Turkey, such as anti-Kurdish discourse in the media and daily life,[66] has been reflected in the Kurdish and Turkish communities in London. For instance, whenever there is a demonstration organised by Kurdish people, some Turkish nationalists organise a demonstration against the Kurds, as stated by Helin:

Demonstrations in London are mainly held by Kurds because the Turks do not have any problems with the state. Turks rarely protested against Kurds. The latest tension between Turks and Kurds is because of *Newroz* – an ancient spring celebration for Kurds and Iranians. Turks do not let Kurds celebrate *Newroz* in Trafalgar Square. These kinds of things happen. [British Kurdish]

The political stands of these groups are also reflected in their social spaces. For example, in some cafes and restaurants in Newington Green there are Turkish nationalist symbols and posters. These political divisions have affected migrants' choices of which areas to settle in London. Although there are political divisions among Kurdish and Turkish communities, economic factors, for instance, working together, transcend the political separation among the communities. The ideological separation between Kurds and Turks is echoed in the politics of community organisations. The Kurdish community, compared to the Turkish community, was more active in establishing community organisations, raising their voices and speaking out about the situation of Kurds in Turkey and their political struggle.[67] Kurds, mainly, are mobilised around community organisations they established to increase the representation of ethnic identity and raise awareness for their political battle with the Turkish state and society over the democratisation of Kurdish people and gaining their right to speak Kurdish and express their ethnic and cultural identity. The community organisations, especially the Kurdish and Turkish Community Centre (Halkevi) and Kurdish Community Centre (KKC) put Kurdish resistance at the centre of their focus.[68] Halkevi is one of the main Kurdish organisations in London, founded in 1984 by the Kurdish community in Stoke Newington, Hackney. Since 1984, Halkevi acts as a substitute for the state, providing social work services, such as health support for the elderly, and organising cultural and social activities. Komkar, the Kurdish Workers Association, was established in 1990 by Kurdish migrants and, like Halkevi, the group aims to facilitate Kurdish cultural expression and, at the same time, support inclusion into the receiving country. Facilitating migrants in the creation of plural attachments can decrease fear of the unknown and fear of losing their roots. Community organisations play a crucial role in protecting ethnic identity and culture among migrants while also encouraging openness to other cultures and promoting inclusiveness. For example, organisations like Day-Mer contribute to the needs of communities by providing information on living in Britain and organising annual festivals that bring together different communities and ethnic groups. According to the director of the Kurdish Advice Centre, such organisations are essential in fostering cultural understanding. Day-Mer also has a political dimension, as stated by the president of the Day-Mer youth committee: 'These people [the members of Day-Mer] were politically active in Turkey; they immigrated to Britain for political reasons and had been involved in political organisations. They wanted to set up parallel structures in London, but some of these have been transformed into organisations tackling urban issues in north London.'

These organisations create a political space for Kurdish and Turkish first-generation migrants who migrated to Britain during the 1980s and 1990s escaping Turkey from violence, torture and imprisonment because of their political stance. The attachment with the country of origin, carrying out political networks with people who share similar political ideology in Britain and Turkey, becomes important for the first generation because they believe one day they will be able to return to a democratic and peaceful Turkey. Mahmut, who migrated to Britain in 1980 as a refugee, said, 'we [people who fight for a free and democratic country] always had a dream that one day we will return to Turkey. So, we always work towards making our country democratic and peaceful even though we are abroad.' However, for some of the first generations, being a member of a transnational community and sharing similar experiences in the settling society makes it difficult to consider returning home. As Ayla stated: 'the majority of Kurdish refugees and Turkish migrants say that they will go back to their country of origin, but they never do. As we are witnessing, many of them live in London for a long time.' Once families have settled in Britain, there seems to be a reluctance to return home. Returning seems difficult for migrants who have built their lives in Britain, and whose children have grown up and adapted to the receiving society. Families who raise their children in different societies and face similar challenges often experience difficulties in communication between parents and children, diverse socialisation processes, and intergenerational conflicts. Regardless of the social group they identify with, parents have strong emotional connections with their country of origin, whereas young people do not.[69]

Kurds and Turks have developed economic, political, social and cultural links that connect the settlement and receiving societies. For instance, there are local Turkish and Kurdish radio stations, free local newspapers published in Turkish, mosques, community organisations, shops selling CDs and books in Turkish, and restaurants and cafes serving Kurdish and Turkish food. Theatre groups and companies from Turkey perform at least once a month in London, and the Arcola Theatre in Hackney, run by Kurdish and Turkish artists, has generated interest, especially among the young. Many of these events are either organised or advertised by community organisations, said Ayşe who attends these socio-cultural events:

> There are many community centres, e.g. Halkevi, Day-Mer etc., and the Arcola Theatre regularly presents plays in Turkish for Turkish-speaking citizens. At the Rio Cinema, every year they hold a Turkish film festival and a Kurdish film festival. I attend the Day-Mer festival every year where they invite artists from Turkey to come and perform and, in the past, Kazım Koyuncu, Siwan Perver, Moğollar, and Kardeş Türküler performed. [British Kurdish]

The first-generation Kurds and Turks have built transnational socio-cultural links between the receiving and sending societies, and the Kurdish community in particular has established transnational networks that pursue their political goals. While the Kurdish community in London

Figure 2.3 Day-Mer's Culture and Art Festival poster. Photo by author.

has been politically active and spoken out about the struggles experienced by Kurdish people in Turkey, the Turkish community has not been actively engaging with the politics of Turkey as Kurds. This is the case in other European countries. As argued by Bahar Baser the Kurdish diaspora in Sweden is politically more active than the Turkish community.[70] Laurence Ossipow *et al.*'s[71] study has also shown that the Kurdish refugees who migrated from Turkey to Switzerland are more politicised than other refugees. Their ongoing battles for their rights and independence have become known especially due to their fight against ISIS in Syria, and the strength of the political mobilisation of Kurds in Europe distinguishes them from other refugees. In contrast to Turkish migrants, Kurds do not have a homeland of their own. While the perception of homeland refers to 'Kurdistan', not 'Turkey',[72] for others it refers to a small town or village.[73] Their transnational ties with the homeland often express their resistance against the Turkish state.

Conclusion

In this chapter, I have discussed the dynamics of the current political context in Britain and Turkey and their impact on the identity of young people with regards to Britishness, Kurdishness and Turkishness. The influence of the political circumstances in both the sending and receiving countries on the sense of belonging and transnational links of young people has in the past been under-examined. Through exploring the contemporary political context in Britain and Turkey, I aim to show how the young people's sense of belonging is shaped by the political context of both countries. As I explore in depth in Chapters 5 and 6, the lives of the children of refugees and immigrants are politicised as a result of the socio-political circumstances of Britain and Turkey. Moreover, I have sketched the historical and social backgrounds of Kurdish and Turkish communities in Britain to show the complexities of these communities divided into opposing groups, which are reflected in everyday life by their settlement patterns, everyday interactions and transnational socio-cultural and political links. In the following chapter, I focus on north London where Kurdish and Turkish communities settled to show what north London represents for young people from Turkey, and I discuss their identity-making practices through their relationship with the community and the neighbourhood.

Notes

1. See Kureishi 1990.
2. See Gilroy 2004: 165.
3. See Gilroy 1990.
4. See Balibar 1991: 47.
5. See Bhattacharyya *et al.* 2021: 21.
6. See De Noronha 2020.
7. See De Noronha 2020.
8. See Kellman 1973: 42–43.
9. See Orwell 1941.
10. See Mackay 2023.
11. See Esen and Gümüşçü 2016; Castaldo 2018.
12. The largest wave of demonstrations and civil unrest in the AKP era of governance in Turkey, which began on 28 May 2013 in protest at the gentrification plans for Istanbul's Gezi Park in Taksim, and then focused on the state of Turkey's democratic regression.
13. See Kirişçi and Sloat 2019.
14. Enoch Powell (1912–98) was a British politician who served as a Conservative Member of Parliament (1950–74) and was Minister of Health (1960–3), and then Ulster Unionist Party (UUP) MP (1974–87).
15. See Hickson 2018: 354.
16. Immigration, as highlighted by the Windrush scandal; written evidence from Faith Osifo (RHR0019). 12 September 2020. https://committees.parliament.uk/writtenevidence/12263/html. Accessed 2 January 2021.
17. See Yuval-Davis *et al.* 2018.
18. See Jones *et al.* 2017; Goodfellow 2019.
19. See Yuval-Davis *et al.* 2018: 229.
20. See Hayward 2020.
21. See Redclift and Rajina 2021.
22. See El-Enany 2016.
23. BBC 2019.
24. See Virdee and McGeever 2017: 1802.

25. See Stephens 2016.
26. See Boffey and Helm 2016.
27. See Yuval-Davis *et al.* 2005: 520.
28. See Beaumont *et al.* 2011.
29. First-generation immigrant.
30. See Back and Sinha 2012.
31. First-generation immigrant
32. See Yuval-Davis *et al.* 2018: 230.
33. See Anderson 2013.
34. See Fanon 1986.
35. See Goodfellow 2019.
36. See Olusoga 2021.
37. See Wallraf 1988
38. See Wallraf 1988.
39. See Kaya 2005.
40. See Boomgaarden and Vliegenthart 2007.
41. See Schain 2018.
42. See İçduygu *et al.*1999; Yeğen 2007, 2009; Saraçoğlu 2009, 2010.
43. See Christofis 2019.
44. See Centre for Preventive Action 2022.
45. See Al Jazeera 2017.
46. See Ibrahim 2022.
47. The People's Defense Units (YPG, also People's Protection Units) is the official army of Rojava–Northern Syria Federation.
48. See Demir 2022: 81.
49. See Demir 2022: 69.
50. See Büyük 2022.
51. See International Commission of Juries 2021
52. See Küçükcan 1999; Aksoy and Robins 2001; Enneli *et al.* 2005; Erdemir and Vasta 2007.
53. See Enneli *et al.* 2005: 54.
54. See Enneli *et al.* 2005.
55. See Atay 2010; Çiçekli 1998.
56. See Küçükcan 1999.
57. See Verkuyten and Yıldız 2009.
58. See Mehmet Ali 2001: 7–8.
59. See Küçükcan 1999.
60. See Enneli *et al.* 2005: 48.
61. See Demir 2015.
62. See King *et al.* 2008: 9.
63. See Demir 2012; Holgate *et al.* 2012.
64. See Mehmet Ali 2001.
65. See Küçükcan 1999; Mehmet Ali 2001.
66. See Saraçoğlu 2009, 2010.
67. See Baser 2014.
68. See Demir 2017.
69. See Küçükcan 1999, 2004; Portes and Rumbaut 2001; Levitt and Waters 2002; Kasinitz *et al.* 2008.
70. See Baser 2014.
71. See Ossipow *et al.* 2019.
72. See Baser 2013; Galip 2014.
73. See Demir 2012.

3
'My north London accent indicates my working-class background': north London, class, ethnicity and community

London is one of the most diverse cities in Europe, both culturally and ethnically, offering a multitude of spaces for minority communities, while retaining its status as a global hub.[1] For instance, Harringay, where many Kurds and Turks settled, has an ethnically diverse population and over 180 languages are spoken by Harringay residents; 30 per cent of Harringay residents do not speak English as their first language.[2]

North London, north of the River Thames, is where migrants from Turkey settled and are concentrated, mostly in the London boroughs of Harringay, Enfield, Waltham Forest, Southwark, Hackney and Islington. The majority of migrants from Turkey live around Green Lanes, which starts in Newington Green and extends to Winchmore Hill. A significant minority live in northeast London, in areas such as Hackney, Harringay, Dalston, Stoke Newington and Tottenham. They have built their lives within the borders of north London by establishing businesses, community organisations, Turkish and Kurdish language schools, shops, restaurants, cafes, and publishing local newspapers in their own languages. 'When we came here, there were not many Turks and establishments run by Turks. We made this place our home by opening Turkish restaurants, community organisations and food centres', said Hüseyin, who migrated to Britain in the early 1980s. As Steven Castles and Alastair Davidson argued, newcomers seek to construct a place that they can again call home.[3]

In understanding the sense of belonging and identities of British Kurdish and Turkish youth in north London, questions concerning their experiences of living within the community, their relationship with other communities in the area, and what north London means to them have become crucial. I contend that while north London, with its many Kurdish and Turkish communities, offers safety, security, and a sense of community for the children of refugees and immigrants, it also results in them being viewed as *Other* by white British people. As a result, the often dismissive 'diversity is so cool' attitude overlooks the experiences of racism faced by these young people. The children of refugees and immigrants frequently reconstruct their identities. These changes in identities are often influenced by how they are seen by others in relation to where they live. In this chapter, I argue that the children of refugees and immigrants living in the neighbourhoods of north London, which are dominated by Kurds and Turks, are constantly being reminded of their working-class and migratory backgrounds.

Class and ethnicity

The relationship between the perceptions and practices of diversity experienced by residents is studied by focusing on how people experience diversity in the neighbourhoods they live in.[4] In these studies, the positive perceptions of diversity are highlighted and diversity is appreciated in the neighbourhood.[5] For example, Susanne Wessendorf points out the notion of 'microspaces of conviviality' where migrants feel a sense of belonging with one another in a diverse neighbourhood on the grounds of shared interests including ethnic backgrounds, religions and languages.[6] This 'diversity is so cool' approach downplays the racism that is experienced by racialised minorities. To comprehend the formation of social relationships in a diverse neighbourhood, it is important to examine the existing hierarchies between racialised minorities and white British individuals, as well as the new hierarchies that are established between the different communities. Les Back explores the complex configurations of difference, naming it 'the metropolitan paradox',[7] by bringing racism to the centre of analysis.

When I asked young people about their experiences of residing in north London, particularly in Harringay, Hackney, Enfield and Tottenham, many referred to commonality rather than diversity. For example, Aydın, who was born and raised in Harringay, touched on the commonality of residents about class:

> The majority of people who live in Harringay, Green Lanes, are poor, and many people here are unemployed. The number of homeless

people in this area is rising. Ethnic minorities living in Harringay experience poverty and social tensions on a daily basis. Although people living in Harringay are from different countries and have different ethnic identities; they are working-class. They understand each other because they know what poverty is. [British Turkish]

Aydın pointed out that the commonality among people living in Harringay is being working-class and having a migratory background. This is not unique to Harringay; the young people living in other parts of north and northeast London touched on their similar experiences and how they are perceived by others. Hackney, in northeast London, is one of the most culturally and religiously diverse neighbourhoods of London, consisting of black, non-British white, and Turkish and Kurdish communities, and has significantly more people of Jewish and Muslim faiths and a higher proportion of people with no religion.[8] According to a recent report published by Hackney Council,[9] nine out of ten Hackney residents say that Hackney is a place where people from different backgrounds get on well together, and 'its diversity and multiculturalism are the main factors contributing to residents feeling proud of the borough'.[10] The positive attitude toward diversity among the residents of Hackney is also highlighted by Wessendorf: 'I noticed that newcomers are not usually asked about their origins, even if they look different or speak with an accent.'[11] This approach to diversity is conceptualised as 'commonplace diversity',[12] which refers to the acknowledgement of differences of origin, language and religion, but class is not mentioned. The valorisation of diversity often dismisses the impacts of socio-economic inequalities and hierarchies of belonging on the everyday lives of racialised minorities. Hackney, for instance, has gone into a regeneration programme that has created and reproduced widening social and economic inequalities and destabilised existing community networks.

Ceren has been living in Hackney for 20 years and remembers the transformations that the neighbourhood has gone through and how these changes have affected how she is perceived:

Hackney is a very different place from what it was 16 years ago. I grew up in Hackney. It is very close to central London. The council estate we live on is quite diverse. There are not just Turks and Kurds but, across the road, there are houses worth millions. So on the one side, there are council houses, and just across the road, there are wealthy people's houses. You can literally see the divide, which is quite weird to see. When walking in the area you can see that the ethnic people and white people position themselves away from each other. That was quite interesting to experience. [British Kurdish]

Explaining how the gentrification process in Hackney has been affecting its residents, Ceren pointed out whiteness as well as class. The experiences of Ceren indicate a clear division between 'white people' and 'ethnic people' in terms of class, race and belonging. Who belongs to Hackney has changed and the division among communities has become much more visible, especially after the gentrification process, which has been happening for some time now. Class becomes one of the most prominent boundaries between people in a diverse neighbourhood. It is also associated with a specific accent that shows that they are working-class.

The studies[13] promoting the positive perceptions of diversity in the neighbourhoods of London do not touch on the experiences of racialised minorities, especially when they commute from their neighbourhood to central London for work and study. However, these young people experience discrimination and racism because of their accent, ethnicity and migratory background when they are in the city of London. Aliza pointed out her experiences of racism after moving out of north London:

> At the secondary school in Enfield I attended there were a lot of Turkish and Kurdish students at that school; of course, there were no white people. I never felt like an outsider at secondary school. At the university, there are groups like Pakistanis, Indians and Somalis. It is so multicultural and I do not feel like an outsider at the university either. Only during boarding school, I felt that. Even at the university, we have 'the white girls', we call them 'the white girls' because they just stick within themselves. I really wanted to be friends with them. I was friends with them at some point, but clearly, they do not want you there, or maybe I feel like I do not identify with them. Black people also live in council estates. They understand why we live there, but you always have to explain to a white person saying that my parents are from here, they came here because of this and so on. You always have to explain yourself to people who are not ethnic. I understand that their background is different as well. I have a level of understanding that they are different people and looking at it from a multicultural background makes us understand things easier and have a level of empathy. But when they are only from one particular background it is not the same. [British Kurdish]

How Aliza makes sense of 'multiculturalism' is about how multiple ethnic groups live in a society and understand each other. The feeling of not being an outsider next to Pakistanis, Indians and Somalis at university was inverted when she was around 'the white girls'. The level of understanding of each other and having an equal relationship without hierarchy has not been reached in multicultural and diverse neighbourhoods of London. The practices of 'everyday multiculturalism'[14] are discussed in line with living together in tolerance despite all the differences.[15] This simplistic understanding of multiculturalism does not challenge its reductionist version of culture, considers its complexity and gives equal weight to the experiences of racism and structural inequalities when thinking of diversity.[16] The children of refugees and immigrants reconstruct their identities in everyday life and these identifications are often influenced by how they are seen by others in relation to where they live. As stated by Alana Lentin, there is a risk of ignoring 'how allied concepts of such as culture and diversity have been incorporated into the denial of the significance of racism'.[17] When young people move out of the segregated multicultural environment and interact with white British people, they feel like an outsider. Multiculturalism does not involve the white majority in its practice. Aliza's experiences show that white British people are not included within multicultural settings, because when she is around them there is a lack of understanding of her background and socio-economic situation, which is opposite to the feeling when she is with 'ethnic minorities' from different backgrounds. This correlates with what Nasar Meer and Tariq Modood argue: 'multiculturalism speaks only to and for minorities'.[18] Aliza is framed as a cultural *Other* as a result of 'encouraging different ethnic or religious groups to form 'parallel societies' and 'the illiberal exclusion of minority ethnic communities'.[19]

The discussions around diversity and multiculturalism do not pay much attention to the role of class when interacting with one another. 'Do you think that class also plays an important role when interacting with white people?', I asked. Aliza replied immediately:

> Yes, white people who do not live on council estates are always seen as richer. When I was born, I was in a council estate. It is because our parents were immigrants who did not have enough money to begin with. Sometimes when you want to invite your white friends to your house, you think that what they are going to think about my house. It should not be like that. I know that our house is lovely; my parents worked so hard for it. But at the same time you are thinking whether they are going to judge me because I have been

> to their house and their house is big. You are thinking about these very small things and this is really about class, then it is also an ethnic thing. These are interlinked. Because when you are white you are middle-class, but when you are ethnic, you are not necessarily middle-class. Also when you go out to eat with them, they say 'are you holding the folk in the right hand?; why do not put a napkin on your lap?' We did not learn these things. We had a spoon to eat whatever was put on our plates. I noticed these things when I went to their house and thought that they are going to judge me. These people know these things; they have grown up with that culture. We are not. Even these little things make you an outsider. [British Kurdish]

Class differences create extra boundaries between whites and racialised minorities. Aliza's intersecting ethnic and class identities made her question her sense of belonging to the neighbourhood, and society in general. Her accent is another signifier of her class background and the neighbourhood where she lives. As she put it:

> I have done my best to make sure that I do not sound like I am from north London. When I was younger at primary school, one girl said 'you have got such an accent'. From that point onwards, I started crying, and I said to myself that I was going to do my best not to have an accent. It still affects me to that day what she said to me. I put on a bit of an accent and I use bigger words. I try to speak with a posh accent. [British Kurdish]

Like Aliza, Ceren also put on an accent and use particular words to sound like the white people because she does not want to sound like the *Other*. She said: 'with Turkish and Kurdish friends, we all make a joke about it. We say "we do not want to sound that we are from Green Lanes". We try to make sure that we do not sound like we are from Green Lanes because it is so obvious that we are from Turkey.' 'Why you do not want to be known that you are from Turkey', I asked Ceren. She replied:

> Because the majority of Turkish, Kurdish people live in north London, a place where is associated as being of lower status. People pick up from my accent where I live, which reveals not only my ethnic background, as everyone knows that North London is where Turkish and Kurdish people live but also my working-class background. [British Kurdish]

Because her socio-economic background and ethnicity are instantly recognisable by white British people as soon as she speaks, she feels like an outsider. Likewise, when Aliza is around white people she does her best to be fluent in English so as not to sound like the *Other,* but when she speaks English at Day-Mer, she said 'I do not care how I am talking.'

From a different perspective, Barbaros stated that his class background reveals commonality with white British young people:

> I was brought up in Muswell Hill. A very middle-class environment. I got to do nice things, got to see nice places. I kept being reminded of how lucky I was. I went to school with white middle-class kids. We had lots of opportunities. Not all kids are getting to horse riding or summer art camps. As a result of going to these places, common memories are created. When you are in a middle-class circle, they say, 'Ohh … you also went to this summer art camp, I did as well.' So, you have these points of discussion and this leads to identity creation as well as strengthens a sense of belonging. [British Turkish]

While belonging to the same class creates commonality through participating in similar lifestyles, religion and ethnicity still play a big role in how he was seen by white British people. Barbaros said:

> I remember my day in year one. I was wearing a small Quran. People asked what is your name? I said 'Barbaros'. They said 'what?'. Then I said 'Barba-ros'. They said 'what is that?' I knew all of a sudden that I will always be different, and I do not want to be different. [British Turkish]

'What does being different mean to you?' I asked Barbaros. After thinking for about two minutes, he responded: 'it means that I will not be fully British, which is scary because I might be discriminated against because of my background, name and religion'.

Yaz also feels different from white British people despite their[20] class background and their posh accent, which they put on in order to be accepted:

> I change my accent where I am depending on the context and to whom I am speaking. I did drama and spent so many years on how to change the way I speak. I am well-trained in copying accents. I can have a posh accent if I am with English people. It helps but also questions what I normally speak. All my English is from school. We

are very middle-class but we did not start as middle-class. We lived in a council flat for a few years. My parents squatted before that. They were granted some sort of social mobility, which meant their experiences shaped how I see money and wealth. I went to a private school, but I was not like the other kids at the school. Class matters a lot, but also it is a difficult thing to understand. [British Turkish]

'Why did you feel different from other children at school?', I asked them. 'It is because I was always asked this question: "Where are your parents from?" and kept reminded that I am the *Other*. It is maybe because of my name or because I am not white enough.'

Even though Yaz and Barbaros belong to the same class background as their white English peers, enjoying access to all resources and opportunities as their white peers and speaking fluent and accentless English, they still feel different. Class matters and is visible in the everyday experiences of young people, but race, ethnicity and religion also have a big impact on how these young people are racialised. While sharing a similar class background with their white peers reveals commonality for Barbaros and Yaz, it also creates boundaries in the case of Aliza and Ceren. The elimination of class differences does not guarantee that these young people will be seen as British as their white peers.

Paying close attention to racism as a powerful attribute of modernity, Stuart Hall indicated that 'late-modern' societies produce differences that are often experienced by racialised minorities.[21] The experiences of young people living in diverse, multicultural neighbourhoods of London demonstrate that they are defined by their cultural origins or as an object, as stated by Ceren: 'You are just seen as an object. White people always ask about our culture and whenever we talk about it, they say "oh my God, that is so cute …." We are more than our cultures.' Understanding the experiences of migrants and minorities in cultural patterns helps create hierarchies and emphasises 'cultural essentialism'.[22] The experiences of young people about living in a diverse and multicultural neighbourhood illustrate 'forms of division and racism within forms of multicultural coexistence'.[23]

Culture and politics

'I never had any English friends. I tried my best, but it is quite difficult in north London because there is not a large English population', said Kemal, British Turkish, highlighting the predominantly Kurdish and

Turkish composition of the neighbourhood when I asked about his experiences of living in north London. Supporting this point, Ali, British Turkish, said: 'North London is like a little Turkey. It is better to know Turkish in north London than English.' He added: 'I enjoy living in north London because I can eat Turkish food, joke about Turkish politics and some of the traditions.' North London is more than a neighbourhood for young people; it offers various cultural resources to Kurdish and Turkish communities, including the local Turkish radio stations, a few local newspapers published in Turkish, mosques including the London Islamic Turkish Association mosque, Süleymaniye mosque, Aziziye mosque, Alevi Cultural Centre and Cemevi, Yunus Emre Institute, AlaTurca (Arcola Theatre's Kurdish and Turkish speaking theatre group), Kurdish and Turkish community organisations, football clubs, shops selling CDs and books in Turkish, food centres, restaurants, cafes, etc.

Theatre groups and companies from Turkey perform at least once a month in London, and the Arcola Theatre in Hackney, run by Kurdish and Turkish professionals, has generated interest, especially among the young. When I asked young people how they describe north London, many referred to the socio-cultural space constructed by the Kurdish and Turkish communities. For example, Ateşcan experiences Turkish culture in Harringay where his father used to own a Turkish restaurant called *Nazar*. He knows most of the Turkish restaurant owners in Harringay through his father, and enjoys spending time in Harringay and eating Turkish food. Another way of practising culture is through speaking Turkish at home, watching Turkish television channels on satellite and listening to Turkish music. As he put it: 'I listen to more Turkish music than English music. My mum is a singer so, when we go somewhere, she was putting on Turkish music and I was listening to it with her. I have also learned the importance of Turkish traditional songs from Alevi culture.'

Like Ateşcan, Harringay represents most of the things about Turkishness for Yaz:

> When I think of north London, Harringay comes to my mind. It is like Little Istanbul. As China Town or Little Italy in New York. It is like here for Turkish people. You walk and you see Turkish lawyers, Turkish bakeries, and Turkish flower shops. For any Turkish needs, you can just go there. It is nice to see and to be there. I think there should be more integration. I understand how these communities operate. I associate again with comfort, food, etc. This kind of life is too superficial. It is not actually my nature. I go to these places with my family to eat. Getting a fix of culture. I have been there

with partners with whom I am in queer relationships. We may hold hands here but when we are there, I actively said 'let's have some distance'. So again, my multiple identities have issues with each other. [British Turkish]

Yaz's description of Harringay as 'Little Istanbul' refers to a space that signifies homogeneity and cultural consumption. Despite its homogeneity, this constructed space offers some sort of comfort for the Kurdish and Turkish communities who live in this neighbourhood and those who are settled in other parts of London – such as being close to food and off-licences, where products from Turkey are sold, *hamam* (Turkish baths), barbers, and so on. These spaces, at the same time, reflect the social and political identities of Turkey. Ateşcan, Yaz and Fatma mentioned their awareness of traditional discourses of the community in their everyday lives and of how they act accordingly. As Ayşe Çağlar states, German Turkish youth accept the ghetto metaphor to define their relationships with places and this leads to negotiation because they do not adopt the concepts of the dominant discourse.[24] Yaz, who is in a queer relationship, found it hard to be able to openly hold hands with her partner in the neighbourhoods where the Kurdish and Turkish communities live. Yaz also highlighted the socio-cultural differences between themselves and the Kurdish and Turkish communities in Harringay. These socio-cultural differences are enhanced by Turkish state policies of polarisation, which cause tension between secular-liberal and religious-traditional people, and leads to the rapid growth of anti-LGBTQ+ rhetoric.

Besides this, Yaz also referred to class as a distinguishing identity category between themselves and the community in London. Similarly, Barbaros also said he finds it difficult to fit in with the Turkish and Kurdish communities in north London due to class differences. He said the following:

> I definitely do not feel similar to the Turkish and Kurdish communities in north London. The types of Turks that my dad is friends with in Turkey are different to the types of Turks I have conversations with within these neighbourhoods. The fact that he is a military kind of guy, he is in different circles. I am placed within different circles. It is not the Turkey I know when I go there. People I know in Turkey are like very *efendi, efendi* [polite and formal]. Always talking in the third person. Definitely, it is different. I am always cherry-picking the culture when I go there. I would say our class backgrounds are different. It sounds terrible to say, but I identify

> with the food but do not identify with the people serving this food to me. That's not the Turkey I am used to. [...] I want to make a point about how space and places make such an important idea about where you grow up. Growing up in Muswell Hill is a bubble, you go to Muswell Hill primary. All relatively similar stuff like housing and then I learned that I am middle-class. When I was visiting working-class areas, I realised that it is a different life. I actively see the kids at my mum's school. They would not like me, they would be swearing and doing crazy things. [British Turkish]

Both Yaz and Barbaros pointed out the class difference between themselves, their families and the Kurdish and Turkish communities in Harringay. As explained in Chapter 2, migrants from Turkey are heterogeneous in terms of language, socio-economic status, cultures, religion, beliefs, migration motivation histories and political ideology. Secular and religious division has increased a lot since the AKP came to power, and this division is reflected in the everyday lives of these groups, which then create polarisation and cause social tensions between the groups, as discussed in Chapter 2. This polarisation in Turkey is mirrored in the everyday lives of Kurdish and Turkish communities in London, and makes most of them feel estranged from each other. Yaz and Barbaros did not grow up in Harringay, Hackney, Enfield or Tottenham. Since they were born they have been living in the middle-class neighbourhoods of north London, which have fewer Kurds and Turks, and no established transnational socio-cultural spaces. Their relationships with the Kurdish and Turkish communities and links to the neighbourhoods where the communities are concentrated are limited to Kurdish and Turkish food consumption.

Apart from being at the centre of Kurdish and Turkish cultural consumption, there is a lot of tension, as in Turkey, between the Kurds and Turks living there together. This is explained by Murat:

> The political debates in Turkey about Kurdish identity or the role of the current government get sort of reflected in north London. There is always tension between Turks and Kurds in Turkey, and this is reflected in the streets and in the schools of north London. These people watch Turkish television, these people do lots of things that the Turkish community does. Unfortunately, friends sometimes split because one is Turkish, and the other is Kurdish. I have seen lots of rows, abuse and even physical fights. [British Kurdish]

Likewise, Ayşe stated:

> There is sometimes tension between Kurdish and Turkish students. Some Kurdish students say that they are from the Kurdish community and do not wish to approach the Turkish community. When I was in secondary school, it was extremely common to have fights between Turkish Cypriots and Kurds. There were not many Turks where I grew up. There were mainly Turkish Cypriots and Kurds. During the rare occasions when they faced each other, they fought the blacks and the Kurds. The norm was to make friends from within your ethnic group. [British Kurdish]

Political and social tensions between Kurds and Turks in Turkey are imported into north London and may increase from time to time depending on Turkey's current political stance towards the Kurds. Transnational media is discerned as the main tool by which young people engage with the Kurdish conflict in Turkey. Even though the political separation between Turks and Kurds is reflected in the structure of the community organisations and settlement patterns, both groups mainly live in north London, close to each other. Murat stated, 'I really enjoy socialising in the Turkish and Kurdish communities.' Similarly, Aliza referred to the importance of being a part of the community in north London:

> As long as you say I am Turkish or Kurdish, people say from north London. I do not think it is a bad thing. It is nice, as we are all here. You want to be close to your family. So one person moved here, and others followed. It is good that the Kurds and Turks live in the same neighbourhood and work together. [British Kurdish]

Aliza's expression of 'close to your family' refers to the social connections, emotional support, friendship and shared experiences of having a migratory background that exist between the Kurdish and Turkish communities living and working in the same urban space. The embeddedness in its local and daily environment transcends their cultural differences and makes it possible for the Kurdish and Turkish populations to bond. In another respect, as a result of living in the Kurdish and Turkish neighbourhoods since an early age, Aliza said that she has constructed close ties, especially, with the Kurdish community from Day-Mer:

> Sadly, I have not made friends with as many different ethnic people as I could have. So, I do feel like I was quite secure in my Kurdish

bubble. A lot of the friends I have now are my friends because our parents met in Day-Mer and our parents continue being friends and then we ended up being friends. It is simply because you can relate to them so much more than anyone else. It is the whole relationship thing. We are all children of refugees from Turkey. Our parents are Kurdish. They [the Kurdish youth] understand. It is so much easier to be around them. At university, I have Kosovan, Lebanese and Pakistani friends. My closest friends are still my Kurdish friends. I wish it was not, but it is how it is. You just feel closer. [British Kurdish]

When Aliza is with other young people who have parents of the same Kurdish background, their shared experiences such as their parents' motivations for migration, status as refugees, and challenges faced as children of refugees make them bond. This understanding and connection are also rooted in their upbringing, cultural practices, and involvement in the Kurdish community through family and community organisations. As Murat noted, they are all 'children of refugees from Turkey' and their shared experiences allow for a deeper understanding and connection:

I have more things in common with friends from the Kurdish and Turkish communities. Our families had immigrated to England in the early 1990s; we all speak Turkish at home, we all probably watch the same Turkish channels, and the ways we grew up are similar, so we have more things in common. We become friends not because we had more things in common. […] I really enjoy socialising in the Turkish and Kurdish communities but also I enjoy living in north London, I am so used to the environment. I would not want to live in Turkey. It is probably just because I have been living in north London since I was born. I believe I should continue living here because I made friends and built a social life here. I am sure if I only lived in Istanbul, I would say the same thing about Istanbul and I would not want to live in north London. [British Kurdish]

Murat's primary identification with north London, where he was raised, still lives and builds his social life, makes this place home for him. This specific urban space plays a crucial role in the everyday life of young people because they have built their social lives and friendships, and have a feeling of comfort and safety there.[25] Besides these positive sides of living in north London, Murat also mentioned the role of shared experiences that are associated with having a transnational background, such as being children of immigrants, watching Turkish television channels, speaking Turkish at home and growing up similarly, in constructing a sense of belonging to a local space. Similarly, Ateşcan identifies with a particular local place in London where he built friendships:

> Grahame Park is where I grew up. It is my home, my identity. I was born in Enfield and then my first house was in Edmonton, a council flat, then Wood Green, and then Grahame Park. There were lots of people my age. I started going to school there. I have a sense of belonging to this place. The place has changed a lot. It was greener in the past now there are lots of buildings. So, I identify more with its greener version. [British Turkish]

Most young people who have been living in north London since they were born or from an early age have constructed their social life in this specific urban district. Friendships were built with the people living in the same area, they have gone to school in the same area and they are familiar with all the shops and institutions established in this specific urban district.

School is a crucial part of the everyday life for young people and a place where they can socialise with their peers, who may or may not come from different backgrounds, and negotiate their participation in the receiving society.[26] Floya Anthias notes that Greek-Cypriot and Asian youths experience a sense of isolation from English youths.[27] This isolation is associated with feeling *Other* and is strengthened by the experiences of racism. Les Back stresses that the experiences of racism among racialised minority youths in a multicultural environment should be taken into consideration.[28] The Kurdish and Turkish youth mostly attend neighbourhood state schools that are close to their homes. In London, these schools are situated in Harringay, Islington and Enfield.[29] The neighbourhood determines both the type of household and the type of schools where children are registered. This structure creates social and cultural homogeneity, which might contradict their 'multicultural' purpose and lead to the reproduction of social inequalities. While Portes and Rumbaut's study[30] show that schools promote diversity by having children from various ethnic backgrounds in certain neighbourhoods, Waters[31], Anthias[32] and Goulbourne *et al.*[33] indicate that the school environment can be homogenous and static.

The homogeneity in schools dictates friendship choices. Many young people have stated that their classmates from the same ethnic background tend to form their own groups. For example, Ali, British Kurdish, who has been living in Enfield, remarked on the importance of having Kurdish friends in school, said: 'When I am with English friends, they do not understand why I need to be at home at a certain time as they think it is weird. I prefer to hang out with friends from my own background because we understand each other better.' Like Ali, Seda also prefers to hang out with her British Turkish friends:

> There are two or three Turkish girls in my classroom; I don't think I would hang out with anyone else. Not to be racist, but you get along better with people from your background. They speak my language, I can sit down and chat with them and share my feelings. What matters is that we speak the same language and nobody can understand us. [British Turkish]

Speaking the same language and sharing similar experiences, such as growing up within similar socio-cultural backgrounds, living in the same neighbourhood and having similarities in life patterns bring these young people together in sharing their 'transnational habitats'.[34] This is a common feeling among young people from a transnational background. They might find it challenging to socialise with people from different backgrounds, as they fear being discriminated against. However, they recreate racial and ethnic boundaries between themselves and members of other groups; Seda's negation 'not to be racist but …' is a symptom of a racist discourse that reflects a structural problem rather than an individual one.

The inability to speak English properly is the most common reason for young people to socialise with people from the same ethnic background. According to Goulbourne *et al.*, 'a shared ethnic background and similarly lived experiences appeared to be the most important factors shaping some of British-Italian closest friendship networks'.[35] Similar experiences, such as mutual understanding, trust, and sharing transnational backgrounds are also some of the reasons invoked by young people in relation to choosing friends from the same ethnic background. This attitude can also be motivated in some cases by exclusion and racism experienced at school, as Anthias argues: 'the more the experiences of exclusion in British society, the greater the likelihood that many young people would construct themselves in ethnic terms'.[36] In other words, feeling a part of a group is a way to overcome discrimination and racism in the school environment, as mentioned by Zeynep, living in Harringay:

> I do not feel that I really fit in at school. With other classmates I get on well, my friends comprise people who are not originally British.

> I did not choose my friends according to their nationality, but it does seem to be the norm for 'foreigners' to stick together. When I was in secondary school, I encountered a racist peer who disliked me because of my background and made jokes about my background, I felt excluded and my education suffered. Since then, I prefer to be friends with people from the same background. [British Turkish]

Similar experiences were also mentioned by Ceren, living in Hackney:

> I went to a state school. I received racist comments from people from ethnic minority backgrounds. Brown and black people make you feel uncomfortable also by saying you are an immigrant. In my school, there are some white middle-class people and everyone else was from different ethnic groups so we were like a token person, a token Muslim girl, a token black person, a token Kurdish girl, a token whatever. I was not friends with any of the white people there. We were never connected. They were not bad people but you could see the differences and how teachers treat children differently. Teachers, for instance, are not in communication with our parents. The white parents were always the classroom governance, they were deciding how things should be done. The little things like not being chosen by the teacher. They had rules about hairstyles which often targets black girls. If I am insecure about my work, never being the smart one, or being chosen by the teacher because always white students were chosen. It continues into the university as well. I cannot break the feeling of being out of place. [British Kurdish]

Zeynep and Ceren felt like outsiders in the school environment because they found it difficult to fit into any established student groups. They experienced what Les Back describes, in the case of Vietnamese youth in London, as a new form of racism that includes new groups who are excluded and marginalised in specific areas.[37] This often occurs, according to Mehmet Ali, through the behaviour of peers and teachers.[38] In their case, the label of 'foreigner' leads them to seek support from their peers of the same ethnic background. Ceren's narrative of being uncomfortable around black and brown people – because of the assumption that she is an immigrant – and how the white students and racialised students are treated differently at school show how belonging is divided hierarchically between racialised students, and a lack of solidarity between the racialised students against the unequal treatment they receive at school. Moreover, both Zeynep and Ceren stressed the difficulty of trying to fit into groups of white people as a result. Aliza also mentioned similar experiences to that of Zeynep and Ceren during her study at a boarding school in London. She said the following:

> I went to a boarding school for two years which was populated by rich white kids. I felt that I am quite confident. I could hold myself if there is racism. But even little things like I was told, such as 'you are a terrorist', 'you do not have a country', were examples of pure racism because they never say these things to each other. I felt if someone has a weaker character, they could not handle it. My parents and brother have always told me that this is who you are and you need to be proud. There are small remarks like 'OMG, you are hairy'. It was a little joke but there were big meanings behind it. […] When I went to their house for example I always felt like an outsider because I am ethnically different from them. Their parents were not engaging in conversations with me that much. I do not speak to anyone from that school. After all, I drifted apart from them because I was different. I do think it is to do with religion. You are a terrorist comment was made because of religion or 'why you are not wearing a hijab'. I am not Muslim, I am an atheist. What are you talking about? It does not matter. Even if I am Muslim they should not be making these jokes. It is an ethnic thing, but it is also the whole Muslim thing. It is the Middle East thing. These kids in boarding school are grown up in a big bubble. They are only friends with each other. Having Turkish or Kurdish going in their community is so foreign to them. I feel like I challenged the ideas of someone like ethnic. Weirdly, that I did not see it as racism at that time but it was racism. [British Kurdish]

Aliza studied in a homogenised environment at school, which she described as a 'white space'. In this space, she was reminded that she is the *Other*, foreign and not British. Forming groups with people from the same background was motivated by the fear of discrimination, as highlighted by Aliza, Murat, Ali, Seda and Zeynep. All of them attended school in the neighbourhoods of Harringay, Hackney, Enfield and Tottenham, which are considered multicultural.[39] However, their experiences of racism, particularly in school, have led them to form friendships with others from their backgrounds for reasons of understanding, security, and solidarity. Ceren, for example, felt excluded due to class differences with her white peers at school:

> I did not choose my friends according to their nationality, but it does seem to be the norm for 'foreigners' to stick together. I am sometimes scared that my name or background will somehow affect my prospects. If I were to encounter a racist person, say a teacher who disliked me because of my background, I would feel bad and my education would suffer. [...] I would feel very angry if they discriminated against me. [British Kurdish]

Ceren discussed the general experiences of Kurdish and Turkish young people in schools, as well as her own experiences of being excluded from resources at school due to their ethnic identity and migratory background. Kurdish and Turkish youth in London fall into disadvantaged groups at school due to their ethnicity and class background.[40] Stressing the difficulty of fitting into the white space as a Kurd, Ceren also referred to class differences as a significant barrier to her inclusion at school. She continued:

> For me being surrounded by white middle-class students at school. We were in one corner of the classroom and they were in another corner. We had a conversation with the teacher saying you should not be in this part of the classroom. She tried to merge it but she made it worse because we were away from the friends we feel close to. The school really changed over time to adjust to the needs of white middle-class students. In the beginning, there were so many free trips to go and do things. By the time I was in year 11 the only trip that was left was skiing in a state school that was not underfunded. Can you pay £500 for a skiing trip? Skiing is not an immigrant consumption, it is a white middle-class consumption, and £500 for a ski trip is a luxury for working-class people. Always white middle-class students went. Consider earning £8 an hour and £500 for skiing is too much. [British Kurdish]

Ceren's experience illustrates that racialised minorities are affected by social inequalities more than others. She pointed to the intersection between migration and class inequalities, especially when saying 'skiing is not an immigrant consumption', and highlighted that belonging to a working-class family and having a migratory background have automatically put the children of refugees and immigrants into the category of *Other*. Ceren added:

> I am working-class and a child of a refugee. Because of my class and migratory background, I am more likely to experience

discrimination and other things which make me start the world from minus one automatically. Most definitely my class background has a massive part of my identity. Even if we get a certain level of income, we will not be able to let go of the cultural side of class. That will always be there. Once I earn a certain amount of income, I categorise myself as a middle-class person. In terms of culture, I have always been working class because I have not grown up with a middle-class income, and I am a minority. I do not know middle-class labels or participate in the social events middle-class people attend. [British Kurdish]

Ceren's experiences highlight the phenomenon of 'the new racism'. This refers to forms of discrimination and prejudice that are based on political discourses about migration and racialised minorities that centre on culture, religion and class rather than skin colour.[41] Ceren pointed out that, as a working-class child of refugees, she will always be perceived as an 'outsider' in British society.

'Some organisations are too radical ... find it difficult to identify with their politics': community organisations at the heart of north London

The community organisations established by the first generation of Kurdish and Turkish migrants play a crucial role in continuing political resilience, connecting people from the same background and keeping young people 'away from the streets'. Community organisations offer different sets of attachments with the country of origin, which could be political, cultural, religious or social, and which influence the relationship with the country of origin. For instance, community organisations with a political background reinforce not only ethnic identity but also political incorporation.[42] Community organisations instil a sense of ethnic identity and provide cultural resources.[43] According to Philip Kasinitz *et al.*, belonging to ethnic organisations is automatically associated with transnational practices, because community organisations are structured to transmit cultural values and the practices of the country of origin to migrants, especially to the 'second generation'.[44] This is illustrated by Goulbourne *et al.* in the case of young Caribbean migrants.[45] The political connotation is particularly prevalent in the case of Kurdish and Turkish communities, as their organisations are structured according to their political ideologies, religions and cultures.

Community organisations solidify transnational links and reinforce solidarity with the people of the country of origin.[46] Goulbourne *et al.* show, for instance, that Italian migrants in London participate in two types of community organisations – Catholic churches and left-wing trade unions – because of a sense of solidarity with other Italians.[47] Both types of organisation run similar activities for Italian migrants. In the case of Italian organisations, a sense of solidarity and socialisation are more crucial than political representation.[48]

There are diverse community organisations within the Kurdish and Turkish communities in terms of their structure, that is political and cultural, but, unlike the Italian community, their activities represent and are linked to their ideologies. The political emphasis of left-wing Kurdish and Turkish and right-wing Turkish organisations compared to other groups such as Italians is more visible and more obviously reflected in their socio-cultural activities. According to Gökçe Yurdakul, Turks in Germany establish politically-oriented associations to support their political standpoint.[49] This can also be said in the case of left-wing Kurdish and Turkish and right-wing Turkish community organisations in London, where political separation among communities is also visible and each organisation reflects their political ideology on a transnational level.

Political representation plays a crucial role in these communities. This political nature of organisations is reinforced in this case by transnational connections created with other organisations established by the Kurdish and Turkish first generation in Europe, especially those in Germany. As explored in Chapter 2, Kurdish and Turkish communities are politically divided, so organisations that are established by these communities also represent different ideological standpoints. Mehmet Ali explains that nationalist Turks establish their organisations and weekend language schools to spread a sense of national identity, whereas Kurds establish their organisations to carry on their resistance for ethnic and cultural rights.[50] The ideological separation between Kurds and nationalist Turks is reflected in their separate structure. While Kurdish organisations hold seminars about Kurdish issues in Turkey and protect their language through Kurdish language courses, Turkish organisations are more likely to promote national culture through language and history courses and the celebration of national days. The organisations were set up to meet the needs of the specific communities, but some have become vehicles for the propagation of various ideologies. Their foundational purposes differ from each other, and each community has its own organisation.

The general aim of community organisations is to strengthen ethnic ties among young people, by making them practise the culture, especially through learning language,[51] and by delivering socio-cultural activities. Community organisations provide different methods of establishing transnational links for migrant communities, such as creating a social environment where they can discuss the social and political issues in the country of origin and the problems that the Kurdish and Turkish communities face in London. Although most of these organisations are orientated toward political activities, some – the Kurdish and nationalist Turkish groups in particular – also combine cultural activities, including language courses. As Russell King *et al.* point out, 'at present, the Kurdish language and identity are largely promoted through community organisations'.[52]

Many community organisations established by the first generation provide Turkish or Kurdish language courses for young people. For instance, the Cyprus Turkish Association was the first community organisation established in London in 1951. It aims to provide Turkish language courses for the children of immigrants, with a mission to promote national identity and culture among the migrant community by transferring this knowledge to the young people.[53] There are currently around 20 Turkish weekend schools located around north and south London, for adolescents between the ages of 10 and 17. Language is thought to be a key element in promoting cultural identity among young people in the case of the Kurdish and Turkish communities.[54] Besides language training, these schools offer classes in Turkish history and culture. Weekend language schools play an important role in spreading nationalist ideology to young people. Esra, British Turkish, used to attend a Turkish language school over the weekend and remarked on its nationalistic standpoint: 'We sing our national song "İstiklal Marşı". We do folk dancing, we have Turkish lessons. We talk about Turkish culture at the Turkish school and it brings Turkish people together.' Her statements emphasise that language schools create a mental relationship with 'Turkishness'.

These organisations and Turkish weekend schools aim to cultivate a sense of Turkish identity and protect it from what some see as the undermining effect of British culture. Aslı expressed her frustration about nationalist Turkish community organisations and weekend language school's attempt to 'glorify' Turkish culture:

Some organisations and weekend schools are annoying; I do not think that they make you a good person or somebody who is more informed about what is going on. There are organisations that try

> to make Turkish and Kurdish people more aware of London. In a Turkish weekend school, one speaker said that all Christian countries will be flooded and the Islamic world will flourish and that will be heaven on earth. She was a teacher and I would not want to have a teacher like her. This was an extreme case. I was very young at the time and do not remember the name of the organisation. Some of the organisations (nationalist ones) harp on what a wonderful culture we have, that we must protect it and not become British. [British Turkish]

Aslı's uncomfortable experience with an organisation imposing its nationalistic views indicates that these organisations aim to circulate religious views and Turkish nationality among young people because they fear that the children of immigrants may lose their cultural heritage.

Apart from Turkish and Cypriot Turkish nationalist organisations, there are also Kurdish organisations that are political and reflect on Kurdish–Turkish conflicts. The activities of Kurdish organisations aim to strengthen ethnic identity among the population, by establishing Kurdish language courses and history courses. Day-Mer, for instance, was set up in 1989 to help Turkish and Kurdish communities with everyday problems in London – for example, filling out the application forms for housing and residency applications – but it also has a political dimension. Members of Day-Mer had been politically active in Turkey and had migrated to Britain as refugees for political reasons, and had been involved in political organisations. Murat has been attending the events organised by Day-Mer since he was a child and said that members of Day-Mer wanted to set up in London political organisations that are similar to those in Turkey, but some of these had been transformed into organisations tackling urban issues in north London. Highlighting the important role of Day-Mer in her life Aliza said:

> I was born in Day-Mer. My parents were involved in the set-up of this organisation in 1989. My brother was one of the first kids coming to Day-Mer. [...] I am glad that there is Day-Mer, so that we can meet with Kurdish youth. I feel more Kurdish because of Day-Mer. I have always been around it. It keeps bringing back my Kurdish identity. If I would not have a community centre, it would be just me and my family, I might not have any Kurdish friends. When I speak to my other friends from other cultures they feel more British because they do not have a community centre that would bring them to their culture. [British Kurdish]

Day-Mer is strengthening Aliza's relation to Kurdishness and is one of the main sites where she socialises with Kurdish people. Through Day-Mer she has constructed a strong connection to the Kurdish community compared to her friends from other ethnic backgrounds who do not have a community centre. She also mentioned different political standpoints of Kurdish community organisations and groups that she negotiates her relation to those organisations:

> When I was younger I tried to integrate myself with Alevi youth but I did not connect with them at all. I wanted to be a part of the Kurdish and Alevi communities, but I could not. The issue is that Day-Mer is politics based rather than ethnicity or religion based, whereas Kurdish is Kurdish and Alevi is Alevi. You learn sema[55] and I cannot identify with it. I can identify more with Day-Mer. [...] When I am around people from the Kurdish community centre I feel different. When I was younger we used to go to demonstrations; I never feel part of that because they were too radical. They were all about Apo [Abdullah Öcalan, leader of the PKK]. I could not identify with that. They were so radical, so crazy. I only care about human rights. I feel like this is the only place I can identify with because people here are politically, religiously and ethnically from the same mindset. Whereas Alevi is too Alevi and Kurdish is too Kurdish for me. I feel closer to people at Day-Mer. [British Kurdish]

Intragroup ideological divisions between the Kurdish organisations in London are negotiated by Aliza by having a one-dimensional focus that is either ethnicity or religion. For Aliza, Day-Mer is an organisation that is based on politics rather than ethnicity or religion; not having a 'too radical' ideology on Kurdish political movements or focusing too much on religion. This differentiates Day-Mer from other Kurdish and Alevi organisations, which makes her associate with Day-Mer more than other organisations.

Ceren also referred to the ideological differences between Kurdish and Turkish organisations in London:

> I used to come to Day-Mer for saz [a Turkish plucked instrument] lessons and do folklore when I was five or six. I started working at Day-Mer a few months ago. To distribute brochures for the forthcoming events at Day-Mer, we used to go to Halkevi and there are all these Kurdish political people, and posters of Abdullah Ocalan, so I felt overwhelmed. We went to Aziziye mosque, which represents

> the ideology of the Turkish government, to hand out leaflets and I felt overwhelmed. It was too much of something. I did not know what to do, or how to ask and was afraid I say something wrong. If I go to a church, I really do not care. When it comes to a mosque I am scared a little bit. [...] My parents never send us to Cemevi or Alevi Federation or Kurdish centres because they were too scared that I could be too much of one thing and Day-Mer was the midpoint. It was perfect. My family is Marxist, so Day-Mer makes sense for that. Day-Mer is an organisation where I learn about Kurdish culture, and I feel more Kurdish because of Day-Mer. It reminds me of my multicultural background rather than a strong ideological standpoint associated with the Kurdish political movement. But some Kurdish organisations have a strong political ideology and I feel like the Kurdish language courses here are from a particular political institution. I would like, for instance, my kids to learn Kurdish but I would not like to send my kids to Kurdish language courses because I do not know what exactly they talk about in these courses. [British Kurdish]

The Kurdish and nationalist Turkish organisations' political and ideological divisions make Ceren feel alienated and she finds it difficult to identify with them. These sharp ideological and religious divisions – on the one hand, the 'radical' approach to the Kurdish movement and, on the other hand, Turkish Islamic nationalism – are reflected in their organisational structure and constructed intra-group division among young people. Both Aliza and Ceren emphasised that they do not identify with the Kurdish organisations that are only based on Kurdish activism and ethnic identity, as for them Kurdishness represents more than those aspects – such as having a multicultural background, a feeling of safety, being a member of a community, friendship and resistance. As they have not experienced political tension like their parents, and have not lived as a racialised minority in Turkey, their understanding of Kurdish activism is different to that of their parents. Pointing out the ideologies of some Kurdish and Turkish community organisations, Ali also mentioned that these organisations are not about being Turkish or Kurdish:

> I cannot say that all of the organisations established by Kurds and Turks are good. Some community organisations try to impose their ideologies on young people. For instance, there are community centres in Newington Green that have a fascist ideology and there are community centres that are Kurdish nationalist. These

organisations do not aim to bring the communities together, they instead create polarisation between the Kurdish and Turkish communities. We, the children of immigrants, have not lived in Turkey and experienced the struggles our families did. So, these ideologies do not mean anything to us. I go to Day-Mer to socialise with Kurdish and Turkish youth and attend activities that bring us together. Socialisation is the main thing for me. [British Kurdish]

Ali's point about not being associated with the ideologies of these community organisations is related to not being directly involved in the political battles of his parents. Similarly, Mehmet also finds the ideologies of some organisations too radical. He used to go to Halkevi to keep out of trouble on the streets and to learn more about the Kurdish political movement, but he realised their values and beliefs are radical. He stopped going to Halkevi after he started questioning his identity. 'What aspects of identity did you question when attending Halkevi?', I asked Mehmet. He said the following:

> Halkevi was an important connection to Kurdishness along with how I learned about my Kurdish identity from my parents. I used to attend a theatre course there, but I learned more about Abdullah Ocalan and PKK than about acting. I was interested in learning drama with other Kurdish young people, together, but I was bombarded with the organisation's nationalist Kurdish ideology. I know that our parents and the Kurds in London had struggled a lot in Turkey – some experienced torture and systemic violence. I understand why they still prefer to fight against the suppression of their cultural rights and to speak Kurdish, but some organisations promote radical ideologies to young people during social activities. I have found it difficult to associate with these ideologies. [British Kurdish]

Like Mehmet, Mustafa, British Kurdish, also said that organisations like Halkevi and the Kurdish Association are like 'guerrilla organisations'. Mehmet and Mustafa stopped attending Halkevi because its ideological viewpoint overwhelmed the social activities. The meaning they give to Kurdishness, which is discussed further in Chapter 6, and how they relate to it is beyond Kurdish political mobilisation and activism. This does not imply that they ignore the Kurdish political struggle, as both stated that they participate in demonstrations and engage in political activism to a certain extent. These community organisations transmit

Kurdish identity, culture and political awareness to young British Kurds, but their involvement and identification with Kurdishness differ from that of their parents and other first-generation refugees.

Community organisations play an important role for young people to construct a sense of belonging, especially for youth who do not feel they belong to British society, as in the case of Elif, British Turkish, who looks for a space where she feels safe and secure. Moreover, community organisations appears to be a safe zone against the experiences of racism in Britain. As Stuart Hall argued: 'identity politics had to do with the constitution of some defensive collective identity against the practices of a racist society'.[56] Like Elif, Nazım also believes that it is hard to live without a community centre: 'These community centres are the backbones of the community itself. It represents our culture. Nonetheless, we should always remember where our parents come from and our culture, because it will guide us.' Community organisations that have transnational links with the social, cultural and political elements of Turkey are also sites that help create a collective spirit among British Turks and British Kurds in London, which makes them strong through unity and offers safety and security. They are the backbone of the community. Young people attend community organisations under the influence of their families, who are members of those organisations; but at the same time, they change organisations or stop participating if it does not correspond to their viewpoints. The main aims of some community organisations are to spread their political ideologies, so some of their political activities for young people reflect political divergences, as stated by some of the young people. But others mainly develop socio-cultural activities for young people to socialise and also build solidarity between each other and other racialised groups. Young people demonstrate their ability to negotiate their relations with community organisations and reject them if they feel uncomfortable with their ideologies, as the ideologies of community organisations do not always match the expectations and perceptions of young people. This is the case with Ateşcan:

> Before university, I was a part of the British Alevi Federation. I was a part of the youth committee. We were going to cultural camps. There were guest speakers about Alevism. We learnt about what Alevism is. All Alevi youth from the UK were joining the camps. Then I started university and gave priority to my education. I sometimes attend Cemevi. I am a proud Alevi. I do not attend other organisations because they have a strong political identity. The British Alevi

> Federation has the least political identity among others. But when Gezi Protests happen we all went to the protest in London because we all had one aim. [British Turkish]

In their everyday lives, young people are engaged in reaffirming their ethnic identity through their relations with families and community, while at the same time being able to create identification across national boundaries. As a result, young people find themselves in a process of constant negotiation in terms of choosing which community organisations to attend and which activities to participate in. While some young people prefer to participate in community organisations that reflect the political struggle, ethnic identities and religious beliefs of Kurdish and Turkish communities, others, such as Barbaros and Yaz, engage with collectives and movements that raise global awareness. For instance, Barbaros is a member of Greenpeace, a couple of other environmental movements and the British Palestinian movement. His reason for choosing to participate in these groups is the issues they are focusing on: 'I have chosen to participate in these groups because they were focused on the issues I was interested in, they educated me, create a plan or gave me avenues of interest to hook, narrow-minded my interests or develop them; helped me validate my opinions, and supported me.' Likewise, Yaz also chooses collectives and groups to be part of based their interests:

> I am a part of LGBTQ+ and various art collectives. I know there is Yunus Emre Institute. I am familiar with some of the north London groups for women especially, but [I am] not part of them. I know that there is an Arcola theatre and they have an Alaturka group. There are so many second-generation people whose parents do not have any English or have little English, so these organisations connect them to society. It is easy for them to get lost, so these organisations hold on to youth. I have not been part of them so cannot speak from experience. These organisations are especially important because the school system generally does not care about these individuals. I think they [schools] do not know enough, they do not have a special interest to know. These organisations pick up a lot of work that schools should be doing. [British Turkish]

Both Barbaros and Yaz are familiar with the community organisations available to the Kurdish and Turkish communities in north London and what these organisations offer to these communities. However, due to their lack of engagement with these communities, they do not attend the activities that the organisations facilitate. They prefer to participate in groups and collectives that are in line with their interests, rather than taking a part in community organisations. Yaz stated that these organisations do a good job of connecting the Kurdish and Turkish people to British society. Yaz also highlighted that these organisations step in when the schools are unable to provide support to the communities.

I also asked young people what their views were about the future of British Kurdish and British Turkish youth and the communities. Their answers indicate that the future for these communities is hopeful. Touching on the importance of continuing education for British Kurdish and British Turkish youth, Ceren stated that 'many of the young people are interested in going to university, getting professional jobs and branching out from what the family business is. I am hopeful as many young people are keen on education.'

Like Ceren, Aliza is also hopeful for the younger generation. She said the Kurdish and Turkish communities had not developed themselves as they should:

> Most of the kids in the community wanted to be off-licence owners. There are still a lot of young people who want to be off-licence owners. This really upsets me because this shows we are not going to develop ourselves as a community. Education is a way to develop ourselves. I have eight cousins and only me and my brother went to university – everyone else has dropped out. This makes me so sad because they have so much potential, but they choose to work at off-licence shops. I believe the younger generation will carry on education, have a profession and be in a better position than their parents. I do have hope. [British Kurdish]

Barbaros also agreed that the Turkish community will improve, especially in starting new businesses. However, Barbaros does not give full responsibility to the community regarding how they should develop; rather, he believes Britain should be more open to acknowledging different cultures:

> It depends on the generation. There will be more integration based on business. Turks will move out of catering, this is already happening. Turks I know working in the restaurant are very business-minded. Some are opening organic vegetarian fruit shops, others open flower shops. That will happen more when Turks are more

comfortable, and become more adventurous. I still think the catering industry will always be there as well as off-licences and cabs. If Britain becomes more open and acknowledges more cultural nuances within the country, then maybe Turks would give up their cultural identities more because they feel less pressure to hold onto them. Perhaps the reason we hold onto them so much is that we want to make sure we do not lose them forever. If it is acceptable, then you do not feel that kind of necessity and pressure to represent two or three generations. [British Turkish]

Thus, pointing out the role of policies in Britain on the future of migrant communities, Barbaros suggests that Britain should be more accepting towards different cultures. This will make Turkish people in Britain move away from their socio-cultural spaces and be more open to change. Similar to Barbaros, Yaz also used the word 'integration' when talking about Kurdish and Turkish communities' transnational socio-cultural spaces in Harringay, without referring to what it means. The nationalist mindset often perpetuates a number of intellectually flawed ideas, one of which is the notion of 'developed nations' versus 'underdeveloped nations', where the 'nation' is arrogantly placed highlighting superiority. This powerful and hierarchical concept leads to a tolerant attitude towards identities seen as inferior or superior, while showing open disdain for those considered inferior. A prime example of this can be seen in popular culture, such as football, where racism, xenophobia, Islamophobia, sexism, anti-Semitism, anti-immigrant sentiment, homophobia, etc., are widespread and visible. While African black football players in Turkey are subjected to racism[57], the situation for a Canadian black football player, for example, is different; he is praised for his professional demeanour, being a good family man, and being a team leader. These exclusionary practices and hate speech clearly reveal prejudices about the origins of immigrants and their children. Even though, the concept of integration is widely used in migration studies to examine the settlement processes of immigrants, it remains unclear.[58] Young people who use the term 'integration' refer to state-mandated processes of integration, which highlights 'assimilation into whiteness'.[59] While Barbaros believes there is a need for integration, Aliza worries that the next few generations might lose their identities, and not learn about and practise Kurdish culture:

> I feel we are breaching our cultures. People are marrying people from other cultures and kids are becoming more English. I am ok with it. I am fine but I also think that the next few generations will

lose all about our culture. I would happily marry someone who is not Kurdish or Turkish – as much as I really want to [marry someone who is Kurdish or Turkish] I could end up with someone who is not. I would not be able to teach Kurdish culture that much. This is sad. [British Kurdish]

All of my participants care about their backgrounds, where their parents came from and what their heritage means to them, and highlighted that if they have a family they want their children to speak the language, know where they come from and what that means, and keep connected with Turkey. One of the main reasons for these young people to hold onto their backgrounds might be that they do not feel fully British, so then they must be Kurdish or Turkish, or at least be competent with these identities. Turkishness and Kurdishness offer an alternative category for self-identification where children of refugees and immigrants do not strongly identify with Britishness or feel less British.

Conclusion

In this chapter, I have examined north London in-depth as a social space where Kurdish and Turkish communities have settled and to show what north London represents for the children of refugees and immigrants and how it affects their identity-making processes. The identity of north London constantly prompts the political and cultural repertoires of Kurdish and Turkish communities. While reaffirming their ethnic identities through attending community organisations established in north London, young people transform traditional discourses of the neighbourhood into their everyday lives; they respond to and negotiate these discourses on their own terms. The narratives of the children of refugees, predominantly of Kurdish origin, say that north London reminds them of their class and migratory backgrounds. Class is one of the most important forms of categorisation that creates boundaries between these young people in a diverse neighbourhood, because when they move out of north London they experience discrimination and racism due to their accent, ethnicity and migratory background. I have discussed these experiences within the context of multiculturalism and have argued that, on the one hand, north London represents safety, security and communality for the children of refugees and immigrants; but on the other hand, their association with the neighbourhood puts them into the category of *Other* in the eyes of the white British people.

Therefore, the 'diversity is so cool' approach dismisses the experiences of racism that these young people face.

After describing how north London affects the way young people are viewed by others, I have explored what north London means for British Kurdish and British Turkish youth, and how they experience living within the community. The polarisation of society in Turkey is mirrored in the everyday lives of Kurdish and Turkish communities in London, and makes most of them feel estranged from each other. Through looking at north London in-depth as a social space that offers transnational elements, I have also looked at the role of community organisations as a crucial transnational resource, which brings the socio-cultural and political aspects of Kurdishness and Turkishness by emphasising their political identity to the identity-making processes of young people. The children of refugees and immigrants find themselves in a process of constant negotiation in terms of choosing which community organisations to attend and which activities they should participate in. While some young people prefer to participate in community organisations that reflect the political struggle, ethnic identities and religious beliefs of Kurdish and Turkish communities, others engage with groups and collectives that raise global awareness of the resistance of Palestinians and LGBTQ+ individuals. Moving from particular neighbourhoods of London, I focus in the next chapter on how the children of refugees and immigrants view London and how they respond to the multicultural discourse they encounter in the social context of London.

Notes

1. See Parkin 1999; Smith 2001; Cattacin 2006; Dahinden 2009.
2. See Harringay Council Report 2021.
3. See Castles and Davidson 2000.
4. See Valentine 2008; Noble 2009, 2011; Wessendorf 2013, 2014.
5. See Wessendorf 2014.
6. See Wessendorf 2016.
7. See Back 1996.
8. See Hackney Council Report 2020.
9. See Hackney Council Report 2020.
10. See Hackney Council Report 2020.
11. See Wessendorf 2013: 411.
12. See Wessendorf 2013.
13. See Vertovec 2007; Wessendorf 2013.
14. See Wise 2009.
15. See Wessendorf 2013, 2014; Wise and Velayutham 2014.
16. See Lentin and Titley 2011; Back and Sinha 2016; Neal et al. 2019.
17. See Lentin 2014: 1270.
18. See Meer and Modood 2011: 13.

19. See Meer and Modood 2011: 33.
20. Non-gendered pronouns are used when referring to Yaz.
21. See Hall 1993.
22. See Hall 1992.
23. See Back and Sinha 2018: 25.
24. See Çağlar 2001.
25. See Zhou 2004; Ehrkamp 2005.
26. See Portes and Rumbaut 2001; Levitt and Waters 2002; Kivisto 2003.
27. See Anthias 2002.
28. See Back 1996.
29. See Mehmet Ali 2001.
30. See Portes and Rumbaut 2001.
31. See Waters 1999.
32. See Anthias 2001; 2002.
33. See Goulbourne *et al.* 2010.
34. See Guarnizo 1997; Vertovec 2001; Wessendorf 2010.
35. See Goulbourne *et al.* 2010: 73.
36. See Anthias 2002: 492.
37. See Back 1996.
38. See Mehmet Ali 2001.
39. See Wessendorf 2014.
40. See Enneli *et al.* 2005.
41. See Goldberg 1990; Balibar 1991; Gilroy 2004; Solomos 2022.
42. See Kibria 1997; Portes *et al.* 1999; Mehmet Ali 2001; Horta 2002; Portes *et al.* 2008.
43. See Mehmet Ali 2001; Takenaka 2009; Goulbourne *et al.* 2010.
44. See Kasinitz *et al.* 2008: 261.
45. See Goulbourne *et al.* 2010: 107.
46. See Küçükcan 1999; Kasinitz *et al.* 2008; Goulbourne *et al.* 2010.
47. See Goulbourne *et al.* 2010.
48. See Goulbourne *et al.* 2010.
49. See Yurdakul 2006.
50. See Mehmet Ali 2001.
51. See Mehmet Ali 2001; King *et al.* 2008.
52. See King *et al.* 2008:19.
53. See Lamb 2001.
54. See Kibria 2002; Goulbourne *et al.* 2010.
55. The whirling dervish ceremony is the inspiration of Maulana Jalaluddin Rumi as well part of Turkish custom, history and beliefs.
56. See Hall 2022: 230.
57. See Şimşek and Sayman 2018.
58. See Robinson 1998; Castles *et al.* 2002; Goksel 2018; Şimşek and Sayman 2018.
59. See Favell 2019.

4
'I enjoy the diversity of London but also feel excluded': London, conviviality and racism

The city of London includes various adjectives in its definition, such as multicultural, global, superdiverse, postcolonial, cosmopolitan and metropolitan. The use of these adjectives and their meanings differ from person to person depending on what sorts of experiences they have gone through about living in London. Similar to other postcolonial cities, London is attractive to migrants from former colonies as well as other countries; however how it is experienced varies. While it represents opportunities and wealth for some, it reminds of poverty and racism for others. London is defined as 'a place of stark contrasts' by Les Back and Shamser Sinha, as they stated:

> London – the United Kingdom's city of migrants – is a place of stark contrasts. It is home to global elites and Kensington oligarchs who buy up to million-pound homes as investment opportunities without any intention of ever living in them, while just a few streets away fugitives from war and poverty from all over the world live in cramped and neglected council estates.[1]

Referring to the unequal experiences of Londoners living in London, Les Back and Shamser Sinha bring another, and often less discussed, aspect of London, that is different from the view that supports how 'diversity is cool', without touching on how diversity and multiculturalism also construct hierarchies of belonging among Londoners and new forms of racism.[2] The hierarchies of belonging create a space for young people to experience racism, which is mentioned by many British Kurdish and British Turkish youth living in London.

In this chapter, I show the experiences of the children of refugees and immigrants living in London, particularly focusing on how they make a home in London and how they respond to the multicultural discourse they encounter in the social context of the city as well as how they negotiate and interpret their experiences of racism in the city. London itself becomes a constant reminder of being 'foreign' for the children of refugees and immigrants who experience racism and exclusion. I argue that young people's experiences in London show the realities of racism that shape everyday life within multicultural conviviality. The multicultural exchanges they experience when interacting with people from other ethnic and racial backgrounds they meet in the shops, parks, cafes and council estates of London do not offer a shared narrative in which their ethnic identities are rendered ordinary. The word multicultural refers to being culturally heterogenous; however, when it meets with -ism, multiculturalism is converted into a political doctrine.[3] The dilemma of multiculturalism claiming both difference and equality within itself is referred to as the 'multicultural question' by Stuart Hall.[4] As discussed in Chapter 3, the main criticisms that multiculturalism has received are its ignorance of the experiences of racism, exclusion of the whites and increased division between 'us' and 'them', which are very much related to the 'multicultural question'.[5]

The dilemma of multicultural London: 'But where are you originally from?'

But where are you originally from?', I hate this question and London is one of the main cities in Britain where I was asked this question. I am not sure if they ask this question because Londoners are from different countries or whether they asked this to make me feel like an outsider and that I am not actually from here. For instance, in London, in the supermarket, at the university, in the restaurant, especially white British people, often ask me where I am from. I say I am from London. Then they say where exactly are you from? I say I am Kurdish. Then they say so you are from north London, aren't you? Everyone knows that Turks and Kurds live in north London. People make jokes about north London, but they had no connection to north London. If a white middle-class person jokes about it, I would not like it; but if someone from a similar background I would be ok with them making a joke about it. [British Kurdish]

Ceren explored how the question of 'where are you from?' makes her feel like an outsider and added 'We are more than our cultures' when referring to how she is seen by white British people she interacts with and the answer of 'I am from London' is never enough; more explanation is always needed. Ceren loves living in London, thinks of having her own house in London in the future. Although she feels London is her home, her belonging to London is being questioned and her existence is reduced to culture, which does not always signify her identity.

This is also experienced by Yaz:

> I went to a bookshop, and I picked up this book on identity. An English guy started talking about it and asked where I am from. I said London. He kept asking about my identity and then I eventually said Turkish. He started talking to me about the Ottoman Empire and showed me a picture of his friend's house in Lebanon. I do not want to see all of this stuff. He asked me a lot of weird questions. Do not talk to me about the Ottoman Empire because I am Turkish. We are strangers at the shop. [British Turkish]

Yaz's narrative indicates that they were put in a specific cultural frame that is not familiar to them. They think that their belonging to London is not acknowledged, as they put it, 'I do not know much about the Ottoman Empire; why I am being associated with this even though I say I am from London.' Like Yaz, other young people also interrogate why their identification with London is not accepted and look for answers to the following questions: 'Can only English people identify with London? If London is home to people from many different backgrounds, why cannot we fully identify with London or be accepted as our main identification?' Young people feel restricted by cultural assumptions that appear reasonable to those questioning their belonging and identities. These cultural assumptions are often linked to where they live in London, as in the case of Ceren, and the history and culture of their parents' country of origin, as in the case of Yaz. Being perceived as a cultural object reinforces the notion that multiculturalism only applies to ethnic minorities and does not include white British people, who are never asked about their cultural identity. Being asked about their origin in the country where they were born, where their personal histories have been constructed, and where they only live, leaves young people confused about what Britishness entails and who is considered British. This question, especially when asked by white British people, only adds to their uncertainty. Despite its multiethnic and multicultural character, even London is a city where the Britishness of racialised minorities has been questioned by others. As Yaz said:

> London is a global city that is very diverse and home to many migrants and offers lots of opportunities. It is very enjoyable to live in London. But it is also very hard to live in a place like London where there are a lot of gangs, drug abuse and street violence. It is a city where you are most likely to experience racism and exclusion. Living in London is not always fun. I have mixed feelings about London. Even in London, a lot of people question where you are from. You drag it out and play that game. Where are you from? London? Really. North or east? They want to find out where your parents are from. What is your ethnicity? Even in London, no matter how multicultural it is, I still have issues where my Britishness has been questioned by others. When I went to New York, people often asked me where I was from. I said British, and this was enough. Whereas in London I have to justify myself to others. I had so many situations in London where they really drag it and questioned where you are from. [British Turkish]

Yaz has lived their entire life in Britain, speaks the language fluently without an accent, has received their education in Britain, and has even performed in English plays, including those of Shakespeare; however, like other children of immigrants, they still face the question of where they are 'really' from, and experiences a constant questioning of their identity. Yet, the cultural assumptions and expectations placed on them as a result of their immigrant background persist. 'White people are not asked this question in a regular social encounter, but we [the children of immigrants] are often asked to explain our identity in Britain', added Yaz.

This persistent reminder of not belonging to London makes them feel what kind of multicultural is being referred to. The state's multicultural approaches create a sense of white exclusion and reduce the identities of minorities to their cultural origins. This then creates segregation, as stated by Aliza:

> We definitely live in a multicultural city. London is one of the most multicultural cities in the world. There is an Asian shop on one corner, a Vietnamese restaurant on the other corner, and a Turkish kebab shop around the corner in London. It is great to have access to these shops and restaurants where we get to learn about other

Figure 4.1 Fusion dish recipes in the window of a Turkish restaurant. Photo by author.

cultures and foods. But on the other side, within multicultural London, we are very separated. While offering access to diverse cultures, London also creates barriers for us to get together with English people, for instance. [British Kurdish]

Aliza experienced and observed forms of division that are constructed within the multicultural city of London. The forms of division are visible in the demographic structure of London's neighbourhoods that produce segregated spaces, as Yasmin Alibhai-Brown writes: 'when many of our forms of multiculturalism have been built on the premise that "immigrants" are so peculiar, so different from mainstream British society that only we can live together is if we keep apart just as much as is possible'.[6] In social encounters every day, hard and hostile boundaries are drawn in England, and London, for migrants, their children and newly arrived refugees. Everyday multiculturalism, which refers to everyday dimensions of living together, is seen as an alternative to state multiculturalism, which reduces its understanding only to cultural origins.[7] However, the experiences of British Kurdish and British Turkish youth show that everyday multiculturalism involves, as stated by Sivamohan Valluvan, 'highly orientalist and exotic accounts of multiculture'.[8] Their lived experiences of multiculture show the processes of racialisation. As stated by John Solomos, 'lived experience of multiculture does not take us "beyond race"⁹ – building on Ash Amin's conceptualisation of 'phenotypical racism'.¹⁰

Barbaros, who was brought up and still lives in Muswell Hill, a predominantly white middle-class neighbourhood in north London, said about his everyday social interactions:

> There is a lot of discrimination in London. I start with my name. In my earliest memory, in year one, I was disgusted by their confusion about Barbaros. The way they say 'Beerb-ros'. I said no but ok. Turks have an unusual name but growing up 13, 14, 15, and 16 was massive for me. Everyone was very small. I was big and hairy. I was different all of a sudden. I was called dirty Turk, hairy Turk, and smelly Turk. They were saying it as a joke, laughing. Ok, we were friends, but I did not feel very comfortable being called dirty Turk. Definitely, that was an example from London. I was called a terrorist at a university in Brighton when we were out at night at a nightclub. After hearing dirty Turk I feel more Turkish, you embrace the role. There is so much to reclaim this term, dirty Turk. After a time, it was confusing more than anything. It is a common insult, why this is so common, and where it comes from. I wonder why the Turks are dirty. It is hard to know where these insults are coming from. [British Turkish]

Yaz, British Turkish, also stated: 'Once I was called a dirty Turk at school. I had this comment from white British calling me a dirty Turk. I did not understand it. People make fun of your parents as well. I started to think why they call Turks dirty.'

These experiences of racism are not limited to interactions between young people from different backgrounds in everyday life. Yaz and Barbaros's experiences demonstrate that the everyday reality of multiculturalism leads to social divisions and that these young people face racism in their social interactions, making it more difficult for them to form meaningful relationships and build a harmonious life. Neither of them understood why Turks are called dirty. This becomes more complicated when they compare Turks with others. For instance, comparing Turks and Greeks Barbaros said: 'Greeks are Mediterranean, too, but they did not receive these insults at the time.' It is not easy to figure out which category or categories 'Turks' fit into – Mediterranean or Middle Eastern or black or European. The colonial and orientalist perspectives in defining the 'Global South', and the identity categories associated with this concept, reconstruct the imaginary divide between the 'Global North' and the 'Global South' along racial lines, as reflected in the daily interactions among young people. For instance, as discussed in Chapter 2, the Leave campaign during the Brexit referendum campaign denigrated Turks by categorising them as (Muslim) thugs or welfare scroungers.

The everyday multiculture also affirms hierarchies of belonging between the children of refugees and immigrants. For instance, Ceren said:

> Multiculturalism can be romanticised, and it depends on how you navigate yourself through it [...] I have fairer skin, I do not experience it much but my hijabi friends always experience some sort of insult or have something thrown at them. I can get away with it because I speak English too. But if I did not have those things, it might not be a safe space for me. [British Kurdish]

Like Ceren, Aliza pointed out the advantages of having fairer skin:

> When I was having an interview to get into a medical school, I really felt the advantage of having a fairer skin, even though I picked up an ethnic category on the form. I know that people who are wearing hijabs or have beards are excluded. Because I have fair skin, I did not experience as much as they did. I definitely feel safer compared to black and brown people. [British Kurdish]

By referring to having a fairer skin colour, both Ceren and Aliza indicated hierarchies of belonging in which people are ranked due to their ethnic and racial backgrounds in multicultural London. The lack of definition based on physical features such as skin and hair makes young people less noticeable in comparison to those with brown or black skin. The young people determine their place in hierarchical structures by comparing their skin colour and non-religious appearance to that of their friends. However, this does not mean that they have not experienced racism. Even though they were not highly noticeable outsiders, being the person who speaks English with a foreign accent, as explored in Chapter 3, makes them suffer from racism in everyday life. As Les Back and Shamser Sinha point out, 'new forms of cultural racism' take new targets, and rank people from different ethnic and racial backgrounds by changing the patterns of power that are constructed on individual and institutional levels.[11] Newcomer refugees from the Middle East are placed at the bottom of a hierarchical structure of belonging. The culture of racism establishes a hierarchy that divides people not by the colour line but by religion, ethnicity and, more importantly, by changing power relations.[12]

Sharing food as a convivial activity

Conviviality is used as an alternative to multiculturalism in exploring everyday diversity in cities. Living together peacefully in a city where the differences become banal and ordinary is one of the main characteristics of conviviality that distinguishes itself from multiculture. Paul Gilroy defines conviviality as follows: 'Conviviality is a social pattern in which different metropolitan groups dwell in close proximity but where their racial, linguistic and religious particularities do not – as the logic of ethnic absolutism suggests they must – add up to discontinuities of experience or insuperable problems of communication.'[13] Gilroy's convivial approach offers an alternative to multiculturalism that eliminates the categorical differences in everyday encounters that coexist with racism.[14] The term conviviality is adopted to explore how people of different ethnic, national, religious and racial identities live together in an urban setting, focusing on social relations in everyday encounters. There are moments when British Kurdish and British Turkish youth enjoy engaging with young people from various backgrounds where living in London becomes their shared interest. In identifying practices of 'everyday multiculture',[15] Yaz noted that getting to know different parts of the city through a friend who is from a different background is also about encountering one another:

> I have a friend who is half Jamaican and half South African. She grows up in Brixton where many Jamaicans live. She has a whole relationship different from mine compared to Brixton and north London. That's a very beautiful relationship we cherish, we speak a lot about London. We grew up very differently, but we connect a lot to the city. We go for drives around London and admire, and eat different kinds of food and I think it is very fulfilling and rewarding to be able to appreciate the city with other people from the city. It helps friendships to be really constructed in your identity formation of the city as well. You could so easily stick to whom you knew at school and when you go beyond that, you start meeting people who did not grow up in north London but also in south, east and west. Living in London is like you can live a certain life and very easily if you wanted you can mix with people from other classes and backgrounds. Even though I went to a private school, there were opportunities, so I did lots of various drama courses where I met with working-class kids. Actually, more working-class kids than middle- and upper-class kids. It is definitely a privilege of living in this city

where we can mix. I do not think this is available in other parts of the UK. [British Turkish]

London is a site for connecting friends through the common experience of living with and in a multicultural complexity. Yaz's experience demonstrates the act of fostering 'an attentiveness and curiosity'[16] to London's complexity. Similarly, Ateşcan appreciates the diversity London offers and makes connections with people beyond his comfort zone and enjoys learning different languages and eating food from around the world: 'not all my school friends are Turkish but are children of immigrants like Albanians. Due to hanging out with people from different backgrounds. I know how to greet in different languages. I even know Albanian enough to start a conversation.' In various spaces throughout London, both Yaz and Ateşcan interact with friends from diverse backgrounds, but despite these differences being unnoticeable, ethnic and racial categories do not become 'banal and ordinary'.[17] They refer to their friends' national and ethnic identities and how spaces are segregated based on ethnic differences when talking about lived experiences in multicultural London. Their experience of multiculture shows that it is difficult to share convivial moments when the main reference is based on the ethnic and racial identities of people rather than their shared lived experiences. Although they are aware of and acknowledge each other's presence, they are still trapped in an inauthentic multiculturalism where individuals emphasise or reference each other's ethnic or racial identities. This prevents the creation of shared spaces where differences are unnoticeable and common experiences of exclusion and racism are not shared. As argued by Sivamohan Valluhan, 'the analysis of convivial multiculture advanced here is not to be understood as suggesting that encounters in London are always, or even most of the time, convivial'.[18]

Despite remarking on ethnic and racial identities within their multiethnic encounter, Yaz and Ateşcan are attentive to understanding and relating to their friends within their social context. Food becomes an important tool to get to know one another. 'Everything connects to food' said Yaz when talking about her experiences of connecting with people in London and getting to know different cultures. Food plays a crucial role in connecting people and sharing common moments. For example, Barbaros said:

London is super-diverse. I like the fact that I can move deep in and out of different cultures. Food is an enormous way and peaceful way of experiencing different cultures compared to politics. I like the fact that I grow up with friends who were literally from different countries. I had one friend who was English. I had a Croatian friend. We were talking about Turkish, Croatian and Serbian connections through food. I think there can be isolation, but I am not aware of this. I have subsequently met people at work who grow up in this kind of environment. You can feel the way they ask certain questions, speak to people, and the phrases they use. There was a Turkish restaurant in Muswell Hill. We used to go to this restaurant to eat kebabs with my English, Croatian and Serbian friends. My English friend told me the best thing about a night out is *ayran* [yoghurt drink] and kebab. [British Turkish]

Taking part in convivial moments through connecting with food in a multicultural city is one of the most repeated common activities shared with friends in London for Barbaros. Food is more than what they eat; it is the rhythm of the city; restaurants are sites for connecting people from different backgrounds within the complexity of London; it is an informal activity of getting to know each other. As Ateşcan put it, 'being in London you experience so many different food cultures. If I go to a different country, I would have some sort of knowledge about their cultures.' Food creates a common space where they share experiences, learn about each other, and find commonalities despite differences; however, it does

Figure 4.2   Window of a kebab shop. Photo by author.

not transgress categorical differences such as national and ethnic identities. Ateşcan continued:

> A lot of Turkish and Kurdish people here get along with Albanians because their culture is so similar. They also make *börek* [filo pastry] and egg with *sucuk* [Turkish sausage]. The best way to connect two cultures is through food. The children of immigrants, regardless of where they are from, automatically connect. I have a Congolese friend who is from Africa. I left him when I was in the nursery. We go to a university now. I still talk to him. [British Turkish]

Through sharing food together, young people create their own convivial moments in which they feel 'connection and closeness'.[19] Foods that Ateşcan referred to as 'similar' and 'common' include ethnic and cultural foods outside of the mainstream among the children of immigrants and puts ethnic and racial identifications and migratory background at the centre. Within the convivial moment that is created through sharing food, racial, ethnic and religious differences do not become 'ordinary, banal and unremarkable'.[20] Food can be a tool for fostering convivial multiculturalism, where the creation of shared spaces lessens the importance of identities and differences. However, conviviality through food does not really eliminate racial and ethnic differences among these young people.

Homogeneous spaces within convivial multiculture

Aliza and Ceren talked about how one of the main things that London offers to them is getting to know about other cultures. Both were brought up in an Alevi community, and they pointed out that knowing about different religions makes them attentive and accepted. Aliza said:

> I become a more open-minded and accepting person because of living in a multicultural city like London. I have become more accepting of different religions and I become so respected that I want to learn. This is simply because of London. I learn about every different religion in this city. I think that is kind of why I developed myself in a way to become a more open-minded person. At the same time, I understand that sometimes you can really feel out of the place. If the majority is white and they want to learn more about you, it is not a problem. My brother lived in Cambridge at one point. I used to go and visit. I like it but I am not sure if I could live there. [British Kurdish]

Similar to Aliza, Ceren also touched on diversity as a positive side of London:

> Diversity is such a gift. I feel so lucky to be able to meet with people from different backgrounds. I do not think I would get that anywhere else in the UK. I learn the most by talking to people about their religions and cultures. When you meet people from different backgrounds, it opens your eyes to a different world you did not know exists. When you go to a seaside town in England, you only see white people. I could live there because I look white, but in terms of my family speaking only Turkish, you get the way they look. This is not something I want to deal with in the future. [...] My friends have been quite diverse. I have always been exposed to that. I feel lucky. This is an advantage of living in London just in the sense that you can meet someone and you can learn so much about what country they are from and what that culture represents for them without having a visit to that country. Going to university with all white people, including the student halls, is hard for me to adjust even though I was living near white people. I can only make friends by attending cultural societies events at the Department of Politics [which] is also very white. So, I find adapting very hard. I guess it is good in terms of preparing for the workplace because it is going to be majority white, anyway. You need to get along with it. [British Kurdish]

Their experiences when visiting different cities in Britain do not capture the openness, attraction and curiosity in what they feel about everyday multicultural life in London. Both Aliza and Ceren compared London to other cities they have visited in Britain and concluded that they could not live in these white and homogenised cities due to fear of racism. Racism provides no room for engaging in various forms of social interaction in homogeneous spaces. Their everyday social encounters with young people from different backgrounds often take place at school, on the street or at the shops; these interactions often do not involve white British people.

For example, Yaz stated that they enjoy the diversity that London offers, but they also highlighted that it is not possible to find inclusive spaces where everyone interacts with each other regardless of their class, racial and ethnic backgrounds:

> London is very diverse and I am very grateful for that. I realised this more when I went to university. The people who had grown

up in different cities of Britain have never met a Turkish person, a black person before. This is absurd to me, but this was their reality. I think I was limited. I am very proud of London. In speaking of homogeneous spaces, I am doing art which is very white and very British and dramatic. I choose the university I went to which is in London because it supposedly majority of black, Asian students, but the whole drama department was very white and British. It is hard to find others as a child of immigrants when studying art. In terms of education in university, that is something I noticed. It is harder to find inclusive spaces. [British Turkish]

Yaz's experiences of living in London show how the intersections of both homogeneous and heterogeneous spaces indicate different features of the city that are often related to its attitudes such as segregation and inclusion. Even within a diverse space like a university, homogeneous spaces are created and kept for the white British people. Yaz and Barbaros studied in private schools for their secondary education. The way they describe the school space is very white, meaning that the space is dominated by upper and middle-class white British students. Yaz went to a small private school where students' parents were rich. Yaz said that they could not really connect with other students at secondary school because of the cultural difference, even though they wanted to connect and bond with them.

Yaz was performing Britishness because of the environment. Barbaros had a similar experience in his secondary school. Like Yaz, he was also studying in a private school in London, but he felt alone because he was around English people, he said. Besides being around white British kids as a determining feature of why such spaces are isolated, both Yaz and Barbaros also referred to class differences between themselves and the white kids. Mete, who studied at Harrow, also did not associate with the school's posh identity:

> I kind of shy away about associated with Harrow. For most people being in Harrow is a big thing about their identity – it shapes their identity. I do not associate with Harrow because my parents are not [as] posh as their parents. When I came to university, I did not really want to tell people that I studied at Harrow because they would judge me. They might say this is a posh kid. After a few weeks, I said I went to Harrow, they said 'no, you did not'. I do not really want to identify with this because it is not me. For me, it is just I went to that school. A lot of my friends' mums and dads are working-class.

> My dad made money later, but he sees himself as a working-class person. Because your class has such a big effect on your culture. I personally feel like culturally I am working-class. Where I and my mum live in London was not a nice place. My mum was never leaving the house at night. She went through a lot of financial struggles. That's why I do not identify with that class. My experience is quite different from most people who went to Harrow. My mindset is also very different from lots of the people went to Harrow. I think there is a massive stigma about going to school like that. A lot of people who go there do turn out not to have a good mindset or are very condescending towards people who are not from that class. [British Turkish]

Like Yaz and Barbaros, Mete also felt isolated around white 'posh' peers at Harrow. His parents were able to send him to Harrow, one of the most prestigious boarding schools in Britain, so he was not very different from the other kids in terms of wealth. However, this was not enough to make him feel not isolated. This feeling of isolation is related to growing up in different socio-economic and cultural environments. Mete's parents gained upward mobility in the later stages of their lives; before that they experienced poverty and stigma. Besides highlighting the socio-economic difference with his peers at Harrow as one of the important factors, Mete also mentioned the role of cultural background, which is related to class as well as the migratory background of his mother. Moreover, growing up in a transnational social space and witnessing the financial struggle and social pressure that his mother experienced as a single mother, Mete negotiates identities and cultures surrounding him within a racialised, gendered, ethnicised and economically stratified society. These experiences led Mete to understand the socio-economic and racial inequalities better than his friends at Harrow, which caused him to feel isolated in the white space.

Touching on the role of class, Ceren, who has always lived in Hackney, highlighted how the gentrification of London neighbourhoods transforms the urban space into a homogenised and less open space, especially for racialised minorities and working-class people. Ceren described her relationship with Hackney:

> Where I live in Hackney, the Hoxton area is getting very expensive. This place attracts middle-class people. I cannot eat out with my parents there, so we go to eat at Newington Green because my parents afford it. These places will keep pushing ethnic minorities

out, excluding working-class people from these areas. So, I do not know what the future of these places will be. These places are developing into better places, but for whom? If I compare, for instance, Glasgow and London, I see many differences. It was nice seeing people, including white British, out protecting the refugee deported in Glasgow. I do not think this would be done in London. If something is going on, there is a fear of going out for demonstrations because of anything that might happen to them. London is very disconnected. They are all in their own bubble. They created segregated places for us. If there is a fight outside of where I leave, I do not get involved in this because I do not know how it is going to impact me. If I have been arrested in the demonstration, I was asked for my DBS; I am scared of being deported, etc. They create fear in us. [British Kurdish]

Ceren's lived experience in Hackney, a neighbourhood that used to be predominantly populated by racialised minorities, and generally in London, highlights that spaces can be conflictual and exclusionary rather than inclusive for all people. Describing how this particular neighbourhood in London has changed, Ceren talked about its exclusion of working-class people. Class differences appear to be a significant factor in accessing some spaces and, due to the segregation, it is harder to create a convivial space where people can establish a way of living together peacefully. In comparing the cities of London and Glasgow in terms of established solidarity, Ceren referred to the disconnected and segregated features of London that make it difficult to build solidarity and convivial spaces and settings.

Similarly, Barbaros pointed out that London has segregated spaces due to the gentrification processes: 'We can mix but at the same time we can isolate ourselves. We can have bubbles. You see, today working-class enclaves like Stoke Newington are basically taken by middle-class people coming in.' Neighbourhood segregation makes the creation of shared common spaces even more difficult for racialised minorities to engage in as they are divided by ethnic and class lines. As Magdalena Nowicka argues, the literature on conviviality is largely silent about class inequalities and focuses too much on human commonality as a way of uniting all people.[21] The experiences of Yaz, Barbaros and Ceren demonstrate that the spaces they encounter in London are segregated and homogenised, not only because of ethnic and racial differences but also due to class differences. There are some convivial moments when solidarity is experienced between young people from different backgrounds.

Solidarity as a basis for conviviality

The children of immigrants bond together because of discrimination and racism in London. It automatically comes down to class. It first starts with passport politics. If you have a British passport you are fine, if you do not you are not. Obviously, racism has always been there. I was born and raised here; however, […] I only speak Turkish at home and learn English at school. My English was not that good until year five. So, automatically people were saying 'are you an immigrant?', 'were you born in this country?' If I see someone going through the same struggle as me, we bond together. […] I have not seen my friend Danial, who is from the Democratic Republic of Congo, for four years. I just came across him on Instagram. He has now become a Boston basketball player. The way we became friends was when we were at nursery there were two white kids and they were pushing him, bullying him. He was very quiet. We were four or five years old. I asked the white kids, 'why are you pushing him?' They said, 'because he is black'. I was bigger because of my family heritage. I beat them up. I went to Danial and asked 'are you ok?', he was crying. I am not black, but it hurt me. I said to him I will be your best friend and always protect you. He looked at me and hugged me. Ever since then, we became friends. He kept me out of bad influences more. […] The children of immigrants, regardless of colour, ethnicity, or religion, who experienced racism are from the same identity. The discriminated against are all the same race. It does not matter what you look like. You can even be white. For example, white gypsies get discriminated against. […] So, ultimately, if I see one person getting bullied, I stand up for this person. Sometimes black kids do this to white kids, saying that in our history, you put us into slavery. Now we are going to do this to you. I am against anyone being discriminated against. The black people in my secondary school were picking on Irish kids and discriminating against them. [British Turkish]

Ateşcan's narrative, pointing out the fact that he has a 'black friend' and he protected him when his 'black friend' was attacked by white peers, could be described as white saviourism. In this case, a friendship between Ateşcan (the white saviour) and Daniel (the black friend) is constructed through the act of the white 'protecting' the black, which is associated with white supremacy, 'the power of whiteness' and racial superiority.[22]

Although Ateşcan does not have as privileged a position as a white person when he is around the white peers, his whiteness was superior next to his black friend. Ateşcan's statement 'the children of immigrants, regardless of colour, ethnicity, or religion, who experienced racism are from the same identity [...] the discriminated against are all the same race' points out the hierarchy between white people and the children of immigrants that occurs due to being a racialised minority. Homogenising experiences of racism among all the children of immigrants dismisses racism that establishes the hierarchies of belonging[23] among them and sees racism as individual prejudice rather than as 'systemic and institutionalized',[24] which was clear when he talked about black people being racist to white people. Ateşcan's statement 'I am not black but it hurt me' highlights the common feeling among the children of refugees and immigrants, which involves empathy and emerges from their experiences of racism, which makes them bond together. Bonding together refers to a closer relationship that involves empathy and the ability to understand someone else's feelings in a shared space. However, being together highlights the ability to live together in difference, referred to by Magdalena Nowicka as a main component of conviviality:

> [It is] a normative idea that relies on the recognition of differences, equal participation, social justice and respect for autonomous individuals. It calls for solidarity between generations and ethnic groups, and for a joint effort in regard to sustainable development. [...] Conviviality is thus concerned with how 'being together' can be successful for all parties involved. [25]

Magdalena Nowicka's definition of conviviality highlights equal participation, social justice and respect, as well as solidarity. What Ateşcan experienced is an example of solidarity, but it is beyond 'being together' – putting oneself into someone else's situation and doing something for the oppressed person that is deeper than collaboration or gift exchanges between ethnically, religiously, culturally and racially different people. Referring to the deportation of members of the Windrush generation, Ateşcan said: 'I disagree with the deportation of the Windrush generation. If it happens to me as a future lawyer, I would fight against this. All migrants in London are alone. If they all come together to protest something, there will be chaos in the UK.' Like Ateşcan, Aliza also indicated the continuing solidarity between migrant communities, not only between Turkish and Kurdish but with anyone oppressed:

> We know how to support each other. If there is some sort of racism going on, I know there would be a support community, whether it is Turkish or Kurdish. With the whole Black Lives Matter protests, there were other communities as well. I do not think this is a Turkish or Kurdish thing. Whoever is being oppressed at that time, you stand up with them. [British Kurdish]

Aliza's account focuses on the practices of bonding together regardless of ethnic, racial, and cultural differences and emphasises the acts of solidarity with oppressed people who are often black, immigrants, working-class people, refugees, and the children of refugees and immigrants. Similar to Aliza, Yaz and Barbaros agreed that there is support and solidarity between people who are oppressed. Yaz stated:

> If there was a racist attack on one group, I think people in the neighbourhood would generally have sympathy and help. I think people would not hesitate to help each other out. I think it comes from helping each other economically and being there for each other when something bad happens. I feel maybe in schools parents would help each other. I remember, even though we did not have Turkish people at school, we were close to Iranian or Moroccan families. I think you can see this support at school. You can stick with each other. [British Turkish]

Highlighting the intersection between solidarity movement and conviviality, Barbaros said:

> I think Palestinian rights protests are a product of conviviality and a kind of mutual support. Also, pro-Palestinian British Jewish-led protests are a product of conviviality conversation and a dialogical environment. Definitely, through Windrush and generations like the 70s, and 80s, you have got more kind of uniform solidarity I would imagine over the kind of homogeneous Caribbean. If you are Turks and Jamaicans, you are probably not that similar, but because government is being oppressive to your lifestyle and your children's lives, then you come together. [British Turkish]

They all pointed out that solidarity takes place between oppressed communities and shared an interesting analysis of what makes them bond together. Mutual understanding among the oppressed and racialised minorities takes place in homogeneous spaces, such as schools and neighbourhoods where racialised minorities share similar experiences of exclusion and racism, as highlighted by Yaz. Barbaros indicated that injustices bring different oppressed communities together to support each other and be in solidarity.

However, convivial moments sometimes get interrupted by tensions or conflict as a result of how transnational homeland politics is reflected on the streets of London. Ceren explained how the Free Palestine protest got very tense, even though it brought racialised minorities together in solidarity with the people of Palestine in London:

> I think sometimes there can be issues with other ethnic groups depending on their homeland politics. For example, I attended the Free Palestine protest. Once I had a scarf on with patterns associated with Kurdish women. I was getting weird looks from Turkish people. There are certain people who have strong opinions about Turkish politics. There was a Somalian man – Somalis love the Turkish government – and he said there are Kurdish rebels who try to ruin Turkey. I did not say anything. I think it depends, but for the most part with people I met, it was positive about other ethnic backgrounds. [British Kurdish]

Ceren is a Kurdish Alevi. As explained in Chapter 2, Kurds have been oppressed by the Turkish state since the foundation of the Turkish Republic in 1923. Kurdish language, culture and names were banned and there is an ongoing Kurdish–Turkish conflict in Turkey. The racialisation of Kurds in everyday life in Turkey has contributed to inter-ethnic tensions and these tensions are reflected in the Kurdish and Turkish communities in Britain and across the borders of nation-states. Ceren's experience highlights the reality of cohabitation in London, which contradicts the concept of conviviality. It demonstrates that living together is not always a success for all involved.[26] This does not mean that there are no convivial moments and situations the young people have experienced, even when racism is present. However, these moments are rare.

As argued by Magdalena Nowicka conviviality is helpful as an analytical lens in understanding how people find commonalities and shared interests at a particular moment in time.[27] Looking back on his experience, Ateşcan said the following:

> When someone picked up again, you show your reaction. When you join a new school, especially in secondary school, if you do

not know anyone, the first people you talk to are people of colour. I changed a lot of schools and, in all schools, this was the case. Even at university, the people I approached are Asian people or black people. I never approached a white person. The children of immigrants automatically approach another child of an immigrant as the first thing because we all experience racism and we connect through this experience. [British Turkish]

Experiencing racism on a daily basis – from peers and teachers at school, people on the street, colleagues and employers at work – makes them bond together and be in solidarity. Racism against the children of refugees and immigrants was prominent in my conversations with British Kurdish and British Turkish young people in London. Besides, they were born in London, they had been given the meaning of *Other*, being the person who is not white British and disliked for that reason. When they share a common experience, their racial, religious and ethnic identities become invisible and they all share an identity of being racialised children of immigrants. As Ateşcan put it: 'The children of immigrants, regardless of colour, ethnicity or religion, experienced racism and are from the same identity. The discriminated against are all the same race.'

What came out consistently in my conversations with young people is that, when empathy intersects with solidarity, there is conviviality.

Figure 4.3 Future Hackney project, Ridley Road Stories Exhibition in Mare Street. Photo by author.

Their accounts do not mention the involvement of white British people in such convivial moments. However, in some cases white British people try to support racialised groups, but they do not support them equally. As Yaz pointed out: 'more and more I see people with t-shirts or stickers writing "I support migrants", in favour of migrants. Very liberal, white, middle-class groups. Within those groups, there are also clashing relationships and competitions even.' The convivial moments shared by these young people do not often involve all parties such as middle-class and white British people, and even if white British people are supportive of migrants and minorities, they do not always fully understand the experiences of these communities.

These accounts of young people illustrate the importance of solidarity and empathy in convivial moments that are forged from their common experience of racism. These young people have formed a bond and show empathy towards each other's situations, being in solidarity with one another when someone is oppressed. This type of connection is more intimate than merely living together in difference, as discussed in studies on conviviality. This offers hope for an urban space where equal participation and social justice can be achieved for everyone.

Is London home?

Home is difficult to define. Is home in our memories? Or where our loved ones are? Or where we have been living all of our lives? Or where we feel safe? The list goes on – more can be added depending on how people feel about home. Avtar Brah poses important questions about how to define home: 'When does a location become home? What is the difference between "feeling at home" and staking a claim to a place as one's own?'[28] What makes someone feel at home differs from person to person, depending on their experiences, especially in a transnational context. The meaning of home changes and stretches between the local context of the country of settlement and transnational ties formed by migration. Sara Ahmed argues home is here not there in the past, and it implies feelings. She states that 'home is sentimentalised as a space of belonging ("home is where the heart is")'.[29] Yaz's heart is in London. When they were describing London, their eyes shone, and they chose their words conscientiously and carefully. Without any hesitance, they said:

> London is my home [...] my heart is in London. I am very attached to the city. I think about my parents and the story they were telling

me about coming here and making it here. I have family members who struggled to come here, to be here. These stories kind of tie me more into the city. I am here, I had this education, I did this, my parents did this, my family went through this and I am proud when I got here I feel a sense of pride. [British Turkish]

Yaz was born in London and has only ever lived in this city. They live with their middle-class family, but their parents were not always middle-class. Their parents squatted and then lived in a council flat for a few years in London. They, then, gained some sort of social mobility. What Yaz feels about London is associated with their parents' struggle and success in London as a migrant. Their parents' and their experiences of living in London are the main sources of their feeling about London, and these feelings make London home for them. They did not mention the opportunities London offers; when I asked about London being home, they talked about their parents' story and experiences and, more specifically, how they feel. As Sara Ahmed states: 'home as "where one usually lives" becomes theorised as the lived experience of locality'.[30] How Yaz experienced the locality of London also has an important role in what makes it home, which also aligns with their belonging. As they put it:

When I went away. I went to a city like London. New York is metropolitan and there are off-licences. When I was there I did not meet any Turkish. It was strange. Off-licences have a huge role in consuming homeland foods for migrants. If I can see certain foods on the shelf I am familiar with a quite specific place of belonging but it is belonging if I see *sucuk* [Turkish sausage] on the shelf, or *gözleme* [Turkish stuffed flatbread]. It is about Turkish British belonging. Where you hang out, and what you do matters. For example, smoking *shisha* as a thing to hang out with is not something white Brits do. I found myself I only ever do it or have done it with friends whose culture is Turkish or Palestinian. With British friends, it would never come up. British people do not do that, but I found myself only doing it with friends whose culture is similar. White British friends never come out to hang out in places like that. [British Turkish]

London is constructed as a space of belonging in which Yaz feels comfortable, familiar and safe; 'home is sentimentalised as a space of belonging ("home is where the heart is")' as Sara Ahmed argued.[31] London as a space of belonging is about their 'lived experience of locality',[32] its Turkish sausages on the shelves of off-licences, and shisha

Figure 4.4 Making *gözleme* [stuffed flatbread] at a Turkish restaurant in Harringay. Photo by author.

smoking places. The home is not the city of London – it is their experiences in London and what they feel as a result of these experiences. The locality blends with senses including what they feel, smell and remember. In this sense, the space of belonging that constructs home is neither British nor Turkish, but it is Turkish British, which reflects their transnational identities. Yaz added:

> Definitely, I feel I belong in London. I feel Londoner hundred per cent. I studied and worked in different parts of London so I feel I am a Londoner. I was born and raised in north London and spent most of my life in north London – but I would just say London. I have only lived in London and I have so many memories from growing up in London and social relations established. [British Turkish]

Rather than a geographical unit, the home includes social networks, experiences and the memories of Yaz. According to Stuart Hall, 'home' and 'belonging' are indicated through symbolic categorisation of place and space.[33] The meaning of home for Yaz, therefore, is closely linked with their parents and their experiences and memories of living in London. The belonging referred to here is not about social identity, but rather emotional attachment and social relations that construct an association with a neighbourhood or city. It is also different from belonging that is affirmed by the nation-state through citizenship. The meaning of home also comprehends the situations and conditions of the place that one associates with feelings, experiences and relationships with people in that particular place and space. Ateşcan identifies with London because there is a sense of community:

> I am a proud Londoner. Here is my home. London is a world of its own. It is a beautiful city not because of its buildings, even because the most discrimination happens in London. I like London because it is a strong city. A city of strong people. To live in London, you need to be strong. Despite all its hardship and discrimination, there is a sense of community here. There is this Nike advert called 'Londoner' where they talk about the hardships in London in terms of gender, race, and class. They say I am proud to be a Londoner. That video perfectly sums up London. It is hard to survive in London but, at the same time, it has a sense of community. Every area has its own community. If I say I am from north London, Turkish people say *hemşehrim* [hometown buddy]. I would not identify as a British Turk, I would identify as a London Turk. There are a lot of immigrants in London, so when people share the same issues and problems, they feel close to each other. If someone is going through the same situation as me, I have empathy. [British Turkish]

Ateşcan's account indicates that the meaning of home is associated with a community. The community he refers to identifies with a sense of solidarity and affinity. His definition of home is closely linked to Doreen Massey's definition of home as a set of social relations in a 'meeting place'.[34] The meeting place, in this case, is north London, a local space that Ateşcan and other Turkish people allude to as a hometown. North London is a space where transnational links are established and where Kurdish and Turkish people engage in transnational activities (see Chapter 3). Both Yaz's and Ateşcan's experiences are lived in a transnational context, and what home means, a space of belonging, also comprises feelings, memories and practices originated across the borders of nation-states and bring transnational socio-cultural aspects into the local space.

Yaz's and Ateşcan's understanding of home encompasses feelings, memories, and practices that transcend national borders. But their multicultural exchanges with individuals from different ethnic and racial backgrounds in daily life are not always positive. Despite London's multi-ethnic and multicultural character, the Britishness of racialised minorities is often questioned by others. The children of refugees and immigrants identify more strongly with London. That is not because London is inclusive and more open to diversity; it is more related to its local and transnational space where their memories and experiences are lived.

London is where they were born and brought up. It is a place they get used to, as all their friendships are formed in London. Their whole life is in London, so London is where they call home. Similarly, focusing on the case of Italians in Switzerland, Susanne Wessendorf argues that 'many second-generation Italians emphasise that home is where they grow up'.[35] Social relations play an important role in the ways home is defined. Doreen Massey highlighted the fact that belonging and home are defined by everyday life experiences and even more precisely by social relations.[36] Taking into account the new practices of migrants across the borders of nation-states within specific places and societies, Doreen Massey argued that these notions are transformed through the experiences of migrants and their negotiation processes. Therefore, such transnational practices make a case for the reconceptualising of home in relation to places where people inhabit with others. Doreen Massey stated that 'social relations exist, necessarily, both in space (i.e. in a locational relation to other social phenomena) and across space. Given that conception of space, a "place" is formed out of the particular set of social relations which interact at a particular location.'[37] Social relations transform a neutral place into a home. Home is a multiple concept that is identified with the social world people live in. According to Nadje Al-Ali and Khalid Koser, a home is a place where personal and social meanings are grounded.[38] In this sense, young people's relation to places and their experiences in these places could make a place 'home'.

The definition of home is a constantly shifting phenomenon in the case of transnational migrants.[39] In this sense, home is not necessarily a fixed and bounded place, it represents relationships with people.[40] In the case of the British Kurdish and British Turkish youth in London, the definition of 'home' is related to where they built their social lives. For some of these young people, home is in London, which is associated with north London; for others, home is London. They feel they belong to London; some of them identify with the identity of London and describe themselves as Londoners, as in the case of Yaz and Ateşcan. Likewise, Ayşe Çağlar argues that Turkish youth living in Berlin consider Berlin as their home – belonging is connected to an urban space rather than a nation and/or ethnic community.[41] Socialising and building a life in London makes it easier for such youth to familiarise themselves with the city and plays a crucial role in defining 'home'. Belonging is challenged and participation in social life in these places is negotiated. Belonging is not based on young people's national entitlement; it is associated with their everyday experiences and the meaning they give to these places and their social world. In other words, the meaning of home has shifted from the old paradigms that connect the issue of belonging with notions of mother tongue and 'fatherland'. Home is now a dynamic concept, which means different things for these young people; but there is one commonality about how they define home as a place where they have their social relations and are familiar with the environment.

Conclusion

London is home to British Kurdish and British Turkish youth. In this chapter, I have presented the experiences of young people who live in London. Their views about London reflect a complex picture that includes both positive and negative experiences. Their multicultural exchanges with individuals from different ethnic and racial backgrounds in daily life are not always positive. Despite London's multiethnic and multicultural character, the Britishness of racialised minorities is often questioned by others. The young people who took part in the research for this book stated that they had experienced racism in everyday social encounters in London and had been asked 'where are you from?', 'where are you originally from?' constantly – not because of curiosity or getting to know more about them, but to indicate that they were different. The accounts of young people highlighted that their answer, 'I am from London', is never enough – more explanation is needed. Moreover, everyday multiculture signifies racism and also affirms hierarchies of belonging among the children of refugees and immigrants. The children of refugees described their experiences of racism as class-specific, particularly based on the neighbourhood they live in, which is associated with a specific accent that affirms their class and migratory background compared to the children of immigrants.

London is not only a site where young people experience racism but also home to many of them. Their memories are formed in London, and they feel comfortable, familiar and safe in the city. The contrasting identities of London – from offering opportunities to experiencing racism – are stated by many British Kurdish and British Turkish youth living in London. In this chapter, I have also delved into the concept of conviviality and focused on the role of experiencing convivial moments in how they make a home in London. Most young people maintained the importance of solidarity and empathy in convivial moments forged from their common experiences of racism.

London is home to these young people. But what about Turkey? How do the children of refugees and immigrants reflect on Turkey through their visits? How do their experiences in Turkey shape their feelings of belonging? I try to find answers to these questions in the next chapter.

Notes

1. See Back and Sinha 2018: 16.
2. See Back and Sinha 2018.
3. See Hall 2000.
4. See Hall 2000.
5. See Alibhai-Brown 2000; Meer and Modood 2011; Back and Sinha 2018.
6. See Alibhai-Brown 2000: 52.
7. See Gilroy 2012; Wise and Velayutham 2014.
8. See Valluvan 2019: 40.
9. See Solomos 2013: 20.
10. See Amin 2012.
11. See Back and Sinha 2018.
12. See Fanon 1986; Back and Sinha 2018.
13. See Gilroy 2006: 40.
14. See Back and Sinha 2016; Tyler 2017.
15. See Wise 2009; Neal *et al.* 2018.
16. See Back and Sinha 2016.
17. See Gilroy 2006: 40.
18. See Valluvan 2019: 205.
19. See hooks 2003.
20. See Gilroy 2006; Back and Sinha 2016.
21. See Nowicka 2019.
22. See Matias 2016; Bonilla-Silva 2006.
23. See Back and Sinha 2018: 17.
24. See Bonilla-Silva 2006: 8.
25. See Nowicka 2019: 21.
26. See Nowicka 2019.
27. See Nowicka 2019.
28. See Brah 1996: 190.
29. See Ahmed 1999: 341.
30. See Ahmed 1999: 341.
31. See Ahmed 1999: 341.
32. See Brah 1996: 192.
33. See Hall 1990.
34. See Massey 1994: 154.
35. See Wessendorf 2010: 377.
36. See Massey 1992.
37. See Massey 1992: 12.
38. See Al-Ali and Koser 2002.
39. See Al-Ali *et al.* 2001.
40. See Wiles 2008.
41. See Çağlar 2001.

5
'Turkey is not my home. I've never lived there': discovering parents' country of origin

Turkey, for some British Kurdish and British Turkish young people, is a country that they visit at least once a year with their parents, their first reference point regarding Turkey and their heritage is their parents. They get to know about Turkey through the memories shared by their parents about their experiences of living in the country. Then, they construct their own memories, thoughts about and experiences in Turkey after spending some time there and being familiar with the socio-political atmosphere in Turkey. Young people raised in Britain, although they have not lived in Turkey and do not have direct ties to the country, form their views about Turkey through their experiences visiting the country and the political transformations happening there.

For Kurdish youth, Turkey represents a place where they feel excluded as Kurds. For example, Aliza explained how she was seen in Turkey as a Kurd: 'Ethnic cleansing is happening against Kurds in Turkey. We are very lucky that being Kurdish is not a crime here [Britain] as it is in Turkey. I want to express my ethnicity freely but need to be careful especially when I am in Turkey.' Referring to racialisation of Kurds in Turkey, Aliza emphasised that Turkey is not a safe country for them. Their relationship with Turkey is constructed through their parents' experiences and the ongoing battle that Kurdish people engage in to be recognised as Kurds in Turkey, to freely speak their own language and mobilise politically.

However, for Turkish youth, Turkey means a holiday place, food and extended family. As Barbaros explained:

> My grandmother used to live in Turkey and my dad is still in Turkey, so I am constantly attached to Turkey. I have lots of family members there and I identify so much with its culture. It is so beautiful for

me. When I go there, I say yes, this is how food should taste like, yes I would like to have a cup of tea, have fresh fruit from the grocery. [British Turkish]

The contrasting narratives of Aliza and Barbaros show that British Kurdish youth build ties with Turkey in a way that differs from British Turkish youth. As mentioned in Chapter 2, Kurds do not have a homeland of their own and, for them, there is no home to return to, as Turkey is not perceived as home. However, for British Turkish youth, Turkey might be perceived as home. The transnational ties of British Kurdish and British Turkish youth with Turkey, therefore, might show some disparities. On the one hand, the children of refugees, predominantly British Kurds, might lose their transnational ties with Turkey because of the racialisation of their families and themselves, and their lack of representation in its politics. On the other hand, the children of immigrants might have stronger transnational ties to Turkey compared to the children of refugees due to their privileged situation that comes from being recognised as white in Turkish society. As argued by Murat Ergin, the hierarchies between 'white' and 'dark' Turks in contemporary Turkey are maintained around culture, class, lifestyle and status.[1] Kurds in Turkey have historically been viewed as lower class, unmodern and less educated in Turkish society,[2] and this assumption still persists today. This type of marginalisation and racialisation is reinforced by the identification of Kurds as 'dark'.

In this chapter, I explore how young British Kurds and British Turks reflect on Turkey, belonging and mobility, and what types of transnational links they construct through their narratives. I argue that their relationship with Turkey is fragile and influenced by the political transformation of the country, which presents a lack of transnational links. These young people do not have a close relationship with Turkey, as their parents do, as they cannot claim their identities based on birth or personal history of residence in their parents' country of origin.[3] In this respect, their relationship with Turkey is limited to the periods they spend there. All my respondents stated that they travel to Turkey once or twice a year with their parents. Their visits to Turkey are fairly short in duration and are focused on visiting family and friends, and tourism. Visiting the parents' country of origin is one of the common transnational activities for the children of refugees and immigrants. Through these visits, they make memories of their own about Turkey. As discussed in Chapter 2, research exploring transnational practices among the children of refugees and immigrants has mainly focused on the socio-cultural aspects of their transnational links.[4] However, the literature on transnational practices among the children of refugees and immigrants often neglects to address their experiences of racism and exclusion, as well as the impacts of the political situations in their parents' countries of origin on their transnational links. In exploring how the children of refugees and immigrants reflect on Turkey through their visits, and how their experiences in Turkey shape their feelings of belonging, this chapter touches on their experiences of exclusion, racism, sexism in Turkey and views about the social and political atmosphere of Turkey, besides showing their transnational social and cultural activities.

Young people give different meanings to their transnational links. Their social ties with relatives in Turkey have interpersonal and emotional dimensions, so sustaining such social ties does not mean the same thing to them. This is illustrated by the fact that they choose whom to communicate with and do not simply construct transnational ties on the basis of kinship. Language plays a crucial role for young people in building social ties with people in Turkey and adapting to the environment. Although Kurdish is traditionally the mother tongue of British Kurdish youth, all British Kurdish participants made it clear that they do not speak Kurdish due to the silencing and suppression in Turkey of the Kurdish language, which is divided into Kurmancı, Zaza and other dialects. Because of the state policies to erase the linguistic identity of Kurds in Turkey, many Kurds have forgotten their language due to not speaking it in everyday life. For example, both Aliza and Ceren stated that they speak Turkish with their parents at home and communicate in Turkish, not Kurdish, with their relatives in Turkey. Even though most British Kurdish and British Turkish young people can express themselves in Turkish, they find it difficult to be in a conversation about politics, for example, and adjust to social rules in the public domain.

Ayşe, Belgin and Ateşcan talked about the struggles they experience when visiting Turkey related to language. Ayşe said:

> Because I do not use much Turkish in London, I have communication problems with people in Turkey. In London, I just talk to my dad in Turkish, so it takes a while to go back to your language. My vocabulary is not extensive, so I sometimes find it difficult to express myself. I need to make an effort. After a while, I adapt to the environment because my family is there. [British Kurdish]

Belgin, British Turkish, stated 'I do not feel very comfortable in the Turkish environment, because I do not feel comfortable with my Turkish and do not want to speak it. When I speak English, they do not understand and everyone gets uncomfortable [...] I am quite lost.' And Ateşcan stated:

> I go to Mersin nearly every year for two weeks and then to Marmaris for holiday. Sometimes, we only go to Mersin. It is good to spend time with my relatives. When I go to Turkey I speak English with my parents but when I am in the UK I speak Turkish with them. It is because people in Turkey speak perfect Turkish and my Turkish is not as good as theirs. [British Turkish]

Besides the lack of language, the socio-cultural unwritten rules and the reflection of politics in everyday life when they visit are also mentioned as important factors. The heterogeneity of Turkish cities with regard to political identities has an important role in the adaptation of young people and how they relate to the country. Yaz tends to go to Bodrum (a tourist holiday town in southwest Turkey) and Istanbul with their family once a year for different kinds of trips, including summer holidays and visiting family. Both Bodrum and Istanbul are considered as liberal cities compared to cities in other parts of Turkey, according to Yaz. Pointing out the importance of the level of language competence in communicating with the members of their family, Yaz mentioned that they want to fully participate in the transnational exchange that takes place between them and the family members in Turkey. Although they want to engage with them more in-depth, to get to know their ideas about Turkish politics and be a part of their conversation, they find it hard to understand or express themselves in Turkish fluently:

> The wheels need to get oiled. From language to temperature. How to greet people, what to say. I feel foreign in Turkey because I cannot speak at the same level, language is a huge one. I do not know the area that well. I do not have the knowledge I have about the UK and London. My behaviours are different. One of my uncles said 'biraz yabancılık var orada' ['there is some foreignness']. I never forgot it. He is right. I do not know how to naturally behave in this space. I always think of my parents leaving Turkey for a reason. They came here, they stayed, and they preferred it here. So, sometimes that helps me when I feel guilty about not understanding Turkey that much. If my Turkish is like my English I would feel much more comfortable. [British Turkish]

Touching on the role of language and their struggles because of not being fluent in Turkish and not having the knowledge about how they should behave in the social environment according to norms, Yaz made it clear that Britain, or London, is where they feel comfortable and most likely at home. They justify that Turkey is not good enough to be 'home' through their parents' decision to migrate to Britain rather than stay in Turkey. Apart from the lack of language adjustment, Yaz also struggled with needing to adjust to gender roles in Turkish society, particularly how they are expected to behave in the social environment as a woman. They said the following:

> It is very frustrating not being able to express yourself. As a woman, I would carry myself again differently; you have to be so *kibar* [polite]. I found this very draining and tiring sometimes. I used to be able to do whatever I want. You can feel labelled on holiday. There is an obligation to see certain people and to behave in certain ways which are contradictory. You are on holiday but you face lots of expectations. I need a Turkish person to brief me and assist me with these things. I worry about getting it wrong. These social rules play a big role in the interactions. If you do not know these social rules it becomes difficult. [British Turkish]

The societal expectations about gender roles make Yaz feel that they cannot be themselves and need to perform according to gender roles and norms. Gender roles construct significant barriers for young people to adapt to society when they visit Turkey regardless of which part of Turkey they go to. For instance, Aliza explained how she is careful about what to wear, even in Istanbul:

> Istanbul sounds like a liberal city but I do not wear shorts there. I do not know why I am scared. I have only been there twice. It is just the news you hear, then you think you should not do it. My parents were grown up in Adana. I was wearing a skirt there, the boys were looking. So, I do not wear a skirt there either. [British Kurdish]

Similarly, Ceren stated that she does not feel comfortable as a woman in Turkey. She said:

> We go to Antep a lot. I do not feel comfortable there in terms of how I dress. I always get told off about the dresses I wear even though I think my dress is not that open. When I go to my village, it is more

liberal. Because everyone from my parent's village lived in Europe, they know what it is like. But when you are in the city it is different, it becomes very conservative. In Mersin, I only wear jeans. The city is populated with Kurdish Sunni and we are Kurdish Alevi. We received weird comments because we are coming from Europe, and we dress more modern. This is a religious thing. I feel less Kurdish in comparison to them because the whole neighbourhood speaks Kurdish and I do not as much. There is a bit like you are too much of this and too little of that. [British Kurdish]

The distinction Ceren made between cities and her parent's village in terms of being conservative and liberal is crucial in displaying the recent political history of Turkey, including the forced migration of Alevi Kurds due to their villages being destroyed by the Turkish government in the southeast and east of Turkey in the 1990s and the rise of conservatism since the AKP came to power in 2002. In her case, being comfortable is associated with acting freely and being accepted in the way she is. Her experience of spending time in the village is rather positive, because Kurdish people there have lived in Europe, and are more liberal and less religious in comparison to Sunni Kurds. However, some of the Kurds in the city of Mersin are conservative because of the influence of religion as well as the Islamist and authoritarian politics of the Turkish government. This creates polarisation in society and affects the everyday lives of people. It also demonstrates the fluidity of the urban/rural divide and how state ideologies are internalised by people in these spaces, as well as the commonality of the experience of living abroad for Kurdish Alevis who were forced to migrate.

Similar thoughts about Turkish politics were shared by Mete:

In terms of Turkey, ever since Erdoğan came into power, he [has] created a massive divide between people like the middle-class, secular and liberal, following secular routes created by Ataturk, and [those who] are culturally Muslim people living outside of cities, who [are] very much related to the religious aspects of politics. This is like a class divide. I see this divide when I go to Turkey. Erdoğan is using this divide in his game and making it more divisive. In the UK, there is more scrutiny, more freedom of the press and political freedom. I was in Turkey when there was a military coup. I thought this would never happen in the UK. I was on the beach with my mum; she said *darbe* [a coup attempt] had happened. The way she said it to me, this is worrying. Erdoğan used it to gain more power. I do not like Turkey to go to this Islamist route, I would like to see cultural progress. I think UK politics is different. [British Turkish]

Mete could not hide his bewilderment, even six years later, talking about his experience of finding himself in the middle of chaos in Turkey, when he was there in 2016 during the coup attempt. He is interested in Turkish politics not only as a politics student but also as a British Turkish youth who, raised in Britain, has emotional attachment with Turkey due to his primary family connection there. Similar to all of my research respondents, he wants Turkey to be a democratic and secular country, as he said he does not like Turkey to go the Islamist route.

Barbaros spent time in various parts of Turkey, including holiday places and more religious places. He used to go to the beaches in Turkey with his mum once every year during the summer. Then, after the age of 16, he used to go with his dad to Konya, Kayseri and Merzifon and to places on the Black Sea coast that are culturally and religiously conservative cities. Talking about his experiences of visiting Turkey, he said:

> When I visited these conservative cities and started to question everything, it is really difficult. You cannot wear every single piece of clothing everywhere in Turkey. If I am wearing comfortable shorts, I cannot go to a village because people might say you are gay. You cannot go walk around with headphones and a super colourful t-shirt because you look different, you look modern. It sounds superficial, but people judge you and you want to fit in. [British Turkish]

Barbaros touched on religion, conservatism, social norms and traditions as a barrier to his belonging in Turkey. His experiences reflect that the ideologies of places clashed with his modern look and liberal views, which makes him feel foreign in Turkey:

> I also find it difficult to adapt because of the language barrier. The first thing I used to get in the taxi is 'Memleket neresi?' ['Which part of Turkey are you from?'] and then all of a sudden the price hikes and the journey takes a bit longer. I do feel foreign in Turkey. Due to my own limitations, it becomes difficult because of not being able to express myself. My experiences are limited due to the lack of interactions. I would not be able to have this kind of conversation in Turkish. So, people kind of talk slightly down to you. I would very rarely be involved in conversation so as not to embarrass my father, because I cannot talk with a certain level of Turkish. The hierarchy there can

be very overwhelming. There are too many layers. For example, I try not to have a conversation about politics in Turkey, I just listen. I try not to get involved in politics which makes me a foreigner. I can read, write and speak in Turkish, but when it gets to a deeper conversation I try not to express my ideas and thoughts. When I speak with my dad about the judiciary system change in Turkey, he uses a massive vocabulary that I do not know. I feel weirdly less Turkish. Apart from that I quite enjoy being from Britain because people see you as favourable, modern. [British Turkish]

Rather than being seen as an incomplete Turk due to the language barrier, Barbaros prefers to be defined as a person from Britain which makes him recognised as 'favourable, modern'. Barbaros does not want to feel foreign in Turkey, so he chooses not to involve in deep conversations with people there. He wants to be identified with a particular collective identity and associates himself with the collective social identity of the West as a form of self-reflection and as being 'favourable, modern'. Stuart Hall wrote that 'identity as a process, as a narrative, as a discourse, is always told from the position of the *Other* […] It is always within the representation. It is that which is narrated in one's own self.'[5] Barbaros's story shows that he discovered he was a foreigner in Turkey and faced challenges adapting to Turkish society, where he was regarded as an outsider. This is similar to the experiences of second-generation Greek Americans when they visit Greece.[6]

'Turkey is not home … People there are racist and sexist'

The meaning of Turkey for the young British Kurdish and British Turkish youth varies depending on their parents' and their own struggles, memories and experiences, and the political transformation of the country over the years. As discussed in Chapter 4, many young people define London as home because they have grounded personal and social meanings in the city. Research on transnational migration, belonging, and home focuses on the multiplicity of homes where migrants have an emotional attachment and feel at home in more than one national and ethnic context.[7] In these studies, home is associated with a place or places where migrants have memories of the past and emotions have been constructed. For example, according to Nadje Al-Ali and Khalid Koser, the definition of home includes national and cultural belonging, but also relates to the contexts in which migrants define home.[8]

Migrants' and their children's emotions about home and what makes a place home are fluid and always in the process of transformation.[9] Home is not always associated with a particular place; it is less spatial in the case of refugees, undocumented migrants and the children of immigrants, especially for displaced people who do not have a home of their own. Instead of placing people in defined geographical spaces contained within national borders, home is defined as a set of social relations, focusing on a variety of experiences of migrants and refugees in the countries of settlement.[10] How home is viewed depends on 'the broader historical and social context',[11] which comprehends the situations and conditions of migrants, and refugees, in both receiving and sending societies, as well as their feelings, emotions about and experiences in both countries.

What home means for the children of refugees and immigrants differs from that of their parents. As discussed in Chapter 4, research shows that many children of refugees and immigrants view home as where they grow up, where their social relations are constructed.[12] The narratives of British Kurdish and British Turkish youth about the complexity of home also display disagreement with how home is labelled as migrants' and refugees' countries of birth or parents' countries of origin. Besides pointing out how social relations, experiences and memories of the children of refugees and immigrants influence how they view home, the narratives of these young people also indicate that having experienced racism in Turkey and the political context of the country has played an important role. Many young British Kurds have shared their experiences of racism, making it difficult for them to view Turkey as home. For example, Aliza discussed her cousin's experiences of the representation of Kurdish identity and experiences of racism in Turkey:

> Your family members and cousins are identified as Turkish and Muslim by the Turkish state and society. And they say 'no you are not Kurdish at all' when you identify as Kurdish. When I was at a protest for Kurdish rights. I posted about it on social media and one of my cousins said when I go there, you are this, you are a terrorist. We had to leave on the second day because I felt very uncomfortable as they were all coming to me. I am not like these crazy radical Kurdish people. I want human rights, that's all. My cousin does not realise that she is Kurdish herself. One of my other cousins has a Kurdish star tattoo on his chest and he was attacked by Turkish people in Ayvalık. They attacked him solely because of his Kurdish star tattoo. They were very violent towards him. You just need to

hold back and there is no way to say that you are Kurdish in Turkey. [British Kurdish]

Aliza's Kurdish identity is challenged by her family who are assimilated into the Turkish identity. Since the foundation of the Republic of Turkey, Kurds in Turkey have been subjected to systematic forced assimilationist practices by the Turkish state.[13] This repression by the Turkish state against the Kurds still continues under the AKP government, which has imprisoned Kurdish activists, removed elected mayors and banned public displays of Kurdish culture and language.[14] Aliza does not feel secure in Turkey as a Kurd. It becomes difficult for her to establish a sense of belonging and acceptance within Turkish society. She touched on how her identities of being Kurdish and Alevi have been oppressed more since the AKP came to power:

> Maybe, the situation of Kurdish Alevis in Turkey was better before the AKP came into power. I am more familiar with the oppression of Kurds and Alevis during the governance of the AKP. I think it is the clash of Alevi and Kurdish as both identities have been rejected by the Turkish state. If you are a Kurdish Sunni, you are probably a bit closer and if you are a Turkish Alevi you are still a bit closer but if you are a Kurdish Alevi, you are totally an outsider. [British Kurdish]

Aliza's relationship with Turkey is undergoing transformation, with her ties to the country becoming weaker as her Kurdish and Alevi identities are oppressed and excluded. Her existence as a Kurd and Alevi is frequently questioned by the state and society. Rojda shared similar feelings about Turkey. She said, 'when I went to Turkey, I never liked it because they have a different mentality. Turkish society is racist. It is difficult to be Kurdish in Turkey. Turkey is not home.' For Rojda, home is a place where she is accepted. Her assertion that 'Turkish society is racist' highlights the fact that if she were to live in Turkey she might face racism due to her ethnic identity as a Kurd.

In contrast to British Kurdish youth, Caribbean young people, participating in transnational networks through visits to their parents' country of origin, construct a sense of belonging and collective membership.[15] Likewise, visits to the parent's country of origin offer a positive basis for the Filipino identity of many children of immigrants.[16] These studies looking into the role of visits to the parents' countries of origin on how the children of immigrants construct a sense of belonging to these places focus on the impacts of mobilisation and dismiss how their experiences of racism, isolation and exclusion make them feel less connected to their parents' countries of origin or whether they can call these places home.

British Kurdish youth do not define Turkey as a space of belonging, comfort and security because of Kurdish people's experiences of racism and how Kurds are labelled in Turkey. Aliza linked the experiences of Kurds with how they have been racialised in the media and by the Turkish president:

> It is more about the media. How the media covers Kurdish people or how the president talks about Kurdish people. Ethnic cleansing is happening in Turkey. You feel like, as a Kurdish person, you cannot be free when you hear the news. The conversation you have with people, especially with nationalist Turkish people, [they] really judge you for no reason. How could I feel safe in a country where my identity is a problem, where Kurds are labelled as terrorists? [British Kurdish]

Referring to the ongoing struggles of Kurdish people in Turkey, their experiences of racism, exclusion and denial of the Kurds' existence in Turkish society, Ceren pointed out that Kurdishness is not only her ethnic identity but also emerges as a political identity:

> I used to feel comfortable saying that I am from Turkey but I do not feel the same way since reading more about the Kurdish issue and the struggles of Kurds, I also met Kurdish people from other countries. There are lots of similarities between other Kurds and Turkish people. If I go to Turkey, I make sure I do not post anything about the rights of Kurdish people and carry a book about Kurdish resistance with me. [British Kurdish]

Ceren's feeling and thoughts about Turkey have changed after getting to know about the experiences of Kurds in Turkey and the suppression of Kurdishness by Turkey. She does not only refer to her own experiences when talking about Turkey, but rather raises the voices of the Kurdish people. The ongoing suppression of Kurds in Turkey strengthens the collective political identity of Kurdishness and constructs a common feeling about Turkey – as an insecure and dangerous place. This insecure place becomes secure only when Aliza is around Kurdish people in Turkey:

> When I go to Istanbul, I do not feel that safe. Where I go to Turkey is mainly where Kurdish people go, so I feel at home there. I go to Altınoluk, Edremit near Izmir which is populated by Kurdish Alevi people. All Kurds in the UK go there for holiday [...] From Germany, France and the UK, Kurdish Alevi people go there. They are very open-minded, liberal people. I feel safe there because I know if anything happens there I have a whole community. [British Kurdish]

Avtar Brah's theorisation of home as 'the lived experience of locality'[17] aligns with Aliza's feelings and memories of a place. As Sara Ahmed puts it: 'the subject and space leak into each other, inhabit each other'.[18] Aliza felt at home in this local space where she encountered Kurds, some of whom also reside in Britain and others in various countries in Europe. This local space signifies commonality, which is not only about sharing the ethnic and political identity of Kurdishness, but also a shared diasporic identity and the experience of living in Europe, which differentiates them from Kurds living in Turkey. The commonality that comes from sharing these identities makes the space secure, familiar and diasporic. Home is not where they originate from but 'how one feels'.[19] Aliza felt safe and comfortable in Altınoluk because she was not excluded, othered or discriminated against in this space, where she found a community spirit. She is a member of the community; she existed there as a Kurd who lives in Britain without being questioned. Being accepted with all her identities made Aliza felt secure and confident. While she felt *Other* in Istanbul and London, she found belonging in the Kurdish diaspora community. The fact that the Kurds do not have a nation, a country of their own, means that the concept of home is not internalised. As explained by Aliza:

> Because we [Kurds] do not have a home, an actual place where we call this our country, we are kind of stuck between Turkey and Britain. I am not British, and I am not Turkish but I am Kurdish. There is no home for me. I do not know where I am from, we do not have a country. It is very sad. I do not feel comfortable in Turkey or England. [British Kurdish]

Aliza referred to home as a physical space, meaning someone's native country, which is associated with boundaries and territory. While not having a physical home has some negative connotations, such as a lack of a sense of belonging and feeling uncomfortable, the construction of a home in a local space – based on mutual experiences associated with the construction of home – has positive aspects, such as safety and comfort. For Aliza and Ceren, Turkey, where racism is directed at Kurdish people, remains only a holiday place – not a home or a place where they feel welcomed. Similarly, for Duygu, British Kurdish, it is difficult to call Turkey home, because of her experiences of exclusion and racism: 'I do not feel at home in Turkey as a Kurdish person and I do not think I could live there. It is not a safe place for me, it is just like a holiday for me. I cannot live under authoritarian Turkish politics and with racist Turkish people.' And Berrin explained:

> I do not really feel at home when I go to Turkey; I feel like an outsider anyway because of my identities. I am a Kurd who was born in the UK and have only lived in this country. My Kurdish identity is not accepted as it is in Turkey and I have never lived in Turkey. So, people assume that you are different and they treat you differently. You have to act accordingly. [British Kurdish]

Their thoughts and feelings about Turkey reflect how they were seen by the Turkish society and state; and their experiences of exclusion and racism. How experiencing racism in both societies impacts the lived transnational experiences of British Kurdish youth is one of the main questions of this chapter and book. Racism as a framing experience in the lives of the children of refugees and immigrants is ignored in the literature.[20] It is, however, one of the most lived transnational experiences of British Kurdish youth both in Turkey and in Britain. Their Kurdish identity has been racialised in Turkey, and they experience racism due to being a racialised minority in Britain, as shown in the previous chapters. The children of refugees from a Kurdish background face otherness, exclusion and racism transnationally – both in Turkey, where their parents used to live before migrating to Britain and where they visit at least once a year, and in Britain, where they were born, have grown up and exclusively lived.

The forms of racism they experience in both settlements are being transformed in relation to the political climate in both countries. For instance, during AKP rule, especially since 2015 after the failure of the 'Reconciliation Process', Turkey's political stance against Kurds has become more authoritarian (see Chapter 2), so the experiences of racism among British Kurdish youth in Turkey took an extreme form. Aliza explained how this political transformation affected the level of the racialisation of Kurds in Turkey:

> I think 10 years ago, Turkey was more modern and democratic. It gets worse every year. You realise this when you read the news or hear what is happening to Kurds when they claim their identity in Turkish society. It is life or death in Turkey, especially for Kurds, LGBTQ+ people and women. Selahattin Demirtaş[21] is in prison. I do feel quite tired and sick of listening to them kill another woman in Turkey. I sometimes feel that I become desensitised to the news; ethnic cleansing in Turkey is always happening. Turkey is getting worse, becoming an Islamic country and as a Kurdish Alevi and a woman I do not feel safe, welcomed and included in Turkish society. I may [have felt] more attached a few years ago but I do not feel the same way now. [British Kurdish]

Aliza's narrative highlights that the figure of the Kurd is seen as a threat and political concern in Turkey, and this has become more intense over the years and affects how she relates to Turkey. In recent decades, especially, her experiences as a woman and Kurdish Alevi in Turkey made her feel more excluded and alienated. Aliza feels lucky that she does not live in Turkey:

> I feel very lucky to be in England than Turkey. People in Turkey cannot escape it as it is not easy. We [the children of refugees] are lucky that we have our British identity so we can escape from Turkey. I also think that we have some family members who are still there. It still impacts a little bit. Indians here, for example, maybe do not have family members there or Somalis have a failed state. So, it does not mean much to them. If I am sent back to Turkey, I can still live a life; but in a place like Bangladesh, or Pakistan, you can never live there. They are so overpopulated, third-world countries, not developed. Turkey is still better compared to these countries. [British Kurdish]

Even though Aliza lacks a connection with Turkey due to her Kurdish and Alevi identities being oppressed, she sees Turkey as a developed country compared to 'not developed' countries and also a country where she could live if she were sent back from Britain. The dilemma of not feeling safe in Turkey but seeing Turkey as an option to live if deported from Britain shows that, although she feels lucky to live in Britain, she does not feel secure. Aliza and other British Kurdish youth's parents' reasons for leaving Turkey and migrating to Britain are political. They are children of refugees. They know the struggles their parents went through because of their ethnic identity and political views while living in Turkey. Having first-hand information about Turkey through listening to their families' experiences makes them aware of the racialisation of Kurds in Turkey. Ceren's parents' reasons for migration were political; they were refugees. Her parents experienced torture and racialisation in Turkey. Their villages were destroyed. Knowing the struggles of Kurds in Turkey and Turkey's discriminatory policies against Kurds made her interested in Turkish politics. She follows the news in Turkey regularly to see if anything has changed there. Keeping up her hopes that Turkey might become a democratic country, she said:

> My friends from other ethnic backgrounds ask me 'why do you guys know so much about what is going on there when you live here?' I completely get where it is coming from. I think because it is so present and what is happening is so painful, we cannot escape it. And because our parents follow the news so much. Turkey could be so much better, but it might get worse. We do not know where Turkey will go. So much injustice in Turkey. It is about life and death there. Other countries are not like that. For my Somali friends, their country is like a failed state. Whatever happens there does not matter to them because they are here now. [British Kurdish]

Both Aliza and Ceren compared Turkey to other countries that have failed states. Even though they mentioned negative experiences such as exile, displacement and racialisation through their families' memories, and racism and exclusion through their own experiences when visiting Turkey, they prefer to keep a connection with Turkey. The connection is deemed necessary because of having some family members who are still living there or because of their parents' continuous social, economic and political links with Turkey. Ceren pointed this out:

> My parents have the idea of going back to Turkey eventually. There will always be a connection with Turkey. I would like to live in Istanbul for a year. I am curious about it, but I would not want to raise my kid in Istanbul. I do not think my parents would allow me to live there as a woman. I would have to hide a lot of who I am; I could not say I am Kurdish, for instance. I think I would hate it in the end. [British Kurdish]

The relationship of Aliza and Ceren with Turkey is constructed through their families' experiences of political persecution and racialisation and then reconstructed through their own experiences of otherness and racism. Both hold Turkish citizenship. I asked them 'how would they feel if their Turkish citizenship is revoked?'. Ceren responded:

> I would be offended. They do not want me to be Kurdish so what's the problem with saying I am Turkish? Are you going to take that away from me as well? It is not like a passport proves anything, but it is for me to show it if they say anything. [British Kurdish]

The Turkish passport does not help construct a sense of belonging but it is a crucial tool that makes her feel safe and legitimised. Aliza stated:

> I would not care if they revoked my Turkish citizenship. The only good thing is I do not need to pay for a visa when I go there every time. I always say if I have a son, I would not like him to have Turkish citizenship because of compulsory military service. Turkey is a beautiful country, aside from politics. So much history, so much culture. That's why I want to go to Turkey. [British Kurdish]

Turkish citizenship connotes just practicality for them when dealing with state bureaucracy in everyday life. Ceren asked a crucial question: 'How do you feel in a country as home when your family and yourself have experienced racism and have to fight for your identity?' This question summarises the feelings of Kurdish young people about Turkey. They are still in search of a home. Ceren went on:

> I do not know where my home is. I think I am still looking for a home. I think I can make home wherever I want to make home. I need people around me that I love. I feel like I will always search for home or maybe home is in me. I do think of London as home but if my family is not here then it is not home to me. I feel Turkey is my route partially and a holiday place. There will be lots of clashes with Turkey if I live there. [British Kurdish]

Aliza said the following:

> I think home is what you make it. I do not have one home. Where my family and my friends are is my home. Turkey is not home. For me, it is a nice summer place that will never be home. I cannot live in Turkey, especially as a woman, Kurdish and Alevi. [British Kurdish]

The relationships of British Kurdish young people with Turkey are complex and constantly evolving. They are shaped by their own experiences of racism, the socio-political circumstances in Turkey, and the impact of authoritarian politics. Turkey is a place where they feel a sense of alienation due to the communal experiences of racialisation and they do not feel a sense of belonging. The children of immigrants whose background is Turkish also do not feel an emotional attachment to Turkey. Similar to the children of refugees whose background is Kurdish, Turkey represents authoritarianism and a lack of democracy, where the gender and religious identities of the children of immigrants are questioned and seen as threats.

As mentioned in Chapter 2, Turkey under the AKP governance has become more authoritarian, conservative and Islamic. In this political environment, ethnic communities, people who do not identify as Sunni Muslims, women and the LGBTQ+ community are defined as dangerous and the state believes they should be controlled. The LGBTQ+ community in Turkey has been experiencing systematic attacks from the Turkish government. For example, Turkey's President Erdogan has argued that LGBTQ+ individuals are perverts; a public health official compared them to paedophiles; and religious authorities warned they spread disease.[22] Discrimination against LGBTQ+ individuals starts at the state level and then moves on to society. Homophobia has increased rapidly in Turkish society, which causes hate crimes and violence, including verbal and physical attacks on LGBTQ+ individuals. Yaz has experienced discrimination because of their sexual identity, and this experience made them change their views on Turkey:

> I have experienced discrimination about queerness in Turkey. When I went on a holiday in Turkey without my family, I choose to go to Marmaris. I was taking my partner at the time. It was my first trip alone to Turkey and I was worried, so I wanted to choose somewhere where English people settled and we would be able to find English stuff as well. It would be easy to do stuff with my partner around English people. I would be scared, and furious, if I had to go to Turkey and live there. That would change everything. I could not do that. That would be horrible. I could not go out at night in Turkey. I cannot be openly queer in Turkey. It would change so much. I love my independence. The queer and women struggle more under the Erdoğan's regime. There was a time when things were different. I do not think independence means to me

> Britishness. I really try to separate the current Turkish government and what I think of Turkey. He [Erdoğan] is not Turkey. So, I try to separate those; but if I had to live in the current context there, I would not want to. [British Turkish]

Yaz's relationship with Turkey is very much influenced by the current government's political stand and policies. Similar to Aliza and Ceren, Yaz also pointed out that Turkey was different in the past. Highlighting the political transformations the country has been experiencing for more than a decade, Yaz believed that they cannot see themselves living in Turkey under the current government. While the authoritarian regime in Turkey detracts Yaz from feeling close to Turkey, they do not distance themselves from Turkey totally, as the political circumstances of the country might change and things might get better.

The idea of home for these young people is not static, but rather a constant process of transformation, as they navigate their transnational identities and negotiate their place in the world. I asked Yaz how they would feel if their Turkish citizenship was revoked. They responded:

> I would not be surprised. I would believe that this could sound right under the Erdoğan's regime. I would then go through a whole different process to go there, to get around there. For me, my Turkish identity is heavily reliant on being able to travel and my family. I can still travel but I need to get a visa. A British passport has a lot more points on it. [...] Seeing my parents get their British citizenship was huge because they have been working hard for it. I remember we went to Paris to celebrate my dad's citizenship. It was a huge deal. Even when talking to someone saying that I am Turkish, I can show you my passport. I am British, I can show you my passport. It sounds like it was legitimised. Bureaucratically belonging definitely. I think a Turkish passport proves something when I get questioned. It is safe and also you can travel around. I use my Turkish *kimlik* [ID card] when I travel to Turkey. I do not use my British passport there. I think already with Turkish I feel powerless because of the government there even though I vote. It is not as democratic as here. I do not trust my vote would count even if I vote here for the Turkish elections. [British Turkish]

The children of refugees' and immigrants' relationships with Turkey are, of course, affected by the political transformations. Depending on these changes, they feel more or less close to Turkey. Home is not static. It is always in the process of transformation. The views, emotions and practices of the children of refugees and immigrants about home are fluid and a lifelong process of making or unmaking, as argued by Alexander Freund.[23] What I argue is that, in the case of these young people, the process of making and unmaking of home or their relationships with their parents' country of origin are not only influenced by their own experiences and emotional connections, but are also related to the sociopolitical circumstances and transformations in the country.

In some cases, the children of immigrants seek to create an artificial home in their parents' country of origin. Barbaros visited the wealthiest neighbourhood of Istanbul, which is more 'modern' than other parts, to feel in England:

> You create the idea of a place around you and home. The longing for simple things like waiting for a bus is not good. I would feel lost because it is ultimately a newer culture than mine. My cultural affiliations, my understanding of communication, my daily language, my use of words, and the way I talk to men and women, are completely different in the whole spectrum of the Turkish population. It is all different so I would feel lost. I spent three months in Turkey once. I went to Bebek [a wealthy neighbourhood in Istanbul] to try to feel I was in England. This is superficially Western. I would hate it. [British Turkish]

Barbaros tried to create a home in Turkey into which he incorporated British elements, but it was not the same. He felt lost in this space that he created because it was too superficial. Home, for Barbaros, represents a place where he gets used to living with its cultural codes, and the daily and political language that is used when communicating with people, and in daily practices. Although his process of making a home in Turkey is not successful, he said that 'I would be disappointed if my Turkish citizenship is taken away from me.' I asked him why. Barbaros responded: 'As my father lives in Turkey, I would feel really upset if my Turkish citizenship is revoked because it makes it hard to get to Turkey. It would affect my identification with Turkish culture because of its accessibility ultimately.' I asked whether he accessed the Turkish culture in London. Barbaros said:

> Yes, I do. But there are things I cannot access in Britain, such as lovely beaches, and holiday places. I would be incredibly sad because you are removing it without giving any rational reasons.

> Turkish culture is a beautiful luxury to have. There is culturally diverse beautiful cuisine, and lovely beaches I can hang on to. With Britishness, the way I think, the way I talk, the way I behave, my interactions are all British and if it is taken away from me, it would be life-changing. [British Turkish]

The process of the making/unmaking of the home involves, for Barbaros, comparison with the alternative option. Where Barbaros feels comfortable in terms of how he behaves and communicates with others without being judged and having any struggles is crucial for his sense of belonging:

> I do not really identify with Turkey. On paper, you kind of identify with names like Eskişehir, where is your grandmother from, where is your father from? *'Nerelisin?'* ['Where are you from?'] People always ask this question, which is such a paradox to me. Where are you from? I am from Muswell Hill. But where is your father from? Oh, yes, Kayseri [a city in central Anatolia, Turkey]. *'Kayserilisin'* ['You are from Kayseri']. I have been to the city twice only and I do not know much about it. How could I feel belong to Kayseri, which I have only visited twice? [British Turkish]

The question 'where are you from?' is often asked to the children of refugees and immigrants both in Britain and Turkey. In both cases, the question is asked to put them into the categories of nation-states, ethnicity and culture. However, many young people did not internalise these categories, except the British Kurdish youth whose ethnic identification becomes a sign of resistance against assimilative policies and exclusion. How British Kurdish and British Turkish youth reflect on Turkey varies depending on their experiences and it is also formed by the political transformations happening in the country and the socio-political circumstances in the country. The meaning they give to the country is changing and will always be in the process of transformation.

Conclusion

In this chapter, I have explored how the young British Kurds and British Turks reflect on Turkey, belonging and mobility, and the types of transnational links they construct through their narratives. How the children of refugees (predominantly British Kurdish) and the children of immigrants

(British Turkish) relate to Turkey is differentiated based on their experiences in Turkey and is influenced by the political context in Turkey. They do not have direct ties to Turkey; they have never lived there, so their views about Turkey are formed through their experiences when they visit Turkey and are influenced by the socio-political context of the country. Turkey represents a place where the children of refugees and immigrants feel excluded for different reasons. As shown by the empirical data, the children of refugees, predominantly Kurdish Alevi, feel excluded because of ethnic, sectarian and gender identities; and the children of immigrants, predominantly Turkish, feel excluded because of authoritarian politics and how women and LGBTQ+ individuals are treated in Turkey. While the children of refugees might have loose transnational ties with Turkey due to being racialised because of their ethnic identity, the children of immigrants have stronger transnational ties with Turkey because of the privileged situation that comes from being recognised as white within Turkish society.

Reflecting on the socio-political changes happening in Turkey throughout time, their views about Turkey and the meanings they associate with Turkey have changed. As I have argued in this chapter, their relationship with Turkey is fragile and influenced by the country's political transformation, which presents a lack of transnational links. Many children of refugees and immigrants referred to their experiences of racism, exclusion and sexism, making it difficult for them to define Turkey as home. For instance, British Kurdish youth do not define Turkey as a place of belonging, comfort and security because of Kurdish people's experiences of racism and how Kurds are labelled in Turkey. British Turkish youth, as women and members of the LGBTQ+ community, also touched on not feeling safe when they are in Turkey, due to increased verbal and physical attacks on women and LGBTQ+ individuals. Turkey remains only a holiday place, not a home or a place where they feel welcomed. In the next chapter, I explore how the young people define themselves and feel about Britishness, Kurdishness and Turkishness.

Notes

1. See Ergin 2016: 8.
2. See Ergin 2014: 330.
3. See Kibria 2002: 301.
4. See Levitt and Waters 2002; Perlmann, 2002; Wessendorf 2007; 2010; Levitt 2009; King and Christou 2010, 2014; Reynolds 2011; Dekker and Seigel 2013.
5. See Hall 2022: 229.
6. See Christou 2006.

7. See Ahmed 1999; Al-Ali and Koser 2002; Boccagni 2020.
8. See Al-Ali and Koser 2002.
9. See Freund 2015; Boccagni 2020.
10. See hooks 1990; Massey 1994; Mallett 2004; Rosello 2020; Şimşek 2022.
11. See Mallett 2004: 3.
12. See Levitt 2002; Christou 2006; Reynolds 2006; Wessendorf 2010.
13. See Yeğen 2009; Loizides 2010; Sagnic 2010.
14. Kowalski and Fidan 2020.
15. See Reynolds 2006.
16. See Wolf 2002.
17. See Brah 1996: 192.
18. See Ahmed 1999: 341.
19. See Ahmed 1999.
20. See Levitt 2009; Portes *et al*. 2009; Wessendorf 2013.
21. Selahattin Demirtaş is a politician, author and former member of the parliament of Turkey, a co-leader of the left-wing pro-Kurdish People's Democratic Party.
22. Yackley 2020.
23. See Freund 2015: 66.

6
'Am I less British because I am a descendant of an immigrant?': citizenship and belonging

Yaz has performed in several London theatres. I have watched Yaz's stage performance before, but this time was different. I watched them play in queer spaces. The play was written collaboratively by the performers. Each performer was written the parts that related to their experiences and identities. Yaz was playing themselves openly talking about the struggles experienced by being someone who self-defines as queer – both in Britain and Turkey. Being seen as an immigrant and Turkish in society, performing as a queer British Turkish among white British performers, gave them confidence in a white space. This is where they felt they belonged with all of their identities. 'My parents, especially my Mum, raised me to be British. I was educated at a prestigious school, brought up and lived in a prosperous area. I speak accentless English better than Turkish. English is my first language. But I still do not feel I fully belong to Britain.' They added:

> Being British is something we fit. It is like Union Jack versus England. You will never say you are in an England flag. I might be in a Union Jack for example. Under all of that, I identify with London more than other cities in the UK. I do not know anything about the UK. I cannot speak for the UK. I could speak more for Turkey than I could for some parts of the UK that are populated by white people. When I say London, my story makes more sense as a child of immigrants raised in London. That's why I say I am from London rather than I am from the UK. Of course, it depends on to whom I am speaking. If a white English person asks me where I am from, I take it as a challenge and say I am from London, ask me more, if an ethnic minority person asks me, I would say British

> but my parents are from Turkey. It is difficult to know if this person tries to make me feel *Other*. There are situations people ask me this question as a form of conviviality – let's talk about something really interesting – or are they trying to *Other* me? In certain moments I feel less British. I am so bad with English TV programmes and this makes me question my Britishness. I have some friends who are really proper English, and I feel so foreign next to them because I did not grow up watching these programmes or going to a pub. But I feel more British next to other friends. It really depends on the social situations. [British Turkish]

Yaz articulated their experiences of Britishness – at different levels and measured within different social situations. Rosemary Sales argues that 'Britishness is too contested as an identity to be a source of unity. The construction of British national identity was based on inequalities between the different parts of the state and between different groups within its borders, and these inequalities are reflected in different levels of identification with "Britishness".'[1] The inequalities between different groups of people within the borders of Britain make it difficult for people like Yaz to identify with Britain. Identification with Britain is deeper than just a sense of familiarity. It is more about being accepted as they are. The question 'where are you from?' draws a line between othering and conviviality. In the case of the former, it reminds them that they are not British, the latter comes out of curiosity. What Yaz referred to, from their own experiences, is the feeling of the *Other* and a constant reminder that *they* are not from this country, especially when this question is asked by a white person. Yaz questions their belonging to Britain because of experiencing otherness and unfamiliarity with accepted British cultural references and history. For example, for Yaz, knowing the popular culture of Britain is pivotal to being British. Yaz has a strong attachment to London. Identifying with London represents Yaz's identity as a child of immigrants raised in London. This identification, however, does not include any reference to nation or culture, it is about their story and experiences. They feel detached from Britishness when they get to know the history of Britain and witness what has been happening in the last ten years in Britain. Vron Ware states that 'Britishness is a concept that travels with heavy global baggage.'[2] This is something that occurred to Yaz when they learned about its history:

> Especially now, people talk too much about empires and colonialism in the UK. This is my answer as someone who has a university degree and is 23 years old. If you ask me years ago maybe I would only focus

on family and travelling. That was a huge thing for me. I do not have that many Turkish family connections in London. Being able to use the language, and talk to my family is important in one's identity. I left secondary school then I started thinking about my identity as a child of immigrants who are Turkish. When I was at school, I was not aware of race and other things too much to understand the role of identity in my life. It was not until I left school. I had a partner at that time who was very supportive. We went to free conferences at SOAS, I was really trying to find answers, subscribing to the magazine which published wonderful things about belonging. In the school system, I was unable to embrace it. Things are different now. Right now it is 2021, and all these social movements like the Black Lives Matter and other global protests, and Brexit happened and all these things make me feel like there is more awareness about foreignness. That also impacts my feeling, so I do not need to hide my Turkishness anymore. Turks typically love astrology. I feel way more comfortable saying that there are so many cultures in the world that use this system as their key to match-making or deciding things, and saying that 'look you cannot just go and say this is bullshit'. I have more knowledge and slightly more understanding maybe. I feel more conscious about saying something from one culture is not wrong. That's something that comes from age, doing a degree, and meeting and talking to a lot of people. [British Turkish]

Yaz's narrative 'I do not need to hide my Turkishness anymore' shows their awareness of the racialisation of minorities and not being seen as British. Even though Yaz did not mention their experience of racism in Britain, they referred to the process of racialisation, racism and nationalism in British politics with reference to debates about colonialism and Brexit. Britishness is an identity that excludes many racialised minorities, including the children of refugees and immigrants who were born in Britain, grew up in Britain, received an education in Britain and have only lived in Britain. This makes it difficult to identify with it. Stuart Hall called this process an 'Identity Politics One' and defined it as:

> one of the main reactions against the politics of racism in Britain. It had to do with the constitution of some defensive collective identity against the practices of a racist society. It had to do with the fact that people were being blocked out of and refused an identity and identification within the majority nation, having to find some other roots on which to stand.[3]

Stuart Hall referred to this act of searching roots and histories 'imaginary political re-identification'.[4] Identities are politicised as a form of resistance and becoming more important in our globalised world. People hold onto their identities to resist their exclusion. Yaz felt less British after learning Britain's history, including lots of undemocratic elements, which examination led them to critically delve in to what Britishness means to them. This does not mean that Yaz feels more Turkish. They do not hide their Turkish identity and experiences of exclusion. The identity of a child of immigrants carries the act of resistance in itself; as Ateşcan stated: 'we, the children of immigrants, regardless of colour, ethnicity, or religion, who experienced racism, are from the same identity. We have an identity called: *Otherness*.'

Identity is difficult to define because it is in constant transformation and always in the process of negotiation. As Stuart Hall argued, 'identity is always an open, complex, unfinished game – always under construction'.[5] As Amin Maalouf argues, 'identity is not given once and for all: it is built up and changes throughout a person's lifetime'.[6] Thus, it is interactive and shaped by experiences of inclusion, exclusion and racism.[7] I prefer to talk about identities rather than identity as identities are not singular including more than one identification. As Stuart Hall put it, 'identity is not something which is formed outside and then we tell stories about it. It is that which is narrated in one's own self.'[8] The notion of identity is complex and historically constructed.

In this chapter, I seek to demonstrate how young people perceive their positioning in society; how racial hierarchies, class, ethnicity and gender are important in one's identity; how the young people's transnational background is reflected in their perception of identity; how the dimensions of the self, the socio-political context of Britain and Turkey influence identity negotiation among the participants; and how the young people feel about being British, Kurdish or Turkish. I argue that the children of refugees and immigrants deidentify themselves from the national identities of Britain and Turkey due to experiencing racism and the impacts of authoritarian politics on their everyday lives. And, as a result, they negotiate these identities in a transnational context. Concentrating on the social and political situations in Britain and Turkey in exploring the formation of identities among the children of refugees and immigrants allows for a wider lens that considers not only what these young people are doing as they cultivate a sense of belonging, but also the often overlooked reasons why. In this sense, the social and political situations in Britain and Turkey that are reflected in the everyday lives of the children of refugees and immigrants become pivotal in understanding the meanings these young people give to the identities surrounding them.

Ceren's relationship with Britain is affected by the anti-immigrant sentiment in and immigration policy of Britain. Ceren did not get citizenship until the age of 11 and experienced anti-immigrant sentiment throughout her life. Her parents sought asylum to Britain when she was two years old in 2002, after the Nationality, Immigration and Asylum Act was introduced. When she was six years old, the family was deported under EU law to Germany because it was the first country they signed in. They stayed there only for two or three weeks and ended up coming back to Britain, because there was a problem with the legislation and the Home Office had been wrong. Ceren explained how a state of limbo, of wanting to be British but being rejected, influences her relation to Britishness.

> It was too expensive to come here to pay for human smugglers already. There were lots of paying. I always joke about it, saying that I was deported. When I go to an airport I always remember this because the first time I was on a plane was when I was deported. This is my trauma. That's the reason why I do not feel British because I am always made to feel that way until a certain point. When growing up we always went to the Home Office, showing that we are here, we did not go anywhere. We could not go back to Turkey, we could not leave the country. It was a constant battle like do we belong here or not, do they send us back or not? I was in a constant state of limbo of wanting to be British but being rejected. For instance, with the Windrush scandal, they sent people back. I do not feel like this is going to happen to me again. Then, I thought about why this would not happen. It is still happening to people. I do not know if this is going to affect me. Then I think that because I have fairer white skin, I do not have dark one, maybe I should not worry about it. [British Kurdish]

Ceren's experience of deportation, being in a constant limbo, of wanting to be British but being rejected, makes her feel that she does not belong in Britain. She is regarded as permanently foreign even though she was granted British citizenship later on. She is not seen as fully British and her belonging in Britain is questioned. Britain has never allowed her to feel that she belongs to the country. Experiencing deportation, the fear of being deported and facing anti-immigrant sentiments have forced Ceren to grapple with anxiety and uncertainty since her childhood.

She is aware that she will always be seen as less British or not British at all, and by referencing the Windrush scandal she highlights that racism against migrants and minorities is rapidly increasing. Nevertheless, before she distinguished herself from black and brown people based on her skin colour which constructs hierarchies of belonging with other communities.

Like Ceren, Aliza also pointed out that how Kurds are seen compared to black people:

> We [Kurds] are quite lucky because we are quite fair-skinned. That's what I realised when I went to get my vaccine they put me down as British. I said no I am Kurdish. I am luckier in that aspect than other brown or black populations because we do not look as ethnic. We are considered more British compared to them. I have just learned certain things like how to use a fork and knife properly because I am not middle-class. [British Kurdish]

Focusing on the differences between Kurds and other racialised minorities, Aliza creates hierarchies based on the level of Britishness. As Les Back and Shamser Sinha suggest, 'new hierarchies of belonging [...] filter and rank people differently, like steps on a staircase'.[9] While some young people feel they belong in Britain, for others belonging has always been questioned. Who is included within the definition of British is filtered through racially hierarchal ways as the use of the term 'British' in British politics often means 'white British'.[10] Her comparison between Kurds and black and brown people in Britain does touch on class as well as race. When she said 'I have just learned certain things like how to use a fork and knife properly', she makes it clear that Britishness is not only about being white but also about class. She feels very British; as she put it:

> I do feel very British. I do feel I picked up the culture here. Sometimes people tell me 'you are whitewashed'. A lot of people are saying that 'she is really white Kurdish' meaning that 'I am more British than Kurdish'. I take things from both cultures as much and I use the ones I like. I try to stay away from the radical Kurdish ideology. I am very Kurdish, I am very proud and I will always stand up for it. but I feel like I cannot be very radical with it. I adopted openness, and liberalism because of the schools I went to. The schools I went to were very white-populated so I guess I picked up these ideologies from there. I am British. [British Kurdish]

Aliza feels more British when she compares herself to other Kurds in Britain, and the distinction she makes between herself and other British Kurds is derived from her interacting more with white British people and British Kurds being stuck in north London and having 'a radical Kurdish ideology' as she put it. The level of Britishness is increased when she moves away from the community and interacts with white British people. However, Ceren feels less British as a result of her challenge to gain British citizenship. She mentioned her experience with the state:

> I do not know if I identify as British. My friends say you are definitely British. I like to reject it myself a little bit. I came here when I was two years old and my family had great trouble getting citizenship. Because I was rejected by the state, I feel that I do not belong in Britain. I fully confirm that I belong in London but I never say that I belong to England. [British Kurdish]

Although Ceren was granted British citizenship after her parents' battle to get it, she is fully aware that her British citizenship is conditional and might be revoked. She does not feel that she belongs in Britain because her ethnic background, rather than her passport, determines her place in Britain. Thus, London offers an alternative to belonging in Britain. Ceren has a strong sense of belonging in London. Belonging comprises an emotional aspect and highlights an association with places including the city, neighbourhood, region or village. As explored in Chapter 4, London is special for the young people presented in this book. London is where they were born and constructed their social lives. Aliza is thankful that her parents migrated to London and said:

> I was born in London. I always felt thankful that my parents came here. I feel so much safer here. I always felt quite lucky to be in London. Here, London is so multicultural, everyone has a different culture. There are so many different cultures. My migratory background is not so much visible in London because people in London are from different backgrounds. I really feel like I am at home here. I might be more excluded if I live in other cities in England. [British Kurdish]

The process of adjustment to the receiving society becomes problematised. Philip Kasinitz et al.[11] state that the tension of 'insider' and 'outsider' status makes identification easier with the city of birth than with their parents' country of origin, as illustrated by Aliza. One of the main reasons why these young people identify more with London is its sociocultural spaces for transnational communities, as Yaz pointed out:

> Seeking out other people who fall into a similar diaspora, in London is very easy for me to do. It is a combination of cultural materials and items, things that I get to do in my day to day. I found a sense of belonging for instance by sharing a meal with another Turkish-British friend in a Turkish restaurant in London. That kind of activity is definitely how British-Turkishness is practised in London. It is very different to having a Turkish meal in Turkey. I think food plays a huge role in who you are and in seeking out those people with whom you can share certain things. When I was abroad in New York, I was homesick. I bought *dolma* [vine leaves] and that makes me feel comfortable. I did not get English food. They had *dolma* everywhere because the Greeks live there. I have never lived in Turkey but I have had many *dolmas* in my life. I enjoy cultural similarities with Middle Eastern people for instance through acts of doing things together. [British Turkish]

London is where Yaz's dual British Turkish membership is practised and where they find similarities with other backgrounds. It reflects Yaz's identification with Britishness and Turkishness. Urban settings represent new forms of identification and cultural references in the case of

Figure 6.1 Turkish tea and *künefe* [sweet cheese pastry].
Photo by author.

British Turkish and British Kurdish youth. Yaz appreciates the diversity in London in terms of knowing other cultures and the spaces it offers for socio-cultural transnational practices, such as sharing a meal with a British Turkish friend at a Turkish restaurant. Yaz switches between different identities, shifting from national to transnational; constructs their own concepts of identities within the global, the local and the native through their experiences, and moves between these identity possibilities.

'I am confused about my belonging and identity': portrayal of complexity

In everyday life, the children of refugees and immigrants enter into different spaces across the borders of nation-states and participate in different cultural and identity positions, at school, at home, in their neighbourhoods, etc. They have different identities, such as British, Kurdish, Turkish, Alevi, women, working-class, queer and so on, and they do not conform entirely to any single category. Floya Anthias argues that the identity formation of young people from racialised minority groups and the impacts of collective identities need to be analysed in relation to location and positionality because this includes the views of individuals about the broader social relations that are constituted in the process of identity construction.[12] Living across more than two socio-cultural spaces reveals the different identity positionings of children of refugees and immigrants. This is seen as problematic in some cases. 'Being in the middle of two cultures' is a phrase used by families and community organisations to describe the 'in between' positioning of the young people. It is argued that not belonging to a particular culture is problematic, which shows that the children of refugees and immigrants have serious identity problems because they are 'between two cultures'.[13] Some scholars refer to the concept of hybridity as the 'third space' between home and host society, to avoid essentialising the identities of the young people by attributing to them a preconceived identity, limited to certain characteristics, and that offers a way to understand the fluidity of these identities and experiences.[14] According to Ayhan Kaya, Turkish youth in Germany employ the conjunction 'and … and … and' in the process of identity formation: for instance, they describe themselves as 'German and Turkish and global and …'.[15] This refers to multiple identifications with different cultures; discourses are constantly intermingled and associated with globalisation.

Mika Toyota argues that multiple identifications are somewhat problematic when situated within the country of origin and the settlement.[16] The concept of 'third space' does not pay much attention to other factors, such as racial discrimination, which may constrain people's experiences of identity.[17] It does not stress the need for creating social networks that transcend ethnic categories and national boundaries[18] and it sometimes reassigns fixed identity.[19]. Defining the identities of the children of refugees and immigrants as in the 'third space' puts them in a category as artificial as the categories of nation and ethnicity. It does not take into consideration that identities are always in the process of transformation, especially within a transnational context when the children of refugees and immigrants position themselves in different places, such as Britain, Turkey, London and north London. Identities are socially constructed and highly complex, connate the process of identification as argued by Stuart Hall.[20] The children of refugees and immigrants' identifications are constructed and transformed through their experiences across the borders of nation-states. For example, Barbaros said that he feels less Turkish after learning about Turkish history and witnessing discrimination against Armenians in Turkey.

> I became less Turkish when I was 15, 16. It was hard. You are fitting into British culture but you have your Turkish culture. At school, they were calling me a Turk, this was my nickname and I was the only Turk in my year. You become the Turkish brand. My good friend Luke is half-Armenian. I became aware of the Armenian genocide when I was 15 after reading about it. I also witnessed the Turks attacking Armenians who use the word genocide in Istanbul. All of a sudden I had to rethink what Turkishness means to me. It is not all about *baklava*, Atatürk, beaches and kebabs. It is also about its history, some of which made me feel less attached to Turkishness. [British Turkish]

Turkishness, like other national identities, has heavy baggage, which includes the Armenian genocide, ethnic cleansing, a pogrom against non-Muslims, and the racialisation of Kurds, Alevis and other minorities. After getting to know and assessing its dark history, Barbaros started to question his relation to Turkishness, which could be related to being ashamed of having 'the Turkish brand' and how non-Turkish people could judge him because of his association with Turkishness.

While Barbaros questions his relation to Turkishness, Ceren thinks about her relation to Britishness and identifies more with Kurdishness.

Ceren's own personal history of experiencing deportation and racism makes her feel less British:

> I do not care if someone tells me you are not that British. It is because I am proud of being Kurdish and being from a multicultural background…Kurdishness for me is very cultural and traditional but in a nice way. I really like that. I never identify as British. I do not know what to say about that. [British Kurdish]

The lack of identification with Britishness is related to Ceren's experience with the anti-immigrant sentiment in Britain, but it is also about experiencing Kurdishness more; as she put it:

> I do not know how to define British culture – for instance, going to a pub. Our parents stuck with what they have brought from Turkey. My parents speak Kurdish but their Kurdish is different […] So, they speak Turkish at home. My parents do not speak English. That's the reason why. I always navigated through them. When I found my own voice it was too late to feel British at that point. It is because I am the second generation and this comes down to that. I do think in the next generations, Britishness will be rooted more […] Also experiencing racism makes me feel less identified with Britishness and more with Kurdishness. Asians, Pakistanis and Indians and the black community have been here for ages, generations and generations. I know some Pakistani families do not teach their children their native tongue. They just teach them English. They are really assimilated into Britishness and Englishness. I assume that part of them is letting go of what is home. Our families are not like that. We are still speaking Turkish and Kurdish, we are quite new here. I do not know if our cultures and mother tongues will let go of. Maybe after a few generations. I hope not. But these communities detach from their homelands and they are the ones who are sent back. They really have no connection. We can still have a life there. [British Kurdish]

Kurdishness represents security besides culture and family for Ceren, especially when she finds it hard to identify with Britishness due to experiencing racism, for instance. Kurdishness is not an alternative to Britishness; it is her main identification, which symbolises resistance to assimilation. It is also easier to identify with as Ceren practises it at home, within the community, and through transnational links in comparison to Britishness. Ceren's experience of being deported from Britain makes her feel less British and not welcomed in Britain, and she has stronger transnational connections and identification with Kurdishness. Research on 'reactive transnationalism' shows that the more children of refugees and immigrants experience discrimination and racism, the more they are transnationally involved in both societies and engage in transnational activities. For example, Eric Snel *et al.* argue that the middle-class Muslim migrants in Rotterdam who experienced discrimination have stronger transnational identifications.[21] In a similar vein, focusing on the case of Bangladeshi-origin Muslims in London, Luton and Birmingham, Victoria Melangedd Redclift and Fatima Begum Rajina show that experiencing racism causes 'protective transnationalism' as a specification of 'reactive transnationalism to increase more especially in line with nationalist politics in the settlement countries'.[22]

As shown in Chapter 5, nationalist politics and racialisation have an important role in the ways the children of refugees and immigrants identify with Turkey and their sense of belonging. Likewise, nationalist politics in Britain and the racialisation of British citizenship make the children of refugees and immigrants identify with Britishness less. For example, the respondents to my research mentioned that, during the Brexit vote and after, they felt the threat because 'they are not white'. Aliza, British Kurdish, stated: 'Brexit happened because they want immigrants out. At the end of the day, the reason I am here is that my parents are immigrants'. Yaz said:

> I have not experienced it as someone yelling at me. But I have friends who have racist parents, which makes me feel uncomfortable. Definitely, hostile energy when you see on the news all these racist things happening that changed a lot. I remember when it happened, there was a sense of fear. Since Brexit, it is increased. They use Turkey in the campaign. I do not agree with the Turkish government, but the image of Turks here is not Erdoğan. It is not fair. [British Turkish]

Barbaros noted:

> In the past, from the eighteenth century onwards, the idea of Turk is used to identify with all Muslims and others. There is a kind of this political element they try to come up against Turks. I could objectively say Brexit may have affected people of colour, black Asian minorities, and Kurdish, which makes them including me feel

unwanted. What we saw there is a product of very toxic Britishness which is still harboured. This is quite embarrassing. There is this imaginary media idea of 'we are going to bring back an idealised Britain where white people play cricket and eat Victorian sponge cakes'. [British Turkish]

The Brexit campaign created an image of Turkey filled with criminals, terrorists and welfare scroungers – that millions of (Muslim) Turks would come to Britain once Turkey joined the EU.[23] The Turkish 'threat' bolsters xenophobia and racism, not only against Turks but also against other racialised minorities residing in Britain, and racism has risen in the wake of the Brexit referendum.[24] The narratives of Aliza, Yaz and Barbaros show that they make a clear distinction between themselves as the children of immigrants and refugees, and the white people who are the subject of an idealised Britain, which is associated with 'white people play[ing] cricket and eat[ing] Victorian sponge cakes', as stated by Barbaros. This distinction between themselves and the white people was strengthened and a 'toxic Britishness' was harboured, during the Brexit campaign and after it happened, which has been experienced by Aliza, Yaz and Barbaros.

The Brexit slogan 'take back control' is rooted in a colonial nostalgia that still informs political discourse in Britain, as stated by Kehinde Andrews.[25] This slogan is associated with an opportunity to limit the numbers of Muslim, Asian and non-white migrants coming to Britain. As explained in Chapter 2, the immigration debate is formed around the fear that Turkey might join the EU and that Muslims – featuring also Syrian refugees as a threat – will enter Britain. A far-right anti-Muslim, anti-Asian, anti-migrant racism during the Brexit vote intersects and is still active in the political discourse today, which impacts the experiences of the children of refugees and immigrants, making them feel like strangers in the country in which they were born. As stated by Barbaros, this very toxic white-only Britishness is still cherished. Experiencing racism and racialisation are barriers to belonging and create unstable feelings of identity in the case of the children of refugees, who are identified as foreigners, despite being citizens of the settlement country and despite their socio-economic status, as in the case of children of refugees in Switzerland, as shown by Laurence Ossipow *et al.*[26]

I asked Barbaros how he identified himself. He said: 'I say British-Turkish. I used to identify more with Turkish. I was raised with my grandmother. After she died, I align more with the British. I would say

British-Turkish, middle-class.' Barbaros stated that, depending on the context, identities transform throughout time:

> Context and age matter. I used to always say Turkish, then something happened and I started saying I am British more. I was a product of my mum who raised me religiously. I used to fast, but I stopped it because of the lack of contact. I was in Brighton and there were no Turks, there was only one *kebapçı* [kebab shop] that used to open at 1 am. It was not practical to fast. The culture around me was validating my actions, it was kind of giving me ownership of the situation in a way because I was constantly getting reminded about why I am doing these things, and other people are reflecting on my actions. […] Superficial things like football make me identify with Britishness. The idea of being British kind of encompasses my values, and my way of life. Because it is not English, it is an umbrella term. It is a less easily distinguishable, more anonymous kind of term that I can fit. In Turkey, I always say Turkish, I never say British. I would say probably, at this moment in time Britishness and then Turkishness and then Islam, being a Muslim. Although I do not practise it, I still emotionally and spiritually believe. I kind of agree with some stories and disagree with others like gender roles. There is an element of spirituality. My grandmothers were telling me it is related to Sufism. [British Turkish]

Figure 6.2 Street art representing John Lennon and Alex de Souza (football player for Fenerbahçe) in Green Lanes. Photo by author.

As Martin Bulmer and John Solomos state, 'each of us lives with a variety of potentially contradictory identities'.[27] These identities change depending on the place, context and living conditions. Barbaros's identification with Turkishness shifted when he was living in Brighton due to a lack of contact with Turkish people and by the loss of his grandmother, who was his reference point to Turkishness. Then, Britishness played a more important role in how he identifies; however, this identification is superficial – it lacks deeper meaning. There seems to be a clear impulse towards straddling both identities: practising Britishness through education and social interaction with peers but at the same time linking the sense of being Turkish to ethnic origin, family and socialisation with other Turkish-origin people in Britain. For example, Barbaros said having close friends who share the same ethnic background is important:

> They help you validate with things you grow up with. Anecdotes of your culture provide more context for people questioning it. It helps you identify more with that culture and teaches you more. Strengthens the links to that culture. Meeting with other middle-class Turkish Brits is good because all other Turks I know are kind of more working-class, grew up in Turkish enclaves and they would not like me at all. [British Turkish]

Barbaros touched on class as a determining factor in choosing friends from the same background. I asked him why he stressed the importance of class. He said the following:

> If you are with people who are like you, you feel this is an environment I am comfortable with and this kind of validates my existence. I lived in a property with my friends who grew up in upper-class families. Their families own castles and, next to them, I felt super foreign. They were visibly different and the anecdotes and the things they engage with are different. They were eating things I never heard of. When you leave the city, you feel you are foreign. But on the other hand, I also feel foreign next to British Turkish or British Kurdish youth who grew up and lived in Harringay within the Turkish and Kurdish communities. [British Turkish]

Barbaros distinguishes himself from British Kurdish and British Turkish youth who live in Harringay, a neighbourhood predominantly populated by Kurds and Turks, based on class stratification and refers to his class background, which differentiates him from his wealthy friends.

This hierarchy based on class also reflects the polarisation in Turkish society – Kurds vs Turks, rural vs urban. Class is a significant identification for Barbaros; as he said, 'it has been something to be proud of, it is something to distinguish me from the rest of British Turks'.

While this shows the reflection of the heterogeneity of the Turkish and Kurdish communities in Britain, it also indicates the hierarchies based on class in diverse socio-cultural spaces these young people enter. Some of these young people are not in contact with the Kurdish and Turkish communities in north London. For example, Yaz stated that it is hard to meet with British Turks in her circle: 'it was hard to meet with other middle-class British Turks. I have not been to that Turkish circle in London. I had not had a chance to meet Turks. I was away from that circle.' In the case of Yaz and Barbaros, Turkishness is practised only through the family and visits to Turkey, and their interaction with the community is limited as they do not participate in events organised by community organisations. Both Barbaros and Yaz referred to a form of socio-spatial segregation between them (middle-class British Turks, the children of immigrants) and working-class British Kurds and British Turks who live in Harringay, predominantly the children of refugees. The children of immigrants who do not live in the neighbourhoods where the Kurdish and Turkish migrants settled have fewer social contacts with the community and differentiate themselves by class from the children of refugees who are predominantly Kurdish, and who are politically engaged with the heritage country context. Moreover, a sense of belonging is articulated through this class hierarchy.

Britishness vs Kurdishness/Turkishness

'How do you define yourself in terms of your identities?', I asked young people. Their varied answers reflect the meanings they give to the identities, and how these identities intersect and are seen by others. For example, Aliza said:

> How I define myself changes with whom I am with. Sometimes I like to say I am Turkish because it is easier for people to understand. But actually I am Kurdish even though I do not speak the language 99 per cent of the time. I am Kurdish but one per cent of it changes. [British Kurdish]

Like Aliza, Ceren's answer changes depending on to whom she is speaking:

> If I speak with Turkish people I say 'oh yes I am Turkish'. When I say Kurdish, they ask what that means, it becomes a long process to explain because when I say Kurdish I make a political statement. It is not only my ethnic identity. I've found out what it means to be Kurdish through my studies – learning about the Kurdish resistance – and through the family. [British Kurdish]

Kurdishness means more than ethnic identity. It represents resistance and political positioning, which goes along with how Stuart Hall defined Black identity as a historical category, a political category and a cultural category, and that was created as a consequence of ideological struggles.[28] Although British Kurdish youth have not lived as a racialised minority in Turkey like their parents, they learn about the Kurdish struggle and resistance from their family, Kurdish community organisations, transnational media and school.

Alevism also depicts a political positioning, especially under the AKP government that has rooted its ideology in Sunni Islamism, against oppression and marginalisation. This is supported by Ceren, British Kurdish: 'I say I am Alevi even though I do not practise it. I feel close to its social identity rather than a religious one. If I introduce myself as Alevi, I do not have much to add to this as I do not know much about Alevism.' Alevism is not just a branch of Shia Islam, it is more than a religious belief for Ceren. It represents resistance and political positioning as Kurdishness. In some cases, the meaning given to ethnic identification assigns the career choices of the children of refugees. For example, Aliza's career choice aligns with her Kurdish identity: 'Even the reason for studying medicine is related to my ethnic identity because not many Kurdish women study medicine.'

Ethnic identification for the children of refugees becomes important even more than before, and this is not only due to their experiences of marginalisation in Britain but also related to their experiences of racialisation in Turkey. In this sense, the meaning that is given to ethnic identification has a transnational connotation that reflects the resistance of Kurds and their experiences in Turkey. Like Ceren and Aliza, Ateşcan also identifies as being Alevi. He said:

> I am Turkish and if people ask if I am Kurdish or not, I expand a little bit because originally I am a Turkmen because my ancestors came

> and settled in Kurdish villages I became Turkmen Kurd. If someone asks me I say Turkmen because I do not know Kurdish culture. I am Alevi as well, which is a very important identification, especially during this time. [British Turkish]

Referring to Aleviness as one of his main identities, Ateşcan relates to it as a cultural and political identity rather than a religious phenomenon. He pointed to the social and political oppression of Alevis under the AKP government when he said 'during this time'.

The children of refugees and immigrants are more than identities that are associated with them, such as black, Muslim, criminal, uncivilised, and so on. Ateşcan touched on the immigration policy of the government to explain how he and other children of immigrants are seen:

> They are bringing in the points system, which is complete bullshit. If someone escapes from war but has a university degree, this person cannot come to this country because of not having enough points. This is ridiculous. English people call Middle Eastern people terrorists and barbarians. When Ukraine refugees fled, they said on BBC news 'we cannot let these high-class, modern people down'. These double standards really piss me off. I experience discrimination. I go to a bank and say I want to put money into my account. They look at me and say where do you get the money from. I say I am a law student and my dad owns a restaurant. They question me because I am darker and have a beard. When I was going to school in north Finchley, a middle-class area, there were all white kids. They were racist. [British Turkish]

This extract indicates what the children of refugees and immigrants, especially from the Middle East, have been feeling in everyday life everywhere in Britain. The process of racialisation that has permeated society – negative stereotyping of Middle Eastern people as terrorists, uncivilised, and harassing women – make young people experience racism more and more in everyday life.

This is, of course, not new. 9/11, the 7/7 London bombings, further terrorist attacks, the 'hostile environment' policy, the refugee movements from the Middle East, Brexit and the Nationality and Borders Bill have aggravated a racist political climate in Britain. Ranking refugees based on their physical appearance on state television is normalised; as the BBC reporter said when reporting about the Russian invasion of Ukraine : 'To me I am sorry it's really emotional for me because I see

European people with blue eyes and blonde hair being healed, children being killed every day with Putin's missiles and his helicopters and his rockets.'[29] Two reporters described Ukrainian refugees as, 'these are not refugees from Syria, these are refugees from neighbouring Ukraine. These are Christians, they are white.' By contrasting Ukrainian refugees with Middle Eastern refugees – civilised vs barbarian, white vs brown, Christians vs Muslims, educated vs uneducated and working vs middle-class – racialised hierarchies are recreated in society. The 'good' and 'bad', 'deserving' and 'undeserving' dichotomy is connected to race and class, and reflects the interrelation between racism and nationalism. Describing the interrelation between racism and nationalism as 'the new racism', Paul Gilroy argues that 'its novelty lies in the capacity to link discourses of patriotism, nationalism, xenophobia, Englishness, Britishness, militarism and gender difference into a complex system, which gives "race" its contemporary meaning'.[30] This highlights that culture and identity become determining factors when discussing 'race'. The Muslimness of the Middle Eastern refugees becomes their race.

Ateşcan's experience of racism is an example of the 'new racism' that sets clear boundaries between who is British and who is not. I asked Ateşcan what he would feel if his British citizenship were revoked? He said:

> If they take away my British citizenship, it is not going to take away the fact that I am British. I was born and raised in this country. If I need to fight against it, I would fight. I know my rights, and I know the steps I need to take. I would become angry and I would do anything to get it back because this is my home. [British Turkish]

Britishness is not something that only needs to be verified by holding British citizenship for Ateşcan, as he will still be British even if he does not hold citizenship. He is British because he was born and raised in Britain; has only lived in Britain; English is his first language; he has been educated in Britain; his friends are in Britain; Britain is unequivocally his home. His relation to Britishness reflects an internalised sense of belonging, and he is ready to fight against the racist framing of Britishness that was designed much earlier and is still apparent today as unattainable for the children of refugees and immigrants, especially those who are black, brown or Muslim.

In 1968 Enoch Powell, who was a Conservative Member of Parliament, made his notorious 'Rivers of Blood' speech in Birmingham, targeting post-colonial settlers, and seeing the immigration of non-whites from the former colonies as a threat to white Britain. Powell's old-fashioned racism has been replaced with new forms of racism against refugees from the Middle East, Muslim migrants and all other racialised minorities. The 'us vs them' rhetoric is still actively used as a way to distinguish not only migrants vs citizens but also white British vs non-white British. Britishness has hierarchical degrees where the difference between full (white) and less (non-white) Britishness is defined by a nation-state that is always seeking a homogeneous, white Britain.

When Aliza answered the question regarding how they would feel if their British citizenship were revoked, she recalled the Shamima Begum case. Aliza stated:

> I never taught about it because I never had to think about it. But they revoked Shamima Begum's citizenship – she does not hold dual citizenship, she is only a British citizen. It is not fair – she was born here, she is a British citizen. It is not fair to put her in a refugee camp and make her stateless. She should be back and put in court and be in prison. All these happen also because she has brown skin. This makes me think whether this might happen to us when we commit a crime. [British Kurdish]

Shamima Begum is a British-born woman who fled Britain aged 15 and joined the Islamic State of Iraq and the Levant and was smuggled into Syria. Begum's British citizenship was revoked in 2019 due to security concerns, which made her stateless as she does not have dual citizenship. The revoking of Shamima Begum's citizenship is a precedent that makes the children of refugees and immigrants worry about their settlement situation in Britain. The Home Office has stated that Begum is eligible to apply for Bangladeshi citizenship because of her heritage. Due to her parents being born in a different country, even though Begum does not hold citizenship of their parents' heritage country, her British citizenship was revoked. Begum's case has attracted media attention which employs othering rhetoric when referring to British citizens who are the *Other*, meaning not white, and the *Other* is presumed as less British.[31]

Ceren pointed out the narrative of the British state about anyone who is not white. Touching on Begum's case she said:

> I understand Shamima Begum was groomed and her citizenship should not be revoked, but when I link it with Kurds, she joined ISIS and they were killing Kurds. I could have been killed. What happened to her is [an] injustice, I get it. It is crazy how they say

to go back to a place [when] you do not have any connection with that place. It applies to all of us. When we commit a serious crime, they deport us. They accepted this as a norm because we are not English. Brexit happened because they do not want immigrants. I do think people are more comfortable voicing an opinion against immigrants. I do feel like people become openly racist. This is why I always need to state where I am originally from because saying London is not considered the right response. [British Kurdish]

Ceren feels less British. This is how many young people feel because Britishness has fully accepted its roots in ideological whiteness, which is now implemented even more with the 'hostile environment' policies and Brexit. The question 'where are you from?' is a constant reminder to go back to where you came from, to 'go home' for the children of refugees and immigrants due to a failure to access a shared British identity.

Ateşcan pointed to the fact that British history has never been homogeneous:

> The old British monarchs were not even English. For example, William the Conqueror was French not English. So, English culture or British history is not English. It is a collection of different cultures. Since the seventeenth and eighteenth centuries, Africans and Asians have been present in Britain. British culture is multicultural including Anglo-Saxons, Germans, Romans and now in London especially there are Turks, and Albanians. So many different cultures into one. [British Turkish]

As Afua Hirsch puts it: 'Britain has no "white history". British history is the multiracial, interracial story of a nation interdependent on trade, cultural influence and immigration from Africa, India, Central and East Asia, and other regions and continents populated by people who are not white.'[32] 'The history of the British Empire is not being taught' said Yaz and added 'I did not learn anything about Turkey at school. I learnt lots of things about Britain. It would have been good to learn about different cultures. We learn good stuff about the monarchy. We did not learn about colonial history.'

Like Yaz, Barbaros and Ateşcan also commented on the British curriculum as not covering the history properly and being inherently Eurocentric. Barbaros, British Turkish, stated: 'It erases so many different cultures. There was very little representation. I did ask my history teacher "why we do not learn about the Ottoman Empire?" She said "it is not important".' Ateşcan, British Turkish, said 'In GCSA history, they do not talk about the battle of Gelibolu, a Turkish battle. It is a massive part of World War One. My teacher said it is not in the module. They do not want to admit that they lost.'

The children of immigrants feel alienated at school; they find themselves under-represented and under-stimulated by the content of the British curriculum. With their histories excluded from the British curriculum, non-white students feel isolated, excluded and alienated in the school environment. They also experience microaggressions, such as people failing to pronounce their names properly after being corrected or commenting about their clothing, which makes them feel alienated and marginalised. For example, Barbaros felt disgusted by the confusion about his name and it being pronounced wrong in year one, as explained in Chapter 4. He also mentioned microaggressions experienced about his appearance and clothing:

> Definitely primary and secondary school played a big part in my identity formation. Conversely, when I used to go to Arabic class. It was not my ethnic identity, but the cultural identity I was representing. Although we were all Muslims on paper, they did not mention a Turkish name but they said 'why do you dress like that?', and 'why is your hair long?'. [British Turkish]

Yaz stated:

> I went to a very small school and I struggled for different reasons, not only because of being Turkish. It was a very atypical kind of secondary school. I did a lot of drama and music. It was great and helped me lots in terms of my confidence. I was doing Shakespeare and these very traditional British plays, it was a very small school, it is hard to say. It would have been very different if I had other Turkish people with me. It was hard to find a balance at school. There are people either completely open to difference to the point where you feel invisible and people who are aware of your identity. My sister went to dinner at her friend's house and her friend's mum came in with a long dress and said 'look, I am Mediterranean'. I dealt with little things like that with my school friends and their parents. [British Turkish]

These microaggressions make young people feeling marginalised, lonely and excluded at school and in other environments when people desire to test each other's differences. In this case, these young people might feel they belong more to their ethnic identity. For example, Ateşcan said that he feels Turkish even though he speaks English better than Turkish. Through his transnational links with people in Turkey, spending some time every year in Mersin, and getting to know the culture and history, he has constructed a close and deeper relationship with Turkishness. Although practising British culture in everyday life makes him feel connected to Britishness, he does not find it as unique as Turkishness. According to Ateşcan, for his sense of belonging, cultural attachment is more important than the practicality of speaking the language well:

> Despite the fact that I am better at English, I know English history, but I still feel Turkish. My parents raised me in a way 'he is going to learn English outside the house but inside the house, he should be speaking Turkish'. With Turkish, I identify with the culture and Turkish identity more but in terms of how I create a sense of belonging to English and British culture, I have to speak English [....] I am very attached to my background, Turkish history. When I go to Mersin I feel very much at home there. I do not feel foreign. Maybe my Turkish is not as good as everyone else and they tell me I am *gurbetçi* [one living away from home] but it does not matter. There is no difference when I go there. It is home to me. [British Turkish]

Ateşcan carried on pointing out the differences between Britishness and Turkishness with reference to cultural aspects. Uniqueness is an important factor in his sense of belonging to these identifications. His understanding of uniqueness in relation to these identities is about representation. Being British does not have a deep meaning for Ateşcan because he thinks it is not unique; it is a combination of different cultures. Whereas being Turkish is more meaningful for Ateşcan as he finds it represented in its history and this brings attachment to the culture even though he experienced *Othering* through the label of *gurbetçi* in Mersin. Like many other children of refugees and immigrants, Ateşcan feels less British, in this sense, Turkishness becomes a safe identity option, one where he will not be rejected even though his Turkish is not as fluent as that of the Turkish and Kurdish residents in Mersin. The representation of Turkishness for Ateşcan is associated with its history and its 'strong' leaders, of which he is very proud:

> With Turkish identity, our history is filled with strong leaders, saying I am a Turk, I am very proud. It is *ayrıcalık* [privilege]. When

people ask 'where are you from?', I say 'I am from London'. Then people say 'Oh, you are British'. Other than that, no one really cares. When I say I am Turkish, people say straight away Ottoman Empire, Atatürk. Turkish identity is strong. Not everyone can achieve what Atatürk and the Ottoman Empire did. I love British culture, it is funny, nice and loose. But I also love Turkish culture. If it comes down to it and I have to pick one, I would pick Turkish identity. November 11 is Remembrance Day when everyone wears the poppy; I do not wear it. So, when I was little I was always interested in Turkish history and Atatürk. I have respect for all the soldiers who died but I am not wearing it. [British Turkish]

Turkishness represents a 'strong' national identity for Ateşcan and being identified with this 'strong' identity that comes from its history, according to Ateşcan, puts him in a safer position, especially when he wants to escape from Britishness. His attachment to Turkishness is strengthened by his family and the community in north London where transnational political practices have been developed. In some cases, these transnational political practices reflect patriotism, long-distance nationalism,[33] especially through glorifying leaders and the Ottoman Empire in the case of the Turkish community. Although Ateşcan represented himself in hybridised ways in which he identifies both with Turkishness and Britishness, he finds comfort and safety in Turkishness, which is to some degree related to his experiences of racism in Britain. When he talked about his experiences of racism, he said that 'we, the children of immigrants, are experiencing racism and we have an identity called: *Otherness*'. How he talks about Britishness and Turkishness, and how these identities are seen by others, are central to his attachment to these identities. The exclusion of racialised minorities, discrimination and racism have become interlaced into the fabric of everyday life in Britain. The children of refugees and immigrants experience this everywhere in Britain and in some cases these experiences make them hold onto their ethnic, and transnational identities as a reaction to being seen as *Other*. This situation is explained in the literature by adopting the concept of 'reactive ethnicity', referring to the fact that migrants and ethnic minorities identify with ethnic identities stronger and engage in transnational activities as a reaction to the experiences of discrimination and racism.[34] However, the children of refugees and immigrants negotiate their positioning with their ethnic identities, especially about how gender is perceived.

Yaz's parents were divorced and they have a younger sister. For years Yaz has been living with her dad, a single parent, raising Yaz and their younger sister. As the older sister, Yaz has caretaking duties around the house and responsibility for taking care of their sister. Yaz feels that English people do not understand these family dynamics, caretaking duties and expectations of females in Turkish society and family. Even though Yaz does not have a traditional family, they stated that there are still expectations around marriage and relationships. Yaz pointed out how gender roles, which have transnational roots, are significant in their everyday life in Britain:

> Turkishness and exoticness here have been fetishised in various relationships, which is common with women. Also, going out would be allowed if I was a boy. My parents would treat me differently if I was a boy. With my queer identity, only recently when I meet with other Turkish queer people, I feel that ok I can be queer and Turkish. I felt more British with the queerness. Queer is a big one for me. Context matters so much. Queer then Turkish and then British. [British Turkish]

Yaz is negotiating their relationship with Turkishness in relation to how gender roles are defined in Turkish society. This also shows that their relationship with Britishness and Turkishness is also defined by how these identities get on with their gender identities and how Yaz feels comfortable. The intersection of Yaz's queer identity with their Turkish and British identities captures the complexity of the existence of these identities together. Yaz stated that they are still learning about Turkishness highlighting their Eurocentric perspective especially when it intersects with queerness. Yaz thought that they would not meet with any Turkish queer because queerness interweaves with the Western approach, and explained how Turkishness and queerness clash in their everyday life:

> I am still learning about Turkishness. For example, I thought I would not meet any Turkish queer. It has huge to be able to find them. Once you know a few, you meet others. Turkish queers are different. For me, these two identities clashed so hard for so many years. [...] I came out to my Dad; he was ok with it. I told myself a story that this is not going to go well for so many years. [...] I had this story in my head, but this was not the case. If I had never seen other Turkish queer people, I would have thought this was banned. Everyone felt

those things could not exist together. It was just refreshing seeing other Turkish queers. [British Turkish]

Yaz's multiple identities conflicting with each other challenge their sense of belonging. Their experience with both Turkishness, which is often associated with Islam, and queerness, which is seen as an example of 'Westernisation', shows that they can claim to belong to these 'conflicting' identities at the same time. While Yaz finds it easier to put Britishness and Turkishness into the same pot as a result of ongoing transnational engagements in Britain and Turkey, they have had difficulties in operating Turkishness and queerness together. As they said: 'there was this white queerness and this like black understanding. Britishness and queerness easily fit with each other. British queer movement is not always inclusive of non-British queer people.' Yaz's identifications interact, intersect and disclaim each other. Their identification as queer is a political act that rejects normative definitions of sexual behaviour and patriarchy, and Turkishness as their ethnic identity disrupts British sovereignty and offers them a space where they find comfort. Depending on the context and place, these two conflicting identities might have things in common; for instance, Turkishness and queerness are both examples of identities that are resisted in Britain. As a Turkish-origin British queer, Yaz has experienced Western-centric perspective of queerness in Britain, which could be discriminatory towards queer people from the Global South. This experience has made them question the inclusivity of queerness in Britain. Yaz questions their relation to both Britishness and Turkishness through practising and performing queerness, and experiences of exclusion as a British Turkish queer from the white queer space and exclusion as a Turkish queer from the authoritarian Islamic space.

How gender roles are defined, perceived and practised in Turkey are also questioned by other young people. For example, on the one hand, in relation to being a male in Turkish society, Barbaros and Ateşcan referred to social expectations of males that create pressure on them in terms of income, success and marriage, and the heteronormativity that is promoted. On the other hand, referring to the conflict they had with their families in relation to gender equality Aliza and Ceren pointed out that even having liberal parents does not guarantee gender equality. Aliza said:

My brother is older but I feel so lucky because he is so chilled. I had a boyfriend, and he knew about it. I experienced heartbreak, he was there. He never commented on anything I wear. He has never been restricted. I think this comes from a socialist background. I have never been restricted from anyone in my family. Even next to my grandad, I wear shorts. [...] My boyfriend came to pick me up from my house. I was in Turkey, Altınoluk. In the opposite house, there was a family we knew, two boys at my age and they had a sister. Their sister was conservative, she went home at 10 pm at the latest. I always socialised with boys because they were my age. I was young, 10, and 11 years old. We had a water fight. My mum was angry. I said to her 'you should not do this. You have a socialist, feminist mindset, you are saying that girls and boys are equal, but you never do this to my brother.' Now, I feel so comfortable that I said these things. Even in London, our parents care what other people think. [British Kurdish]

Ceren also touched on gender roles in her family:

In my family, my brother is younger than us. He is completely open. It is pretty ok, but I have heard comments from other people saying that if you are a Kurdish girl you should not drink or go out. It is attached to being Kurdish and having a Muslim background as well. It is not the same for other Kurdish girls. For example, I am going on a year abroad, my Kurdish friends are shocked because my parents let me go. It is sad because their parents might not support this. I know I am lucky but I had to fight a lot with my parents to do what I want. As much as my parents say they are liberal, they do not practise it. There were a lot of fights and a lot of arguments about what I wanted. They do not want to let go of what has been taught to them back home. [...] I think they are also scared that we are becoming English. There is this idea that European culture is bad because people feel comfortable with their identities. So, there is a constant thing of what if we let go of who we are or whom they want us to be. [British Kurdish]

The experiences of these young people show how broader social identities play a crucial role in their sense of belonging to their parents' country of origin. These traditional gender roles are not only taken seriously in Turkey; they are moving transnationally and practised by the children of refugees and immigrants during their socialisation process in Britain, as stated in Chapter 5. Their accounts reveal that heteronormativity, which is associated with patriarchal structures, gender norms and stereotypes is being challenged in a transnational space. For example, while some young people commented on how they face sexism when they visit Turkey, others mentioned how gender norms in Turkish culture affect their everyday lives in Britain, which is related to how these gender norms are reproduced. As highlighted by Ceren, one of the reasons why their parents reproduce these gender roles is the fear of their children becoming English. This parental concern over the children of refugees and immigrants is also experienced by first-generation parents in America, and this fear is a part of the paradox of the immigrant experience.[35] The first generation overcomes obstacles to give their children the chance to become English, especially through education and academic success, but at the same time parents are uncomfortable with their children becoming English. They fear that their children are losing their cultural roots.

The representatives of Kurdish and Turkish community organisations in London who are also parents highlighted this feeling and the correlated fear of losing the ability to guide and influence their children. The director of Gik-Der revealed: 'we are losing our children [...] they are becoming English [...] they should know who they are and where they come from'. The first generation who migrated to Britain due to political and socio-economic reasons would like to provide a better future for their children but, at the same time, they do not want their children to lose their background and become British.

For young people who are growing up with such a dual frame of reference, however, remaining close to their parents' country of origin becomes difficult: they interact with different cultural repertoires in everyday life. The children of refugees and immigrants feel alienated from their families and, in their account, alienation happens when parents and children possess dissonant cultural views about appropriate ideas and behaviours.[36] The everyday social experiences of children of refugees and immigrants in a transnational context help widen their understanding of identity, which is constantly in the process of negotiation, beyond commonalities and enables them to engage with identities at an individual level. Floya Anthias offers the term 'transnational positionality' instead of 'identity', which refers to the claims and attributes that individuals make about their position in the social order, their views of where and what to belong to and what not belong to, as well as broader social relations that constitute this process.[37]

How the children of refugees and immigrants position themselves within a range of social positionings in relation to gender, ethnicity and class is always in a process of negotiation. For instance, Yaz negotiates how queerness is practised both in Turkey and Britain; their transnational positionality is constructed through the lived experience in which gender is performed in both locations, and they position themselves beyond commonality. Yaz's practice of performing gender in Turkey and how it links with their ethnic identity clashes:

> I do understand Turkish as an ethnic identity. Here I say Turkish, I specify where my family is from Turkey. I did not grow up as Turkish, my family were not loud about Atatürkçü. I grow up with parents, especially my mum who embraced Britishness so much. She tried actively to form a British child. Turkishness is there but you cannot change it. I feel like it would be easier for men to find space to bond in Turkishness. There are cafes men go to, and when you get to a certain age you go to these places, to watch a football match. But with women, it would be a different process to bond or seek out these people. [...] Queer is a big one for me. Context matters so much. Being queer is difficult in Turkey. [British Turkish]

Yaz's transnational positionality is beyond ethnic and national identifications, and takes gender identifications into account; in some cases, Yaz's sense of belonging to Turkey and Britain is constructed in line with the representation of their gender roles. Yaz's relationship with Turkishness is in a constant process of negotiation throughout their socialisation process. Turkishness is referred as a family thing; values and attitudes play a big role in this identification for Yaz. As they put it:

> Even in London, I feel pressure to get married from the Turkish community. There is pressure to get into a relationship for women in Turkey. I went to a Turkish off-licence here, and the woman who works there said, 'ok, you finished your study, you can now get married'. Everyone knows everyone's business. [British Turkish]

Yaz felt pressure for gender conformity from their parents even though they were raised as British:

> Turkish parenting in this country still means you cannot go out this time. Going out was harder. If you want to have a drink, go out. You might need to lie to your parents. Why Ryan's mum allows everyone to drink, and why my mum does not? I was confused seeing these Brits – what is it about British parents that are so widely different? When mum raised me as a British child, all the Britishness is very superficial, but then being a Turk is something they cannot escape. For instance, my dad is very modern, super modern, accepting

> whatever, but he still comes from a very male-oriented Turkishness background, unconsciously I guess. This is how they grow up. It is clear how widely differently we grow up from our parents. England is being more individualist and Turkey is being more collectivist. [British Turkish]

Yaz pointed out the socio-cultural context of Turkishness and Britishness that have an impact on individuals. Turkishness comprises gender-based social roles that affect Yaz's sense of belonging with Turkishness, which is not correlated with how their gender identity is represented in Britain.

Like Yaz, Barbaros also thinks that Britishness is superficial compared to Turkishness which is more about family, and community, and has a deeper meaning. For Barbaros, people in Turkey are warmer compared to people in England, where no one really cares about each other. He links this with the culture of welcoming people that is extended to everyday interactions, and compares Turkey with Britain, referring to the historical reference: 'If you look at British colonialism, [it] is about using the area, perching the area. Turks are rinsing the area.'

How the children of immigrants practise Turkishness is different from how Turkish people practise it in Turkey. For example, Serkan pointed out that not being raised in Turkey makes claiming Turkishness difficult.

> I am British. My parents are Turkish. My background is Turkish. That makes me a Turk. Because I was born in this country, I am British in some way. If I was born in Turkey, I would have a lot of things to say about Turkishness. But to me, Turkishness in this country is just being a Turk. It is just a family thing. Food I eat at home. In my home, I eat Turkish food and chat with my family in Turkish. This is Turkishness. There is nothing I can add to it basically. If we come to Britishness, because I was born in this country, I have more things to say about Britishness. I think I am more British than Turkish. I was raised in this country. I was kicked out of Turkey for five years. I lived there for my education. But it was really bad and I didn't like it. I am so used to British culture. I was born here then I went to school. Everything was English, chatting in English, eating your mashed potatoes. [British Turkish]

The context is important in understanding how these young people view where and to what they belong, and how they position themselves within a range of locations and dislocations in relation to gender, ethnicity, national belonging and class.[38] 'It is all about London' said Yaz, when referring to their established connection with British Kurdish and British Turkish friends. They added: 'My friend and I had conversations together speaking both English and Turkish. This builds a great sense of belonging. To be able to speak with people who speak English and Turkish is great. That connects you because they know the context.' The commonality of experiencing being a child of immigrants, living across the borders of nation-states, mixing English and Turkish while talking and creating words that include Turkish and English within itself, constantly being asked 'where are you originally from?' and reminded that they are not fully British, bring the children of refugees and immigrants into a similar space where their transnational identity, the shared identity of living in a transnational context, beyond 'territorially bounded notions of nation, culture and ethnicity',[39] is practised. For Yaz, identity has so much to do with home and comfort and, when they feel worried or anxious, they seek the culture they get comfort from. Yaz was longing for *dolma* in New York, even though they have never lived in Turkey, because they have eaten *dolmas* at a Turkish restaurant in north London, and in Turkey. Longing for *dolma* is an example of transnational positionality.

Conclusion

Being British is unclear to many children of refugees and immigrants. However, so also is defining what it means to be Kurdish or Turkish. In this chapter, I have sought to demonstrate how young people perceive their positioning in society; how their transnational background is reflected in their perception of identity; how the dimensions of the self, the socio-political context of Britain and Turkey influence identity negotiation among the participants; and how the young people feel about being British, Kurdish or Turkish. The children of refugees and immigrants stated that they feel less British because of feeling excluded by having a lack of knowledge about British culture and its identity, and not affiliating with Britain's colonial past. They are trying to figure out what kind of Britishness they can belong to.

Nevertheless, Kurdishness means more than ethnic identity for the children of refugees as it represents resistance and political positioning. For that reason, they stated that they are proud of their Kurdishness and feel more Kurdish than British. In this sense, identity is defined as a political category, as argued by Stuart Hall.[40] Kurdishness is also stated as easier to identify with in comparison to Britishness due to the ongoing transnational socio-cultural and political links, and through their families and community.

Turkishness is associated more with family, holiday and food. In a similar exploration of Britishness, being Turkish is also questioned in relation to history and political circumstances. Many of my respondents pointed out that norms around gender and sexuality are deeply ingrained in Kurdish and Turkish societies and they have felt the pressure for gender normativity not only when they visit Turkey but also from their parents and from the Kurdish and Turkish communities in London. These young people negotiate gendered identities, which find space within Kurdishness and Turkishness.

I have argued that the socio-political context in Britain and Turkey shapes how young people make sense of their identities and negotiate them in a transnational context. The experiences of racism among the children of refugees and immigrants have an impact on how they define their Britishness, Kurdishness and Turkishness. They all experience racism, but Kurds experience it transnationally in both settings. There is little research into how experiencing racism in both the immigrant and emigrant society influences their transnational ties and sense of belonging and how those ties can change over time in line with political and socio-economic shifts. As shown in this chapter, Britain's 'hostile environment', the post-Brexit landscape and Turkey's authoritarian and anti-Kurdish landscape impact on how young people construct transnational identities.

Notes

1. See Sales 2012: 49.
2. See Ware 2007: 4.
3. See Hall 2022: 230.
4. See Hall 2022: 231.
5. See Hall 1993: 362.
6. See Maalouf 2000: 20.
7. See Chimienti *et al.* 2019.
8. See Hall 2022: 230.
9. See Back and Sinha 2016: 151.
10. See Bhambra 2017.
11. See Kasinitz *et al.* 2002; 2004.
12. See Anthias 2002.
13. See Watson 1977; Anwar 1998.
14. See Bhabha 1990; Featherstone 1994; Kaya 2002.
15. See Kaya 2002: 58.
16. See Toyota 2003.
17. See Song 2003.

18. See Toyota 2003.
19. See Hutnyk 2005.
20. See Hall 1996; 2022.
21. See Snel *et al.* 2016.
22. See Redclift and Rajina 2021.
23. Stephens 2016.
24. Booth 2019.
25. Andrews 2021.
26. See Ossipow *et al.* 2019.
27. See Bulmer and Solomos 1998: 826.
28. See Hall 2022: 232.
29. 'European people with blue eyes and blonde hair being killed" what a BBC interviewee commented'. Arab News. https://www.youtube.com/watch?v=pU-8gKaUO_Y
30. See Gilroy 2006: 42.
31. See Smith 2016.
32. See Hirsch 2018: 83.
33. See Anderson 1998.
34. See Portes and Rumbaut 2001; Herda 2018; Snel *et al.* 2016.
35. See Kasinitz *et al.* 2008.
36. See Portes and Rumbaut 2001.
37. See Anthias 2002: 512.
38. See Anthias 2002: 502.
39. See Song 2003: 115.
40. See Hall 2022.

7
Conclusion

The self-proposed question 'Am I less British?' was asked by almost all the young people who were interviewed for this book. It is not even a question for the children of refugees and immigrants; it is more of a reply. Most discussions of Britishness at the policy level fail to include the children of refugees and immigrants within its 'shared culture' and, because of this, these young people are often associated with their parents' country of origin, even though they have never lived there. The identities that the children of refugees and immigrants accept, reject, negotiate and make in a transnational context contradict and also restore each other.

Am I Less British? has addressed these contradictions and restorations by offering a perspective on the questions of identity and belonging beyond the category of culture in a transnational context that differs from the common definitions and debates in the literature on the identity formation of the children of refugees and immigrants. The identities of these young people are primarily defined as being 'between two cultures'[1] and/or experiencing hybridity as the 'third space'.[2] By defining the children of refugees and immigrants as being 'between two cultures' or in a 'third space' these scholars put young people into the categories of identity. By contrast, this book has explored the identity-making processes of young people through everyday life experiences, taking into account the diverse positioning of individuals in understanding the broader social relations that are constituted in these processes. Defining the identities of these young people as 'between two cultures' restricts identities only to culture, and ignores the thoughts, feelings and responses of young people to the identities to which they belong through citizenship and ethnicity, and political resistance in the case of Kurdish youth.

Am I Less British? has paid attention to the various versions of identifications, including the collective social identities of class, gender, ethnicity, religion and nation, and has shown that the political contexts of the countries to which these young people are linked transnationally influence their processes of identification. I have argued that the children of Turkish immigrants deidentify themselves from national identities, such as Turkish and British, due to their experiences of racism and exclusion transnationally. As a result, they find themselves in a constant process of negotiating their identity. However, the children of Kurdish refugees identify more with their Kurdishness as a response to racism in a transnational context, both in Turkey and Britain.

Furthermore, the importance of the everyday life experiences of these young people in a transnational context has been discussed. As such, the main aim of this book has been to critically approach and discuss the concepts of identity and belonging in a transnational context with the help of the theoretical perspectives of transnational identities, and an explicit focus on individual perceptions and experiences. The experiences of racism and exclusion faced by the children of refugees and immigrants in both Britain and Turkey shape their perceptions and relationships with these countries. The socio-political context of both countries plays a significant role in shaping the identities of these young people and their sense of belonging.

The concept of transnationalism cannot fully explain their experiences, and its limitations have been highlighted in this book. Through a conceptual tool, I have demonstrated how racism and exclusion in a transnational context cause these young people to deidentify themselves from national identities and to have a lack of social and economic engagement. I have argued that the experiences of the children of refugees and immigrants must be understood within the context of the political and socio-economic circumstances in the countries they engage with transnationally. My argument in *Am I Less British?* questions the existing knowledge in the literature on the identities of the children of refugees and immigrants and contributes to a broader understanding of identities and belonging in a transnational context by finding answers to questions about how the children of refugees and immigrants position themselves within a range of locations where they face racial and class hierarchy, racism and discrimination; how they make sense of their identities and belonging within the contemporary political context in Britain and Turkey, and what it means to be a citizen of Britain and Turkey. I hope that the findings presented in this book contribute to an understanding of the meaning of identities in our globalised world.

In this concluding chapter, I want to summarise what I have learnt from the accounts of the children of refugees and immigrants. The analytical framework I have presented in this book offers four insights into the relationships between young people and their respective nationalities, cities and identities.

First, how the children of refugees and immigrants relate themselves to identities in a transnational context differs depending on the meaning they give to identities. As shown in this book with regard to the children of refugees, British Kurdish young people predominantly identify with Kurdishness more compared to how British Turkish young people define themselves with Turkishness, because Kurdishness represents the history of resistance and a political positioning against racialisation, violence and denial. The children of refugees experience racism transnationally, both in the receiving and sending societies, due to their Kurdish identity.

The literature on the transnational activities of the children of immigrants explores the positive impacts of being involved in transnational links with their parents' country of origin, especially when they experience racism in the settlement country, but ignores the experiences of racism in general and their experiences as the children of refugees specifically.[3] Focusing on the experiences of racialisation and racism among the children of refugees and immigrants in the settlement country, Switzerland, in a comparative way, Laurence Ossipow *et al.*'s research shows that the children of refugees are daily racialised and identified as foreigners in Switzerland, despite holding Switzerland citizenship, compared to the children of immigrants, and shows that the class and the refugee status of their parents have an impact on their racialisation.[4] Similar to their findings, my research also shows that the children of refugees whose parents belong to the working-class and who have settled in the neighbourhoods of north London that are populated predominantly by people from migratory and working-class backgrounds experience racism in Britain more than the children of immigrants who are from a middle-class background. However, in contrast, my findings support the conclusion that, despite their privileged class status, the children of immigrants also feel excluded from and feel less belonging to British society because they were constantly reminded of their parents' migratory background. For instance, both Barbaros and Yaz mentioned that, even though they are from a middle-class background and live in affluent neighbourhoods, they were still discriminated against because of their background, religion and name.

Examining the experiences of racism among the children of refugees and immigrants in Turkey, my findings suggest that while the children of refugees, and British Kurdish youth experience racism in Turkey, the children of immigrants, and British Turkish youth do not experience racism during their visits to Turkey, which supports the findings of Alice Bloch and Shirin Hirsh[5] that 'experiencing racism during visits to the heritage country reinforced the specificity of the refugee context that led to their parents' migration'. This has caused the children of refugees to engage in transnational social and economic activities less in comparison to the children of immigrants, however strong transnational political engagement as a result of ongoing exclusion and racialisation in Turkey. Most of the studies only focus on the outcomes of experiencing racialisation and racism in the case of the children of refugees either in the sending or the receiving societies, rather than exploring the consequences of these experiences in both settings on their senses of belonging, and transnational links in both settings. By deploying the transnational perspective in exploring the experiences of racism among the children of refugees and immigrants, which have a big impact on how they relate to identities and construct senses of belonging, this book has focused on such experiences in both the sending and receiving societies. Therefore, I have shown, in this book, that, as in the case of the children of refugees, the children of immigrants experiencing racism in both societies makes them deidentify themselves from national identities; they feel they belong less to both societies and have a lack of social and economic transnational engagements. This makes them feel they identify with London, particularly north London, where they have established social networks, and where they feel safe and comfortable. With its particular focus on the experiences of racism in a transnational context, this book has contributed to the literature on transnational identities and the children of refugees and immigrants, and demonstrated that such experiences have an impact on their transnational engagement and identifications.

Second, this book has indicated that diversity and multiculturalism reconstruct hierarchies of belonging and new forms of racism in line with Les Back and Shamser Sinha's study.[6] The multicultural exchanges the children of refugees and immigrants experience when interacting with people from other ethnic and racial backgrounds in their everyday lives – on the streets, in shops, parks, cafes, and council estates, and so on – do not offer a shared narrative in which their ethnic identities are rendered ordinary. The children of refugees and immigrants interviewed for this book stated that they are often in London asked the question 'where are you originally from?', which is a persistent reminder that they do not belong to London, and makes them wonder what kind of multiculture is being referred to. London is a multicultural city where the Britishness of the children of refugees and immigrants has been questioned by white

British people and, in some cases, by other racialised minorities. This book has contributed to the literature on conviviality by showing that class inequalities among the children of refugees and immigrants limit the convivial moments these young people experience. However, it has also revealed that the shared experiences of being the children of immigrants and experiencing exclusion and racism makes them bond together and has constructed convivial moments comprising solidarity and empathy.

Third, the literature on the identities of the children of refugees and immigrants mostly explores their belonging(ness) only through referencing national and ethnic identities that reconstruct artificial categories. The literature is largely silent about the role of intersectionality in the identification processes of these young people. I have shown that adopting an intersectional lens in exploring the sense of belonging and identities of these young people is crucial to have a deeper understanding of the complexity of their lives in changing socio-political circumstances in a transnational context. The accounts of the young people presented in this book have shown that particularly the intersections of class, gender and ethnicity indicate complex experiences, and these experiences have been interpreted differently depending on the socio-political circumstances of the countries. For example, British Kurdish young women have faced exclusion and racialisation based on their ethnic and gender identity in Turkey and within the community in north London; they also have faced exclusion and racism based on their ethnicity, class and parent's migratory status in Britain. Ceren does not feel excluded because of her class identity in Turkey, but she feels *Other* in Britain due to her class identity: 'people pick up from my accent where I live, which reveals not only my ethnic background, as everyone knows that north London is where Turkish and Kurdish people live, but also my working-class background'. Their accounts have also designated that their lived experiences of identity-based oppression vary depending on the socio-political circumstances of the countries they engage with. For instance, the children of immigrants who belong to the LGBTQ+ community do not feel secure and safe in Turkey due to the anti-LGBTQ+ policies of the AKP government and the reflection of these policies in society. Nevertheless, they feel safer in Britain but experience different levels of exclusion and discrimination within the white LGBTQ+ community in Britain due to their background. As Yaz stated 'there was this white queerness and this like black understanding. Britishness and queerness easily fit with each other but British queer movement is not always inclusive of non-British queer people.' While Yaz feels excluded in the white queer space because of their Turkish identity in Britain, they also feel excluded in Turkey because of being queer. They experience different types of exclusion and discrimination depending on how their oppressed identities are seen by others in diverse settings; as Floya Anthias states, 'belonging has become a term that can no longer be linked to a fixed place or location but to a range of different locales in different ways'.[7]

Fourth, I have sought to change the ways identities of the children of refugees and immigrants are discussed in a transnational context, which has associated identities in-betweenness, here and there, and within the categories of the nation-state. This book has highlighted the role of racism in shaping the identities of the children of refugees and immigrants in a transnational context. The experiences of racism, exclusion and class inequalities have a significant impact on the sense of belonging and the identity-making processes of these young people. The literature on transnationalism has focused mainly on the connection between receiving and sending societies however, this book sheds light on the experiences of racism and their effects on the construction of identities. This is related to the fact that the concept of transnationalism does not offer a sufficient analysis of migrants' experiences beyond the nation-states, as it does not take into account how colonial legacies and racial hierarchies are relevant to our time when positioning itself as an alternative to nationalism. I have shown that the children of refugees and immigrants experience racism in a transnational context, and their identity-making process is not only influenced by the British context where they live, but also by the political atmosphere in their parents' country of origin, and race and racism that are shaping the nation-states have an impact on the lives of these young people. For example, the young people stated that even though they were born in Britain and are British citizens they do not feel as British as white British youth due to British state's practices of *Othering* including – anti-migrant racism in the context of 'hostile environment' immigration policies and Brexit. In the Turkish context, British Kurdish young people stated that they tend to reaffirm their Kurdish identity through participating in cultural and political activities and taking part in Kurdish political movements as a reaction to anti-Kurdish racism in Turkey. Their experiences of racism have a direct relationship with racism bolstered by the states both historically and currently. The shared experiences of oppression and exclusion lead to convivial moments, solidarity and empathy among the children of refugees and immigrants, resulting in the deidentification from national identities and the reinforcement of oppressed identities, such as Kurdishness and LGBTQ+.

The children of refugees and immigrants presented in this book feel less British because Britishness has been defined by its roots in ideological whiteness, and has been implemented strongly with the 'hostile environment' policies and Brexit. 'Go back to where you came from' is a synonym of the question 'where are you from?' for the children of refugees and immigrants, due to a lack of access to a shared British identity. Their relation to Britishness shows an ongoing struggle. Their relation to Turkishness and Kurdishness indicates different struggles based on ethnicity and gender, which is also related to acceptance and inclusion. How they experience Turkishness and Kurdishness is different from how Turkish and Kurdish people experience these identities in Turkey. For example, Turkishness for Yaz is related to the food they eat in north London and to family, which does not have the national connotation that it has in Turkey. She said:

> I found a sense of belonging, for instance by sharing a meal with another Turkish-British friend in a Turkish restaurant in London. That kind of activity is definitely how British-Turkishness is practised in London. It is very different to having a Turkish meal in Turkey. I think food plays a huge role in who you are and seeking out those people whom you can share certain things with.

While highlighting a distinction between practising Turkishness in London and in Turkey, Yaz also referred to their sense of belonging as Turkish-British. Similar to Yaz, other children of immigrants and refugees have found a sense of belonging through their identity as the children of refugees and immigrants; so being both Turkish and British or Kurdish and British is what they identify with.

The stories of the young people shared in this book are good examples of resisting and challenging the essentialist understanding of identity and its categories. Without addressing the root causes of racism in the nation-states, which are reflected in their policies, it is not possible to have inclusive and equitable societies. In *Am I Less British?*, I have sought to suggest different ways of thinking about the identity problem by portraying the lives of the children of refugees and immigrants in London. The narratives of the children of refugees and immigrants demonstrate that experiencing racism transnationally makes new forms of resistance emerge. Accordingly, deidentifying themselves from national identities and holding onto the oppressed identities appear as new forms of resistance in response to racism and exclusion. These young people are not making identities; they are resisting how their identities are oppressed and articulated in relation to how they are seen by others. The complex and dynamic social life of these young people, their responses to identity categories and how belonging is denied and approached by the young people in their everyday lives suggest that there is still hope for the future.

Notes

1. See Anwar 1998.
2. See Bhabha 1990; Kaya 2002.
3. See Wolf 2002; Wessendorf 2007, 2010; Fokkema *et al.* 2013; White and Goodwin 2021.
4. See Ossipow *et al.* 2019.
5. See Bloch and Hirsh 2018: 16.
6. See Back and Sinha 2016.
7. See Anthias 2016: 183.

Bibliography

Ahmed, Sara. 1999. 'Home and Away: Narratives of Migration and Estrangement', *International Journal of Cultural Studies* 2(3): 329–47. doi: 10.1177/136787799900200303.

Aksoy, Asu. and Kevin Robins. 2001. 'From Spaces of Identity to Mental Spaces: Lessons from Turkish-Cypriot Cultural Experience in Britain', *Journal of Ethnic and Migration Studies* 27(4): 685–711. doi: 10.1080/13691830120090458.

Al Jazeera. 2017. 'Turkey's Failed Coup Attempt: All You Need to Know', *Aljazeera English*, 15 July, https://www.aljazeera.com/news/2017/7/15/turkeys-failed-coup-attempt-all-you-need-to-know. Accessed 3 March 2022.

Al-Ali, Nadje and Khalid Koser. 2002. 'Transnationalism, International Migration and Home'. In Nadje Al-Ali and Khalid Koser (eds.) *New Approaches to Migration: Transnational Communities and the Transformation of Home*. London: Routledge, pp. 1–14.

Al-Ali, Nadje, Richard Black and Khalid Koser. 2001. 'The Limits to "Transnationalism": Bosnian and Eritrean Refugees in Europe as Emerging Transnational Communities', *Ethnic and Racial Studies* 24(4): 578–600. doi: 10.1080/01419870120049798.

Alibhai-Brown, Yasmin. 2000. *After Multiculturalism*. London: Foreign Policy Centre.

Amin, Ash. 2012. *The Land of Strangers*. Cambridge: Polity Press.

Anderson, Benedict. 1998. 'Long-Distance Nationalism'. In B. Anderson (ed.) *The Spectre of Comparisons: Nationalism, Southeast Asia and the World*. London: Verso, pp. 58–74.

Anderson, Bridget. 2013. *Us & Them? The Dangerous Politics of Immigration Control*. Oxford: Oxford University Press.

Andrews, Kehinde. 2021. '"Take Back Control": How Colonial Nostalgia Still Informs Political Discourse'. 24 February, https://www.penguin.co.uk/articles/2021/02/kehinde-andrews-brexit-uk-colonial-history-racism-politics. Accessed 10 March 2021.

Anthias, Floya. 2001. 'New Hybridities, Old Concepts: The Limits of "Culture"', *Ethnic and Racial Studies* 24(4): 619–41. doi: 10.1080/01419870120049815.

Anthias, Floya. 2002. 'Where do I Belong? Narrating Collective Identity and Translocational Positionality', *Ethnicities* 2(4): 491–515. doi: 10.1177/1468796802002004030.

Anthias, Floya. 2016. 'Interconnecting Boundaries of Identity and Belonging and Hierarchy-Making Within Transnational Mobility Studies: Framing Inequalities', *Current Sociology* 64(2): 172–90. doi: 10.1177/0011392115614780.

Anwar, Muhammad. 1998. *Between Cultures: Continuity and Change in the Lives of Young Asians*. New York: Routledge.

Atay, Tayfun. 2010. '"Ethnicity within Ethnicity" among the Turkish-Speaking Immigrants in London', *Insight Turkey* 12(1): 123–38. http://www.jstor.org/stable/26331147. Accessed 19 January 2021.

Back, Les. 1996. *New Ethnicities and Urban Culture: Racisms and Multiculture in Young Lives*. London: UCL Press.

Back, Les and Shamser Sinha. 2012. 'New Hierarchies of Belonging', *European Journal of Cultural Studies* 15(2): 139–54. doi: 10.1177/1367549411432030.

Back, Les and Shamser Sinha. 2016. 'Multicultural Conviviality in the Midst of Racism's Ruins', *Journal of Intercultural Studies* 37(5): 517–32. doi: 10.1080/07256868.2016.1211625.

Back, Les and Shamser Sinha. 2018. *Migrant City*. London: Routledge.

Balibar, Étienne. 1991. 'Racism and Nationalism'. In Étienne Balibar and Immanuel Wallerstein (eds.) *Race, Nation, Class: Ambiguous Identities*. London: Verso, pp. 37–67.

Basch, Les, Nina Glick Schiller and Cristina Szanton-Blanc. 1994. *Nations Unbound: Transnational Projects, Postcolonial Predicaments and Deterritorialized Nation-States*. New York: Gordon and Breach.

Baser, Bahar. 2013. 'Diasporas and Imported Conflicts: Turkish and Kurdish Second-Generation Diaporas', *Journal of Conflict Transformation and Security* 3(2): 105–25. http://hdl.handle.net/1814/30817.

Baser, Bahar. 2014. 'The Awakening of a Latent Diaspora: The Political Mobilization of First and Second Generation Turkish Migrants in Sweden', *Ethnopolitics* 13(4): 355–76. doi: 10.1080/17449057.2014.894175.

Batainah, Heba. 2008. 'Issues of Belonging: Exploring Arab-Australian Transnational Identities'. In Helen Lee (ed.) *Ties to the Homeland: Second Generation Transnationalism*. Newcastle: Cambridge Scholars Press, pp. 151–67.

BBC. 2019. 'Brexit "Major Influence" in Racism and Hate Crime Rise'. BBC News, 20 June. Available at: https://www.bbc.co.uk/news/uk-wales-48692863. Accessed 6 July 2023.

Beauchemin, Cris and Mirna Safi. 2020. 'Migrants' Connections Within and Beyond Borders: Insights from the Comparison of Three Categories of Migrants in France', *Ethnic and Racial Studies* 43(2): 255–74. doi: 10.1080/01419870.2019.1572906.

Beaumont, Peter, Jasmine Coleman and Sandra Laville. 2011. 'London Riots: People are Fighting Back. It's Their Neighbourhoods at Stake', *The Guardian*, 10 August, https://www.theguardian.com/uk/2011/aug/09/london-riots-fighting-neighbourhoods. Accessed 10 February 2021.

Berggren, Niclas, Ljunge, Martin, and Nilsson, Therese. 2019. 'Roots of tolerance among second-generation immigrants', *Journal of Institutional Economics* 15(6): 999–1016. doi:10.1017/S1744137419000316.

Bhabha, K. Homi. 1990. *Nation and Narration*. London: Routledge.

Bhambra, K. Gurminder. 2017. 'The Current Crisis of Europe: Refugees, Colonialism, and the Limits of Cosmopolitanism', *European Law Journal* 23: 395–405. doi: 10.1111/eulj.12234.

Bhattacharyya, Gargi, Adam Elliott-Cooper, Sita Balani, Kerem Nişancıoğlu, Kojo Koram, Dalia Gebrial, Nadine El-Enany and Luke de Noronha. 2021. *Empire's Endgame: Racism and the British State*. London: Pluto Press.

Bloch, Alice and Shirin Hirsch 2018. 'Inter-Generational Transnationalism: The Impact of Refugee Backgrounds on Second Generation', *Comparative Migration Studies* 6(30): 1–18. doi: 10.1186/s40878-018-0096-0.

Boccagni, Paolo. 2012. 'Revisiting the "Transnational" in Migration Studies: A Sociological Understanding', *Revue européenne des migrations internationales* 28(1): 33–50. doi: 10.4000/remi.5744.

Boccagni, Paolo. 2020. 'Advancing Transnational Migration Studies Through Home: a Conceptual Inquiry'. HOMInG Working paper no. 11_2020. https://erchoming.files.wordpress.com/2020/11/homing-wp-11_2020.pdf. Accessed 18 June 2021.

Boffey, D. and Toby Helm. 2016. 'Vote Leave Embroiled in Race Row over Turkey Security Threat Claims', *The Guardian*, 22 May, https://www.theguardian.com/politics/2016/may/21/vote-leave-prejudice-turkey-eu-security-threat. Accessed 2 March 2021.

Bonilla-Silva, Eduardo. 2001. *White Supremacy and Racism in the Post-Civil Rights Era*. Boulder: Lynne Rienner.

Bonilla-Silva, Eduardo. 2006. *Racism Without Racists: Color Blind Racism and the Persistence of Racial Inequality in the United States*. Second Edition. New York: Rowman & Littlefield Publishers.

Boomgaarden, G. Hajo and Rens Vliegenthart. 2007. 'Explaining the Rise of Anti-Immigrant Parties: The Role of News Media Content', *Electoral Studies* 26(2): 404–17. doi: 10.1016/j.electstud.2006.10.018.

Booth, Robert. 2019. 'Racism Rising Since the Vote, Nationwide Study Reveals', *The Guardian*, 20 May, https://www.theguardian.com/world/2019/may/20/racism-on-the-rise-since-brexit-vote-nationwide-study-reveals. Accessed 10 March 2021.

Brah, Avtar. 1996. *Cartographies of Diaspora: Contesting Identities* London: Routledge.

Bulmer, Martin and John Solomos. 1998. 'Introduction: Re-thinking Ethnic and Racial Studies', *Ethnic and Racial Studies* 21(5): 819–37. doi: 10.1080/014198798329667.

Bulmer, Martin and John Solomos. 2018. 'Migration and Race in Europe', *Ethnic and Racial Studies* 41(5): 779–84. doi: 10.1080/01419870.2018.1426872.

Büyük, F. Hamdi. 2022. 'Femicide Remains Major Problem in Turkey, Report Warns', *Balkan Insight*, 25 November, https://balkaninsight.com/2022/11/25/femicide-remains-major-problem-in-turkey-reportwarns/#:~:text=In%202022%20so%20far%2C%20116,or%20to%20break%20up%20with. Accessed 1 December 2022.

Çağlar, Ayşe. 2001. 'Constraining Metaphors and the Transnationalisation of Spaces in Berlin', *Journal of Ethnic and Migration Studies* 27(4): 601–13. doi: 10.1080/13691830120090403.

Castaldo, Antonio. 2018. 'Populism and Competitive Authoritarianism in Turkey', *Southeast European and Black Sea Studies* 18(4): 467–87. doi: 10.1080/14683857.2018.1550948.
Castles, Steven and Alastair Davidson. 2000. *Citizenship and Migration: Globalisation and the Politics of Belonging*. New York: Routledge.
Castles, Steven, Maja Korac, Ellie Vasta and Steven Vertovec. 2002. Integration: Mapping the Field. Report of a Project carried out by the University of Oxford *Centre for Migration and Policy Research and Refugee Studies Centre*, contracted by the Home Office Immigration Research and Statistics Service, Home Office Online Report 28/03.
Cattacin, Sandro. 2006. 'Why Not "Ghettos"? The Governance of Migration in the Splintering City'. *Willy Brandt Series of Working Papers in International Migration and Ethnic Relations*, 2(6). Malmo University. Sweden. https://www.diva-portal.org/smash/get/diva2:1409930/FULLTEXT01.pdf. Accessed 11 April 2021.
Centre for Preventive Action. 2022. 'Conflict Between Turkey and Armed Kurdish Groups', Centre for Preventive Action, 3 August, https://www.cfr.org/global-conflict-tracker/conflict/conflict-between-turkey-and-armed-kurdish-groups. Accessed 10 August 2022.
Chimienti, Milena, Alice Bloch, Laurence Ossipow and Catherine Wihtol de Wenden. 2019. 'Second Generation from Refugee Backgrounds in Europe', *Comparative Migration Studies* 7(40): 1–15. doi: 10.1186/s40878-019-0138-2.
Christofis, Nikos. 2019. 'The State of the Kurds in Erdoğan's "New" Turkey', *Journal of Balkan and Near Eastern Studies* 21(3): 251–9. doi: 10.1080/19448953.2018.1497750.
Christou, Anastasia. 2006. 'Deciphering Diaspora – Translating Transnationalism: Family Dynamics, Identity Constructions and the Legacy of "Home" in Second-Generation Greek-American Return Migration', *Ethnic and Racial Studies* 29(6): 1040–56. doi: 10.1080/01419870600960297.
Çicekli, Bülent. 1998. *The Legal Position of Turkish Immigrants in the European Union: A Comparison of the Legal Reception and Status of Turkish Immigrants in Germany, the Netherlands, and the UK*. Ankara: KarMap.
Correa, J. Michael. 2002. 'The Study of Transnationalism Among the Children of Immigrants: Where We Are and Where We Should Be Headed'. In Peggy Levitt and Mary C. Waters (eds.) *The Changing Face of Home: The Transnational Lives of the Second Generation*. New York: Russell Sage, pp. 221–41.
Crul, Maurice, Jens Schneider and Frans Lelie. 2012. *The European Second Generation Compared. Does the Integration Context Matter?*. Amsterdam: Amsterdam University Press.
Dahinden, Janine. 2009. 'Are We All Transnationals Now? Network Transnationalism and Transnational Subjectivity: The Differing Impacts of Globalization on the Inhabitants of a Small Swiss City', *Ethnic and Racial Studies* 32(8): 1365–86. doi: 10.1080/01419870802506534.
Dahinden, Janine. 2017. 'Transnationalism Reloaded: The Historical Trajectory of a Concept', *Ethnic and Racial Studies* 40(9): 1474–85. doi: 10.1080/01419870.2017.1300298.
De Noronha, Luke. 2020. *Deporting Black Britons: Portraits of Deportation to Jamaica*. Manchester: Manchester University Press.
Dekker, Bram and Melissa Siegel. 2013. 'Transnationalism and Integration: Complements or Substitutes?'. No 2013-071, *MERIT Working Papers*, United Nations University – Maastricht Economic and Social Research Institute on Innovation and Technology (MERIT). https://ideas.repec.org/p/unm/unumer/2013071.html. Accessed 11 May 2021.
Demir, Ipek. 2012. 'Battling with Memleket in London: The Kurdish Diaspora's Engagement with Turkey', *Journal of Ethnic and Migration Studies* 38(5): 815–31. doi: 10.1080/1369183X.2012.667996.
Demir, Ipek. 2015. 'Battlespace Diaspora: How the Kurds of Turkey Revive, Construct and Translate the Kurdish Struggle in London'. In Anastasia Christou and Elizabeth Mavroudi (eds.) *Dismantling Diasporas: Rethinking the Geographies of Diasporic Identity, Connection and Development*. Farnham: Ashgate, pp. 71–84.
Demir, Ipek. 2017. 'Shedding an Ethnic Identity in Diaspora: De-Turkification and the Transnational Discursive Struggles of the Kurdish Diaspora', *Critical Discourse Studies* 14(3): 276–91. doi: 10.1080/17405904.2017.1284686.
Demir, Ipek. 2022. *Diaspora as Translation and Decolonisation*. Manchester: Manchester University Press.
di Giovanni, Julian, Francesc Ortega and Andrei A. Levchenko. 2015. 'A Global View of Cross-Border Migration', *Journal of the European Economic Association* 13(1): 168–202. http://www.jstor.org/stable/24539137. Accessed 9 May 2021.

Eckstein, Susan. 2002. 'On Deconstructing and Reconstructing the Meaning of Immigrant Generations'. In Peggy Levitt and Mary C. Waters (eds.) *The Changing Face of Home: The Transnational Lives of the Second Generation*. New York: Russell Sage, pp. 211–15.

Ehrkamp, Patricia. 2005. 'Placing Identities: Transnational Practices and Local Attachments of Turkish Immigrants in Germany', *Journal of Ethnic and Migration Studies* 31(2): 345–64. doi: 10.1080/1369183042000339963.

El-Enany, Nadine. 2016. 'Brexit as Nostalgia for Empire', https://criticallegalthinking.com/2016/06/19/brexit-nostalgia-empire/.

El-Enany, Nadine. 2020. *Bordering Britain: Law, Race and Empire*. Manchester: Manchester University Press.

Elo, Maria, Florian A. Täube and Per Servais. 2022. 'Who is Doing "Transnational Diaspora Entrepreneurship"? Understanding Formal İdentity and Status', *Journal of World Business* 57(1): 101240. doi: 10.1016/j.jwb.2021.101240.

Enneli, Pınar, Tariq Modood and Harriet Bradley. 2005. *Young Turks and Kurds: A Set of Invisible Disadvantaged Groups*. York: Joseph Rowntree Foundation.

Erdal, B. Marta. 2020. 'Theorizing İnteractions of Migrant Transnationalism and İntegration Through a Multiscalar Approach', *Comparative Migration Studies* 8(1): 1–16. doi: 10.1186/s40878-020-00188-z.

Erdemir, Aykan and Ellie Vasta. 2007. *Differentiating Irregularity and Solidarity: Turkish Immigrants at Work in London*. Oxford: Compass.

Ergin, Murat. 2014. 'The Racialization of Kurdish Identity in Turkey', *Ethnic and Racial Studies* 37(2): 322–41. doi: 10.1080/01419870.2012.729672.

Ergin, Murat. 2016. *Is the Turk a White Man?: Race and Modernity in the Making of Turkish Identity*. Leiden, Boston: Brill.

Esen, Berk and Şebnem Gümüşcü. 2016. 'Rising Competitive Authoritarianism in Turkey', *Third World Quarterly* 37(9): 1581–606. doi: 10.1080/01436597.2015.1135732.

Faist, Thomas. 2000. 'Transnationalization in International Migration: Implications for the Study of Citizenship and Culture', *Ethnic and Racial Studies* 23(2): 189–222. doi: 10.1080/014198700329024.

Faist, Thomas. 2010. 'Diaspora and Transnationalism'. In Rainer Bauböck and Thomas Faist (eds.) *Diaspora and Transnationalism: Concepts, Theories and Methods*. Amsterdam: Amsterdam University Press, pp. 9–34.

Falcke, Swantje, Christoph Meng and Romy Nollen. 2020. 'Educational Mismatches for Second Generation Migrants: An Analysis of Applied Science Graduates in the Netherlands', *Journal of Ethnic and Migration Studies* 46(15): 3235–51. doi: 10.1080/1369183X.2020.1738211.

Fanon, Frantz. 1986. *Black Skin, White Mask*. London: Pluto Press.

Favell, Adrian. 2019. 'Integration: Twelve Propositions after Schinkel', *CMS* 7, 21. doi:10.1186/s40878-019-0125-7.

Favell, Adrian and Ettore Recchi. 2019. 'Social Transnationalism in an Unsettled Continent'. In Ettore Recchi, Adrian Favell, Fulya Apaydın, Roxana Barbulescu, Michael Braun, Irina Ciornei, Niall Cunningham, Juan Díez Medrano, Deniz N. Duru, Laurie Hanquinet, Steffen Pötzschke, David Reimer, Justyna Salamońska, Mike Savage, Janne Solgaard Jensen and Albert Varela (eds.) *Everyday Europe: Social Transnationalism in an Unsettled Continent*. Bristol: Policy Press, pp. 1–33.

Featherstone, Mike. 1994. *Global Culture, Nationalism, Globalisation and Modernity*. London: Sage Publications.

Finn, Victoria. 2020. 'Migrant Voting: Here, There, in Both Countries, or Nowhere' *Citizenship Studies* 24(6): 730–50. doi: 10.1080/13621025.2020.1745154.

Fokkema, Tineke, Eralba Cela and Elena Ambrosetti. 2013. 'Giving from the Heart or from the Ego? Motives Behind Remittances of the Second Generation in Europe', *International Migration Review* 47(3): 539–72. doi: 10.1111/imre.12032.

Forest, Adam. 2022. 'Rishi Sunak Says "Racism Must Be Confronted" After Royal Family Row', *The Independent*, 1 December, https://www.independent.co.uk/news/uk/politics/rishi-sunak-racism-royal-family-b2237229.html.

Freund, Alexander 2015. 'Transnationalizing Home in Winnipeg: Refugees' Stories of the Places Between the "Here-and-There"', *Canadian Ethnic Studies* 47(1): 61–86. doi: 10.1353/ces.2015.0006.

Galip, Ö. Belçim. 2014. 'Where is Home?: Re-visioning "Kurdistan" and "Diaspora" in Kurdish Novelistic Discourse in Sweden', *Nordic Journal of Migration Research* 4(2): 82–90. doi: 10.2478/njmr-2014-0009.

Gilroy, Paul. 1990. 'Nationalism, History and Ethnic Absolutism', *History Workshop Journal* 30(1): 114–20. http://www.jstor.org/stable/4289014. Accessed 19 January 2021.
Gilroy, Paul. 1993. *The Black Atlantic: Modernity and Double Consciousness*. London: Verso.
Gilroy, Paul. 2004. *After Empire: Melancholia or Convivial Culture?*. London: Routledge.
Gilroy, Paul. 2006. 'Multiculture in Times of War: An Inaugural Lecture Given at the London School of Economics', *Critical Quarterly* 48(4): 27–45. doi: 10.1111/j.1467-8705.2006.00731.x.
Gilroy, Paul. 2012. '"My Britain is Fuck All": Zombie Multiculturalism and the Race Politics of Citizenship', *Identities* 19(4): 380–97. doi: 10.1080/1070289X.2012.725512.
Glick Schiller, Nina. 2003. 'The Centrality of Ethnography in the Study of Transnational Migration: Seeing the Wetland Instead of Swamp'. In Nancy Foner (ed.) *American Arrivals: Anthropology Engages the New Immigration*. Santa Fe, NM: School of American Research Press, pp. 99–128.
Goksel, Gulay, U. 2018. *Integration of the Immigrants and the Theory of Recognition: 'Just Integration'*. Switzerland: Springer International Publishing.
Golbert, Rebecca. 2001. 'Transnational Orientations from Home: Constructions of Israel and Transnational Space Among Ukrainian Jewish Youth', *Journal of Ethnic and Migration Studies* 27(4): 713–73. doi: 10.1080/13691830120090467.
Goldberg, T. David. 1990. 'Racism and Rationality: The Need for a New Critique', *Philosophy of the Social Sciences* 20(3): 317–50. doi: 10.1177/004839319002000303.
Goldring, Luin and Patricia Landolt. 2012. 'Transnational Migration and the Reformulation of Analytical Categories: Unpacking Latin American Refugee Dynamics in Toronto'. In Anna Amelina, Devrimsel D. Nergiz, Thomas Faist and Nina Glick Schiller (eds.) *Beyond Methodological Nationalism: Research Methodologies for Cross-Border Studies*. New York: Routledge, pp. 41–65.
Goodfellow, Maya. 2019. *Hostile Environment: How Immigrants Became Scapegoats*. London: Verso.
Goulbourne, Harry, Tracey Reynolds, John Solomos and Elisabetta Zontini. 2010. *Transnational Families. Ethnicities, Identities and Social Capital*. London: Routledge.
Green, L. Nancy and Roger Waldinger. 2016. 'Introduction'. In Nancy L. Green and Roger Waldinger (eds.) *A Century of Transnationalism: Immigrants and Their Homeland Connections*. Urbana: University of Illinois Press, pp. 1–31.
Guarnizo, Luis Eduardo. 1997. 'The Emergence of a Transnational Social Formations: The Mirage of Return Migration Among Dominican Transmigrants', *Identities* 4(2): 281–322. doi: 10.1080/1070289X.1997.9962591.
Guarnizo, Luis Eduardo and Michael Peter Smith. 1998. 'The Locations of Transnationalism'. In Michael P. Smith and Luis E. Guarnizo (eds.) *Transnationalism From Below*. Piscataway, NJ: Transaction, pp. 3–35.
Hackney Council. 2020. 'Population'. https://hackney.gov.uk/population. Accessed 17 June 2022.
Hall, Stuart. 1990. 'Cultural Identity and Diaspora'. In Jonathan Rutherford (ed.) *Identity, Community, Culture, Difference*. London: Lawrence and Wishart, pp. 222–37.
Hall, Stuart. 1992. 'Cultural Studies and Its Theoretical Legacies'. In Lawrence Grossberg, Cary Nelson and Paula Treichler (eds.) *Cultural Studies*. New York and London: Routledge, pp. 277–94.
Hall, Stuart. 1993. 'Culture, Community, Nation', *Cultural Studies* 7(3): 349–63. doi: 10.1080/09502389300490251.
Hall, Stuart. 1996. 'Introduction: Who Needs "Identity"?'. In Stuart Hall and Paul du Gay (eds.) *Questions of Cultural Identity*. London: Sage Publications, pp. 1–17.
Hall, Stuart. 2000. 'Conclusion: The Multicultural Question'. In Barnor Hesse (ed.) *Un/settled Multiculturalisms: Diasporas, Entanglements, Transruptions*. London: Zed Books, pp. 209–41.
Hall, Stuart. 2022. 'Old and New Identities, Old and New Ethnicities'. In Les Back and John Solomos (eds.) *Theories of Race and Racism*. Third Edition. London: Routledge, pp. 227–35.
Harringay Council. 2021. 'State of the Borough'. https://www.haringey.gov.uk/local-democracy/about-council/state-borough/haringey-census-2021-statistics-about-borough#:~:text=In%20Harringay%2C%20the%20population%20size,and%20for%20England%20(7%25). Accessed 16 June 2022.
Hayward. Katy. 2020. 'What Brexit Means for Britain's Borders', *UK in a Changing Europe*, 31 December, https://ukandeu.ac.uk/what-brexit-means-for-britains-borders/. Accessed 3 January 2021.
Herda, Daniel. 2018. 'Reactive Ethnicity and Anticipated Discrimination Among American Muslims in Southeastern Michigan', *Journal of Muslim Minority Affairs* 38(3): 372–91. doi: 10.1080/13602004.2018.1524136.

Hickson, Kevin. 2018. 'Enoch Powell's "Rivers of Blood" Speech: Fifty Years On', *Political Quarterly* 89(3): 352–7. doi: 10.1111/1467-923X.12554.

Hirsch, Afua. 2018. *Brit(ish): On Race, Identity and Belonging*. London: Vintage Publishing.

Hobsbawm, J. Eric. 1990. *Nations and Nationalism Since 1780: Programme, Myth, Reality*. Cambridge: Cambridge University Press.

Holgate, Jane, Janroj Keles and Leena Kumarappan. 2012. 'Visualizing "Community": An Experiment in Participatory Photography Among Kurdish Diasporic Workers in London', *The Sociological Review* 60(2): 312–32. doi: 10.1111/j.1467-954X.2012.02075.x.

hooks, bell. 1990. *Yearning: Race, Gender, and Cultural Politics*. London: Turnaround.

hooks, bell. 2003. *Teaching Community: A Pedagogy of Hope*. London: Psychology Press.

Horta, P.B. Anna. 2002. 'Transnational Networks and the Local Politics of Migrant Grassroots Organising in Post-Colonial Portugal', ESRC Transnational Communities Programme: Working Paper Series 3, https://core.ac.uk/download/pdf/303039823.pdf. Accessed 4 October 2021.

Husband, Stuart. 2002. 'Little Istanbul', *Evening Standard*, https://www.standard.co.uk/hp/front/little-istanbul-7223100.html. Accessed 2 June 2021.

Hutnyk, John. 2005. 'Hybridity', *Ethnic and Racial Studies* 28(1): 79–102. doi: 10.1080/0141987042000280021.

Ibrahim, Arwa. 2022. 'What Was Turkey's Failed Coup About – and What's Happened Since?', *Aljazeera English*, 15 July, https://www.aljazeera.com/news/2022/7/15/turkeys-failed-coup-attempt-explainer. Accessed 25 July 2022.

İçduygu, Ahmet, David Romano and Ibrahim Sirkeci. 1999. 'The Ethnic Question in an Environment of Insecurity: The Kurds in Turkey', *Ethnic and Racial Studies* 22(6): 991–1010. doi: 10.1080/014198799329215.

Innes, Alexandria. 2019. *Colonial Citizenship and Everyday Transnationalism: An Immigrant's Story*. London: Routledge.

International Commission of Juries. 2021. 'Turkey's Withdrawal from Istanbul Convention a Setback for Women and Girls' Human Rights', Advocates for Justice and Human Rights, 1 July, https://www.icj.org/turkeys-withdrawal-from-istanbul-convention-a-setback-for-women-and-girls-human-rights/. Accessed 7 July 2021.

Itzigsohn, José and Silvia G. Saucedo. 2002. 'Immigrant Incorporation and Sociocultural Transnationalism', *International Migration Review* 36(3): 766–98. http://www.jstor.org/stable/4149563. Accessed 12 June 2021.

Itzigsohn, José and Silvia G. Saucedo. 2005. 'Incorporation, Transnationalism and Gender: Immigrant Incorporation and Transnational Participation as Gendered Processes', *International Migration Review* 39(4): 895–920. http://www.jstor.org/stable/27645557. Accessed 19 July 2021.

Jones, Hannah, Yasmin Gunaratnam, Gargi Bhattacharyya, William Davies, Sukhwant Dhaliwal, Emma Jackson and Roiyah Saltus. 2017. *Go Home? The Politics of Immigration Controversies*. Manchester: Manchester University Press.

Kasinitz, Philip, John H. Mollenkopf and Mary C. Waters. 2002. 'Becoming American/Becoming New Yorkers: Immigrant Incorporation in a Majority Minority City', *International Migration Review* 36(4): 1020–36. doi: 10.1111/j.1747-7379.2002.tb00116.

Kasinitz, Philip, John H. Mollenkopf and Mary C. Waters. 2004. *Becoming New Yorkers: Ethnographies of the New Second Generation*. New York: Russell Sage Foundation.

Kasinitz, Philip, John H. Mollenkopf, Mary C. Waters and Jennifer Holdaway. 2008. *Inheriting the City: The Children of Immigrants Come of Age*. New York: Russell Sage Foundation.

Kaya, Ayhan. 2001. *Constructing Diasporas: Turkish Hip-Hop Youth in Berlin*. Bielefeld: Transcript Verlag.

Kaya, Ayhan. 2002. 'Aesthetics of Diaspora: Contemporary Minstrels in Turkish Berlin', *Journal of Ethnic and Migration Studies* 28(1): 43–62. doi: 10.1080/13691830120103921.

Kaya, Ilhan. 2005. 'Identity and Space: The Case of Turkish Americans', *The Geographic Review* 95(3): 425–40. http://www.jstor.org/stable/30034246. Accessed 19 January 2023.

Kellman, C. Herbert. 1973. 'Violence Without Moral Boundaries', *Journal of Social Studies* 29(4): 29–61.

Kibria, Nazli. 1997. 'The Construction of 'Asian-American: Reflections on Intermarriage and Ethnic Identity Among Second-Generation Chinese and Korean Americans', *Ethnic and Racial Studies* 20(3): 523–44. doi: 10.1080/01419870.1997.9993973.

Kibria, Nazli. 2002. 'Of Blood, Belonging and Homeland Trips: Transnationalism and Identity Among Second-Generation Chinese and Korean Americans'. In Peggy Levitt and Mary

C. Waters (eds.) *The Changing Face of Home: The Transnational Lives of the Second Generation.* New York: Russell Sage Foundation, pp. 295–311.

King, D. Anthony. 2009. 'Postcolonial Cities', *Online Elsevier Encyclopedia.* http://www.elsevierdirect.com/brochures/hugy/SampleContent/Postcolonial-Cities.pdf. Accessed 21 March 2021.

King, Russell and Anastasia Christou. 2010. 'Diaspora, Migration and Transnationalism: Insights from the Study of Second-Generation "Returnees"'. In Rainer Bauböck and Thomas Faist (eds.) *Diaspora and Transnationalism: Concepts, Theories and Methods.* Amsterdam: Amsterdam University Press, pp. 167–84.

King, Russell and Anastasia Christou. 2014. 'Second-Generation "Return" to Greece: New Dynamics of Transnationalism and Integration', *International Migration* 52(6): 85–99. doi: 10.1111/imig.12149.

King, Russell, Mark Thomson, Nicola Mai and Yılmaz Keleş. 2008. '"Turks" in the UK: Problems of Definition and the Partial Relevance of Policy', *Journal of Immigrant and Refugee Studies* 6(3): 423–34. doi: 10.1080/15362940802371895.

Kirişçi, Kemal and Amanda Sloat. 2019. 'The Rise and Fall of Liberal Democracy in Turkey: Implications for the West'. *Brookings*, February, https://www.brookings.edu/research/the-rise-and-fall-of-liberal-democracy-in-turkey-implications-for-the-west/. Accessed 8 January 2022.

Kivisto, Peter. 2001. 'Theorising Transnational Immigration: A Critical Review of Current Efforts', *Ethnic and Racial Studies* 24(4): 549–77. doi: 10.1080/01419870120049789.

Kivisto, Peter. 2003. 'Social Spaces, Transnational Immigrant Communities, and the Politics of Incorporation', *Ethnicities* 3(1): 5–28. doi: 10.1177/1468796803003001786.

Klingenberg, Annemarie, Johannes M. Luetz and Ann Crawford. 2021. 'Transnationalism – Recognizing the Strengths of Dual Belonging for Both Migrant and Society', *Journal of International Migration and Integration* 22: 453–70. doi: 10.1007/s12134-019-00744-2.

Kowalski, Philip and Umut Can Fidan. 2020. 'Erdoğan Continues Repression of Kurdish Political and Cultural Rights', *Ahval News*, 9 November, https://ahvalnews.com/turkish-kurds/erdogan-continues-repression-of-kurdish-political-and-cultural-rights. Accessed 14 April 2023.

Küçükcan, Talip. 1999. *Politics of Ethnicity, Identity and Religion: Turkish Muslims in Britain.* Aldershot: Ashgate.

Küçükcan, Talip. 2004. 'The Making of Turkish-Muslim Diaspora in Britain: Religious Collective Identity in a Multicultural Public Sphere', *Journal of Muslim Affairs* 24(2): 243–58. doi: 10.1080/1360200042000296645.

Kureishi, Hanif. 1990. *The Buddha of Suburbia.* London: Faber & Faber.

Kwon, Jungmin. 2022. *Understanding the Transnational Lives and Literacies of İmmigrant Children.* New York: Teachers College Press.

Lamb, Terry. 2001. 'Language Policy in Multilingual UK', *Language Learning Journal* 23(1): 4–12. doi: 10.1080/09571730185200031.

Lawrence, Paul. 2005. *Nationalism: History and Theory.* Harlow: Pearson Longman.

Lee, Helen. 2011. 'Rethinking Transnationalism Through the Second Generation', *The Australian Journal of Anthropology* 22(3): 295–313. doi: 10.1111/j.1757-6547.2011.00150.x.

Lee, Helen. 2016. '"I Was Forced Here": Perceptions of Agency in Second Generation "Return" Migration to Tonga', *Journal of Ethnic and Migration Studies* 42(15): 2573–88. doi: 10.1080/1369183X.2016.1176524.

Lentin, Alana. 2008. *Racism: A Beginner's Guide.* Oxford: One World Publications.

Lentin, Alana. 2014. 'Post-Race, Post-Politics: The Paradoxical Rise of Culture After Multiculturalism', *Ethnic and Racial Studies* 37(8): 1268–85. doi: 10.1080/01419870.2012.664278.

Lentin, Alana and Gavan Titley. 2011. *The Crises of Multiculturalism: Racism in a Neoliberal Age.* London: Zed Books.

Levitt, Peggy. 2001. 'Transnational Migration: Taking Stock and Future Directions', *Global Networks* 1(3): 195–216. doi: 10.1111/1471-0374.00013.

Levitt, Peggy. 2002. 'The Ties that Change: Relations to the Ancestral Home over the Life Cycle'. In Peggy Levitt and Mary C. Waters (eds.) *The Changing Face of Home. The Transnational Lives of the Second Generation.* New York: Russell Sage Foundation, pp. 123–44.

Levitt, Peggy. 2009. 'Roots and Routes: Understanding the Lives of the Second Generation Transnationally', *Journal of Ethnic and Migration Studies* 35(7): 1225–42. doi: 10.1080/13691830903006309.

Levitt, Peggy and B. Nadya Jaworsky. 2007. 'Transnational Migration Studies: Past Developments and Future Trends', *Annual Review of Sociology* 33(1): 129–56. doi: 10.1146/annurev.soc.33.040406.131816.

Levitt, Peggy and Mary C. Waters. 2002. 'Introduction'. In Peggy Levitt and Mary C. Waters (eds.) *The Changing Face of Home: The Transnational Lives of the Second Generation*. New York: Russell Sage Foundation, pp. 1–30.

Loizides, G. Neophytos. 2010. 'State Ideology and the Kurds in Turkey', *Middle Eastern Studies* 46(4): 513–27. doi: 10.1080/00263206.2010.492987.

Maalouf, Amin. 2000. *On Identity*. London: Harvill Press.

Mackay, Neil. 2023. 'Prince Harry's Afghan Killings Show "The Man is Morally Numb"'. *Herald Scotland*, 6 January. https://www.heraldscotland.com/opinion/23234143.prince-harrys-afghan-killings-show-the-man-morally-numb/. Accessed 9 January 2023.

Mahler, J. Sarah. 1998. 'Theoretical and Empirical Contributions Toward Research Agenda for Transnationalism'. In Michael P. Smith and Luis E. Guarnizo (eds.) *Transnationalism From Below*. Piscataway, NJ: Transaction, pp. 64–100.

Mallett, Shelley. 2004. 'Understanding Home: A Critical Review of the Literature', *The Sociological Review* 52(1): 62–89. doi: 10.1111/j.1467-954X.2004.00442.x.

Massey, Doreen. 1992. 'A Place Called Home? The Question of Home', *Journal of Culture, Theory, Politics* 17: 3–15. https://journals.lwbooks.co.uk/newformations/vol-1992-issue-17/. Accessed 16 April 2021.

Massey, Doreen. 1994. *Space, Place, and Gender*. NED-New Edition. Minneapolis: University of Minnesota Press.

Matias, Cheryl E. 2016. 'White Skin, Black Friend: A Fanonian Application to Theorize Racial Fetish in Teacher Education', *Educational Philosophy and Theory* 48(3): 221–36. doi: 10.1080/00131857.2014.989952.

Mavrommatis, George. 2021. 'Nativism and Second-Generation Migrants in Greece: Differentiating Between Ethnic and Civic Elements of Citizenship', *Ethnic and Racial Studies* 45(12): 2289–308. doi: 10.1080/01419870.2021.2006735.

Meer, Nasar and Modood, Tariq. 2011. 'How Does Interculturalism Contrast With Multiculturalism?', *Journal of Intercultural Studies* 33(2): 1–22. doi: 10.1080/07256868.2011.618266.

Mehmet Ali, Aydın. 2001. *Turkish Speaking Communities and Education: No Delight*. London: Fatal Publications.

Midtbøen, H. Arnhinn and Marjan Nadim. 2019. 'Ethnic Niche Formation at the Top? Second-Generation Immigrants in Norwegian High-Status Occupations', *Ethnic and Racial Studies* 42(16): 177–95. doi: 10.1080/01419870.2019.1638954.

Neal, Sarah, Katy Bennett, Allan Cochrane and Giles Mohan. 2018. *Lived Experiences of Multiculture: The New Social and Spatial Relations of Diversity*. London: Routledge.

Neal, Sarah, Katy Bennett, Allan Cochrane and Giles Mohan. 2019. 'Community and Conviviality? Informal Social Life in Multicultural Places', *Sociology* 53(1): 69–86. doi: 10.1177/0038038518763518.

Noble, Greg. 2009. 'Everyday Cosmopolitanism and the Labour of Intercultural Community'. In Amanda Wise and Selvaraj Velayutham (eds.) *Everyday Multiculturalism*. Basingstoke: Palgrave Macmillan, pp. 46–65.

Noble, Greg. 2011. 'Belonging in Bennelong: Ironic Inclusion and Cosmopolitan Joy in John Howard's (Former) Electorate'. In Keith Jacobs and Jeff Malpas (eds.) *Ocean to Outback: Cosmopolitanism in Contemporary Australia*. Crawley: UWA Press, pp. 150–74.

Nowicka, Magdalena 2019. 'Convivial Research Between Normativity and Analytical Innovation'. In Mette Louise Berg and Magdalena Nowicka (eds.) *Studying Diversity, Migration and Urban Multiculture*. London: UCL Press, pp. 17–35.

O'Flaherty, Martin, Zlatko Skrbis and Bruce Tranter. 2007. 'Home Visits: Transnationalism Among Australian Migrants', *Ethnic and Racial Studies* 30(5): 817–44. doi: 10.1080/01419870701491820.

Olusoga, David. 2021. *Black and British: A Forgotten History*. London: Picador.

Orwell, George. 1941. 'England Your England'. *The Lion and the Unicorn: Socialism and the English Genius*, 19 February. https://orwell.ru/library/essays/lion/english/e_eye. Accessed 21 January 2023.

Ossipow, Laurence, Anne-Laure Counilh and Milena Chimienti. 2019. 'Racialization in Switzerland: Experiences of Children of Refugees from Kurdish, Tamil and Vietnamese Backgrounds', *Comparative Migration Studies* 7(19). doi: 10.1186/s40878-019-0117-7.

Özkırımlı, Umut. 2010. *Theories of Nationalism: A Critical Introduction*. Second Edition. Basingstoke: Palgrave Macmillan.

Parkin, Robert. 1999. 'Regional Identities and Alliances in an Integrating Europe: A Challenge to the Nation-State?', *ESRC Transnational Communities Programme: Working Paper Series 7*, https://ora.ox.ac.uk/objects/uuid:50223e63-9a19-4874-93d4-03548b92d382/download_file?file _format=application%2Fpdf&safe_filename=Regional%2Bidentities%2Band%2Ballian ces%2Bin%2Ban%2Bintegrating%2BEurope%3A%2Ba%2Bchallenge%2Bto%2Bthe%2Bnat ion%2Bstate%3F&type_of_work=Record. Accessed 22 December 2021.

Perlmann, Joel. 2002. 'The Intermingling of Peoples in the United States: Intermarriage and the Population History of Ethnic and Racial Groups Since 1880', Levy Economics Institute of Bard College, Annandale-on-Hudson, NY.

Portes, Alejandro. 1996. *The New Second Generation*. New York: Russell Sage Foundation.

Portes, Alejandro. 2001. 'Introduction: The Debates and Significance of Immigrant Transnationalism', *Global Networks* 1(3): 181–93. doi: 10.1111/1471-0374.00012.

Portes, Alejandro and Rubén G. Rumbaut. 2001. *Legacies: The Story of the Immigrant Second Generation*. Berkeley: University of California Press.

Portes, Alejandro, Cristina Escobar and Renelinda Arana. 2008. 'Bridging the Gap: Transnational and Ethnic Organisations in the Political Incorporation of Immigrants in the United States', *Ethnic and Racial Studies* 31(6): 1056–90. doi: 10.1080/01419870701874827.

Portes, Alejandro, Luis E. Guarnizo and Patricia Landolt. 1999. 'The Study of Transnationalism: Pitfalls and Promise of an Emergent Research Field', *Ethnic and Racial Studies* 22(2): 217–37. doi: 10.1080/014198799329468.

Pries, Ludger. 1999. *Migration and Transnational Social Spaces*. Aldershot: Ashgate.

Redclift, Melangedd Victoria and Fatima Begum Rajina. 2021. 'The Hostile Environment, Brexit, and "Reactive-" or "Protective Transnationalism"', *Global Networks* 21(1): 196–214. doi: 10.1111/glob.12275.

Reynolds, Tracey. 2006. 'Caribbean Families, Social Capital and Young People's Diasporic Identities', *Ethnic and Racial Studies* 29(6): 1087–103. doi: 10.1080/01419870600960362.

Reynolds, Tracey. 2011. 'Caribbean Second-Generation Return Migration: Identities, Transnational Family Relationships and "Left Behind" Kin in Britain', *Mobilities* 6(4): 535–52. doi: 10.1080/17450101.2011.603946.

Riccio, Bruno. 2001. 'Disaggregating the Transnational Community: Senegalese Migrants on the Coast of Emilia-Romagna'. University of Oxford. Transnational Communities Programme.

Robinson, Vaughan 1998. 'Defining and Measuring Successful Refugee Integration'. *Report of Conference on Integration of Refugees in Europe*. Antwerp 12–14 November. Brussels: European Council on Refugees and Exiles.

Rogers, Alisdair. 2004. 'A European Space for Transnationalism?'. In Peter Jackson, Philip Crang and Claire Dwyer (eds.) *Transnational Spaces*. London: Routledge, pp. 165–85.

Rosello, Mireille. 2020. 'Autobiography of a Ghost: Home and Haunting in Viet Thanh Nguyen's The Refugees'. In Emma Cox, Sam Durrant, David Farrier, Lyndsey Stonebridge and Agnes Woolley (eds.) *Refugee Imaginaries: Research Across the Humanities*. Edinburgh: Edinburgh University Press, pp. 519–32.

Sagnic, Ceng. 2010. 'Mountain Turks: State Ideology and the Kurds in Turkey'. *Information, Society and Justice* 3(2): 127–34.

Saini, Rima, Michael Bankole and Neema Begum. 2023. 'The 2022 Conservative leadership Campaign and Post-Racial Gatekeeping', *Race & Class*, 0(0). doi: 10.1177/03063968231164599.

Sales, Rosemary. 2012. 'Britain and Britishness: Place, Belonging and Exclusion'. In Waqar I. U. Ahmad and Ziauddin Sardar (eds.) *Muslims in Britain: Making Social and Political Space*. London: Routledge, pp. 42–61.

Saraçoğlu, Cenk. 2009. '"Exclusive Recognition": The New Dimensions of the Question of Ethnicity and Nationalism in Turkey', *Ethnic and Racial Studies* 32(4): 640–58. doi: 10.1080/01419870802065226.

Saraçoğlu, Cenk. 2010. 'The Changing Image of the Kurds in Turkish Cities: Middle-Class Perceptions of Kurdish Migrants in İzmir', *Patterns of Prejudice* 44(3): 239–60. doi: 10.1080/0031322X.2010.489735.

Savage, Mike, Niall Cunningham, David Reimer and Adrian Favell. 2019. 'Cartographies of Social Transnationalism'. In Ettore Recchi, Adrian Favell, Fulya Apaydın, Roxana Barbulescu, Michael Braun, Irina Ciornei, Niall Cunningham, Juan Díez Medrano, Deniz N. Duru, Laurie Hanquinet, Steffen Pötzschke, David Reimer, Justyna Salamońska, Mike Savage, Janne

Solgaard Jensen and Albert Varela (eds.) *Everyday Europe: Social Transnationalism in an Unsettled Continent*. Bristol: Policy Press, pp. 35–60.

Schain, Martin. 2018. 'Shifting Tides: Radical-Right Populism and Immigration Policy in Europe and the United States', *Transatlantic Council on Migration, Migration Policy Institute*, August, p. 25. https://www.migrationpolicy.org/research/radical-right-immigration-europe-united-states. Accessed 21 January 2023.

Şimşek, Doğuş. 2021. 'Winners and Losers of Neoliberalism: The Intersection of Class and Race in the Case of Syrian Refugees in Turkey', *Ethnic and Racial Studies* 44(15): 2816–35. doi: 10.1080/01419870.2020.1854812.

Şimşek, Doğuş. 2022. 'What Makes a Place a Home?'. In Tamar Mayar and Trinh Tran (eds.) *Displacement, Belonging, and Migrant Agency in the Face of Power*. Abingdon and New York: Routledge, pp. 225–37.

Şimsek, Doğuş and Yusuf Sayman. 2018. *'Çabuk Çabuk': Africans in Istanbul*. Istanbul: Pencere Yayınları.

Smith, C. Robert. 2002. 'Life Course, Generation, and Social Location as Factors Shaping Second-Generation Transnational Life'. In Peggy Levitt and Mary C. Waters (eds.) *The Changing Face of Home: The Transnational Lives of the Second Generation*. New York: Russell Sage Foundation, pp. 145–67.

Smith, J. Heather. 2016. 'Britishness as Racist Nativism: A Case of the Unnamed "Other"', *Journal of Education for Teaching* 42(3): 298–313. doi: 10.1080/02607476.2016.1184461.

Smith, P. Michael 2001. *Transnational Urbanism: Locating Globalization*. Oxford: Blackwell.

Snel, Eric, Margerita T. Hart and Marianne van Bochove. 2016. 'Reactive Transnationalism: Homeland Involvement in the Face of Discrimination', *Global Networks* 16(4): 511–30. doi: 10.1111/glob.12125.

Solomons, Adam. 2022. 'Sangita Myska Dismantles Caller's Claim that Rishi Sunak "Isn't Even British"'. https://www.lbc.co.uk/news/sangita-myska-dismantles-callers-claim-that-rishi-sunak-isnt-even-british/. Accessed 24 October 2022.

Solomos, John. 2013. 'Strangers, Identities and Belonging', *Identities* 20(1): 18–23. doi: 10.1080/1070289X.2013.763039.

Solomos, John. 2022. *Race, Ethnicity and Social Theory*. Abingdon and New York: Routledge.

Sommer, Elena 2020. 'Transnational Entrepreneurial Activities (TEA)'. In Elena Sommer (ed.) *Social Capital as a Resource for Migrant Entrepreneurship: Self-Employed Migrants from the Former Soviet Union in Germany*. Wiesbaden: Springer, pp. 237–81.

Song, Miri. 2003. *Choosing Ethnic Identity*. Cambridge: Polity Press.

Soysal, N. Yasemin. 2000. 'Citizenship and Identity: Living in Diasporas in Post-War Europe?', *Ethnic and Racial Studies* 23(1): 1–15. doi: 10.1080/014198700329105.

Soysal, N. Yasemin. 2015. *Transnational Trajectories in East Asia: Nation, Citizenship, and Region*. Abingdon: Routledge.

Spiro, Peter J. 2019. 'The Equality Paradox of Dual Citizenship', *Journal of Ethnic and Migration Studies* 45(6): 879–96. doi: 10.1080/1369183X.2018.1440485.

Stephens, Philip. 2016.'The Brexiters' Ugly Campaign to Vilify Turks', *Financial Times*, 9 June, https://www.ft.com/content/f264be32-2cc6-11e6-bf8d-26294ad519fc. Accessed 10 February 2021.

Takenaka, Ayumi. 2009. 'How Diasporic Ties Emerge: Pan-American Nikkel Communities and the Japanese State', *Ethnic and Racial Studies* 32(8): 1325–45. doi: 10.1080/01419870701719055.

Toyota, Mika. 2003. 'Contested Chinese Identities Among Ethnic Minorities in the China, Burma and Thai Borderlands', *Ethnic and Racial Studies* 26(2): 301–20. doi: 10.1080/0141987032000054448.

Tyler, Katherine. 2017. 'The Suburban Paradox of Conviviality and Racism in Postcolonial Britain', *Journal of Ethnic and Migration Studies* 43(11): 1890–906. doi: 10.1080/1369183X.2016.1245607.

Valentine, Gill. 2008. 'Living with Difference: Reflections on Geographies of Encounter', *Progress in Human Geography* 32: 323–37.

Valluvan, Sivamohan 2019. 'The Uses and Abuses of Class: Left Nationalism and the Denial of Working-Class Multiculture', *The Sociological Review* 67(1): 36–46. doi: 10.1177/0038026118820295.

Varshaver, Evgeni, Anna Rocheva and Nataliya Ivanova. 2022. 'E-namus? Social Networking Sites and Conservative Norms of Romantic Relationships among Second-Generation Migrants in Russia', *Journal of Ethnic and Migration Studies* 48 (13): 3240–58. doi: 10.1080/1369183X.2021.1883423.

Verkuyten, Maykel and Asli A. Yıldız. 2009. 'Muslim Immigrants and Religious Group Feelings: Self-Identification and Attitudes among Sunni and Alevi Turkish-Dutch', *Ethnic and Racial Studies* 32(7): 1121–42. doi: 10.1080/01419870802379312.
Vertovec, Steven. 1999. 'Conceiving and Researching Transnationalism', *Ethnic and Racial Studies* 22(2): 447–62. doi: 10.1080/014198799329558.
Vertovec, Steven. 2001. 'Transnationalism and Identity', *Journal of Ethnic and Migration Studies* 27(4): 573–82. doi: 10.1080/13691830120090386.
Vertovec, Steven. 2007. 'Super-Diversity and Its Implications', *Ethnic and Racial Studies* 30(6): 1024–54. doi: 10.1080/01419870701599465.
Vertovec, Steven. 2009. *Transnationalism*. New York: Routledge.
Vickerman, Milton. 2002. 'Second Generation West Indian Transnationalism'. In Peggy Levitt and Mary C. Waters (eds.) *The Changing Face of Home: The Transnational Lives of the Second Generation*. New York: Russell Sage Foundation, pp. 341–66.
Vink, Maarten, Arjan H Schakel, David Reichel, Ngo Chun Luk and Gerard-René de Groot. 2019. 'The İnternational Diffusion of Expatriate Dual Citizenship', *Migration Studies* 7(3): 362–83. doi: 10.1093/migration/mnz011.
Virdee, Satnam and Brendan McGeever. 2017. 'Racism, Crisis, Brexit', *Ethnic and Racial Studies* 41(10): 1802–19. doi: 10.1080/01419870.2017.1361544.
Wallraff, Günter. 1988. *Lowest of the Low: The Turkish Worker in West Germany*. London: Methuen.
Ware, Vron. 2007. *Who Cares About Britishness? A Global View of the National Identity Debate*. London: Arcadia Books.
Ware, Vron and Les Back. 1994. 'White/Whiteness', *Paragraph* 17(3): 281–91. http://www.jstor.org/stable/43263449. Accessed 10 March 2021.
Waters, C. Mary. 1999. *Black Identities: West Indian Immigrant Dreams and American Realities*. Cambridge, MA: Harvard University Press.
Watson, L. James. 1977. *Between Two Cultures: Immigrants and Minorities in Britain*. London: Blackwell Publishing.
Wessendorf, Susanne. 2007. '"Roots Migrants": Transnationalism and "Return" Among Second-Generation Italians in Switzerland', *Journal of Ethnic and Migration Studies* 33(7): 1083–102. doi: 10.1080/13691830701541614.
Wessendorf, Susanne. 2010. 'Local Attachments and Transnational Everyday Lives: Second-Generation Italians in Switzerland', *Global Networks* 10(3): 365–82. doi: 10.1111/j.1471-0374.2010.00293.x.
Wessendorf, Susanne. 2013. 'Commonplace Diversity and the "Ethos of Mixing": Perceptions of Difference in a London Neighbourhood', *Identities* 20(4): 407–22. doi: 10.1080/1070289X.2013.822374.
Wessendorf, Susanne. 2014. *Commonplace Diversity: Social Relations in a Super-Diverse Context*. Basingstoke: Palgrave Macmillan.
Wessendorf, Susanne. 2016. 'Settling in a Super-Diverse Context: Recent Migrants' Experiences of Conviviality', *Journal of Intercultural Studies* 37(5): 449–63. doi: 10.1080/07256868.2016.1211623.
White, Anne and Kinga Goodwin. 2021. 'Invisible Poles and Their Integration into Polish Society: Changing Identities of UK Second-Generation Migrants in the Brexit Era', *Social Identities* 27(3): 410–25. doi: 10.1080/13504630.2020.1859361.
Wiles, Janine. 2008. 'Sense of Home in a Transnational Social Space: New Zealanders in London', *Global Networks* 8(1): 116–37. doi: 10.1111/j.1471-0374.2008.00188.x.
Wimmer, Andreas and Nina Glick Schiller. 2002. 'Methodological Nationalism and Beyond: Nation-State Building, Migration and the Social Sciences', *Global Networks* 2(4): 300–30. doi: 10.1111/1471-0374.00043.
Wise, Amanda. 2009. 'Everyday Multiculturalism: Transversal Crossings and Working-Class Cosmopolitans'. In Amanda Wise and Selvaraj Velayutham (eds.) *Everyday Multiculturalism*. Basingstoke: Palgrave Macmillan, pp. 21–45.
Wise, Amanda and Velayutham, Selvaraj. 2014. 'Conviviality in Everyday Multiculturalism: Some Brief Comparisons Between Singapore and Sydney', *European Journal of Cultural Studies* 17, 406–43. doi: 10.1177/1367549413510419.
Wolf, L. Diane. 2002. 'There's No Place Like "Home": Emotional Transnationalism and the Struggle of Second-Generation Filipinos'. In Peggy Levitt and Mary C. Waters (eds.) *The Changing Face of Home: The Transnational Lives of the Second Generation*. New York: Russell Sage Foundation, pp. 255–94.

Woolf, Stuart (ed.). 1996. *Nationalism in Europe, 1815 to the Present: A Reader*. London: Routledge.
Yackley, J. Ayla. 2020. 'Turkey's LGBTIQ+ Community at Risk Amid Rise in Homophobic Rhetoric', *Politico*, 24 July. https://www.politico.eu/article/turkey-lgbtq-community-risk-rise-in-homophobic-rhetoric/. Accessed 17 February 2021.
Yeğen, Mesut. 2007. 'Turkish Nationalism and the Kurdish Question', *Ethnic and Racial Studies* 30(1): 119–51. doi: 10.1080/01419870601006603.
Yeğen, Mesut. 2009. '"Prospective-Turks" or "Pseudo-Citizens": Kurds in Turkey', *The Middle East Journal* 63(4): 597–61. http://www.jstor.org/stable/20622956. Accessed 11 April 2021.
Yıldız, Erol and Marc Hill. 2017. 'In-Between as Resistance: The Post-Migrant Generation Between Discrimination and Transnationalization', *Transnational Social Review* 7(3): 273–86. doi: 10.1080/21931674.2017.1360033.
Yurdakul, Gökçe. 2006. 'State, Political Parties and Immigrant Associations in Berlin', *Journal of Ethnic and Migration Studies* 32(3): 435–53. doi: 10.1080/13691830600555244.
Yuval-Davis, Nira, Floya Anthias and Eleonore Kofman. 2005. 'Secure Borders and Safe Haven and the Gendered Politics of Belonging: Beyond Social Cohesion', *Ethnic and Racial Studies* 28(3): 513–35. doi: 10.1080/0141987042000337867.
Yuval-Davis, Nira, George Wemyss and Kathryn Cassidy. 2018. 'Everyday Bordering, Belonging and the Reorientation of British Immigration Legislation', *Sociology* 52(2): 228–44. doi: 10.1177/0038038517702599.
Zhou, Minglang. 2004. 'Minority Language Policy in China: Equality in Theory and Inequality in Practice'. In Minglang Zhou and Hongkai Sun (eds.) *Language Policy in the People's Republic of China: Theory and Practice since 1949*. Boston: Kluwer, pp. 71–95.

Index

accent 5, 23, 55, 56, 58, 59, 82, 88, 91, 110, 173
Ahmed, Sara 105, 106, 124
Alevis 21, 31, 42, 122, 144, 152
   Kurdish 118, 122
Alevism 78, 151
attachment(s) 5, 14, 47, 71, 136, 157, 158
   cultural 157
   emotional 107, 119, 120, 129
authoritarian 39, 41, 125, 129, 138, 160, 166
authoritarianism 31, 32, 38, 129
   competitive 31
   politics 22, 32, 40, 118, 129, 133, 138
   regime 15, 22, 130

Back, Les 16, 24, 35, 54, 66, 68, 85, 91, 140, 172
Begum, Shamima 1, 4, 154
Brexit 15, 19, 22, 32, 34, 36, 37, 137, 146, 152, 155, 174, 175
   Britain 3, 4, 38
   campaign 34, 147
   post-Brexit 38, 41, 166
   referendum 4, 30, 33, 34, 91, 147
British curriculum 155, 156
Britishness 6, 82, 87, 97, 132, 136–140, 145, 146, 148, 149, 153–5, 157, 158, 163, 164, 169, 174, 175
   level of Britishness 140, 141
   racialised hierarchy(ies) of Britishness 1, 2, 4
   of racialised minorities 88, 108, 110
   toxic Britishness 147
bonding together 101, 102

citizenship 2, 4, 9, 21, 23, 25, 30, 108, 139, 141, 153, 154, 169
   British 1, 2, 4, 36, 130, 139, 141, 146, 153, 154
   dual 8, 154
   Turkish 128, 130, 131
class 54–7, 82, 98, 114, 140, 149, 150, 153, 162, 165
   background 58, 59, 60, 70, 71, 82, 110, 149
   difference(s) 58, 60, 62, 63, 69, 70, 97, 99
   hierarchy 3, 150, 170
   identity (ies) 16, 58, 173
   inequalities 70, 99, 173, 174
   middle-class 58, 59, 60, 63, 68, 70, 71, 97–9, 105, 106, 118, 140, 148, 171
   stratification 149
   working-class 54–6, 58, 63, 70, 71, 97–9, 149, 150, 171, 173
   upper-class 92, 149

colonial history 40, 155
colonial legacies 9, 10, 22, 174
community 18, 62, 80, 108, 124, 150, 158, 164, 166
   Kurdish 21, 44, 46, 47, 48, 54, 64, 65, 75, 151
   transnational 48
   Turkish 21, 35, 46, 49, 54, 63, 64, 80, 158, 163
community organisations 19, 21, 23, 45, 47, 48, 53, 71–3, 77–80, 82, 83, 143
   Kurdish and Turkish 21, 61, 76, 162
   local community organisations 17
   politics of 46
   scope of 45
   socio-cultural activities of 21
   structure of 64
conservatism, rise of 118
convivial(ity) 16, 24, 92, 95, 99, 101–5, 110, 136, 173
   moments 24, 93–5, 99, 103, 105, 110, 111, 173, 174
   multiculture/multiculturalism 93, 95
   space(s) 99
coup attempt 39, 118, 119

dehumanising of immigrants 31
deportation(s) 30, 101, 139, 145
diaspora(s) 7, 142
   Kurdish 40, 49, 124
displacement 127
diversity 24, 45, 54–7, 66, 83, 85, 92, 93, 96, 109, 143, 172

emotional attachment 107, 119, 120, 129
empathy 24, 56, 101, 104, 105, 108, 111, 173, 174
ethnic cleansing 113, 123, 126, 144
exclusion 3, 6, 13, 24, 25, 30, 38, 40, 57, 67, 86, 123, 125, 127, 133, 138, 160, 170, 172–5
   common experiences of 93
   of Kurdish identity 5
   legal exclusion of Black Britons 31
   processes of exclusion 11
   of racialised minorities 158
   sense of white exclusion 88
   of working-class people 99

Fanon, Frantz 11, 36
family connection(s) 119, 137
food(s) 93–5, 142, 164, 175
    Turkish 48, 61, 63, 164

gender 162, 163, 166, 173, 175
    conformity 163
    difference 153
    equality 160
    identity(ies) 133, 159, 164, 173
    norms 161, 162
    roles 117, 148, 159, 160, 161, 162, 163
gentrification 98
    process(es) 56, 99
Gezi Park protest 39
Gilroy, Paul 11, 16, 24, 29, 92, 153
Global North 9, 90
Global South 90, 91, 160
Green Lanes 16, 17, 19, 44, 53, 54, 58; *see also* Harringay

Hall, Stuart 60, 78, 86, 107, 120, 137, 138, 144, 151, 165
Harringay 16, 17, 19, 44, 45, 53–5, 61–3, 81, 149; *see also* Green Lanes
hate crime(s) 30, 31, 41, 129
heteronormativity 160, 161
hierarchy(ies) of belonging 24, 33, 35, 55, 85, 91, 101, 110, 140, 172
Home Office 4, 36, 139, 154
homeland 9, 13, 37, 49, 106, 114
    politics 103
hostile environment 4, 30, 32, 33, 35, 36, 152, 155, 174, 175
hybridity 143, 169

integration 9, 13, 14, 15, 20, 61, 80, 81
Islamophobia 30, 37, 81
Islamophobic 34
isolation 37, 66, 94, 98, 123

Justice and Development Party (AKP) 31, 32, 39, 40, 63, 118, 122, 125, 129, 151, 152, 173

Kurdish identity 5, 11, 16, 63, 74, 77, 78, 121, 122, 125, 151, 171, 174
Kurdish question 18, 38
Kurdish resistance 47, 123, 151
Kurdishness 5, 25, 75–8, 83, 123, 124, 145, 151, 165, 170, 171, 175
Kureishi, Hanif 29

LGBTQ+ community 40, 129, 133, 173
LGBTQ+ individuals 30, 31, 41, 83, 129, 133
London riots 34, 35

Massey, Doreen 108, 109
methodological nationalism 7
metropolitan 85, 92, 106
metropolitan paradox 16, 54
microaggressions 156
Middle East 69, 91, 152, 154
migrant(s) 29, 54, 105, 106, 109, 120, 121, 154
    bad 35
    deserved 36
    good 35
    transnational 9, 109
    undeserved 34, 35, 36
migratory background(s) 3, 6, 55, 56, 64, 70, 82, 95, 98, 110, 141, 171
multicultural 16, 56, 66, 69, 85, 86, 88, 141, 155
    background 56, 76, 145
    Britain 6, 29
    character 108, 110
    city 88, 89, 94, 95, 172
    complexity 93
    conviviality 24, 86
    discourse 24, 83, 86
    environment 57, 66
    exchanges 86, 108, 110, 172
    London 16, 89, 91, 93
multiculturalism 24, 30, 55, 57, 82, 85, 86, 87, 89, 90–3, 172
    convivial 95
    everyday 57, 89
    state 89
multiethnic 87, 93, 108, 110

Nationality and Borders Bill 4, 15, 152

oppressed communities 102, 103
Orwell, George 31
othering/otherness 35, 125, 128, 136, 138, 154, 157, 158, 174
Ottoman Empire 39, 40, 87, 155, 158

polarisation 62, 63, 77, 83, 118, 150
political struggle 47, 77, 79, 83
postcolonial 16, 85
poverty 55, 85, 98
Powell, Enoch 32, 153, 154
process(es) of racialisation 5, 11, 40, 89, 137, 152
protective transnationalism 12, 146

queer/queerness 62, 129, 135, 143, 159, 160, 162, 163, 173, 174
    identity 159
    movement 160, 173
    space(s) 135, 160, 173

race 3, 4, 11, 56, 60, 90, 100, 101, 104, 108, 137, 140, 153, 174
racial hierarchies 7, 9, 25, 30, 35, 138, 174
racialisation of Kurds 103, 113, 125, 127, 144
racialisation of Kurdish identity 16
racialisation of minorities 137
racialised minority 66, 76, 101, 125, 143, 151
racism 10–12, 29, 60, 96, 101, 104, 110, 125, 154, 171, 174
    cultural 35, 91
    dynamics of 36
    new form(s) 68, 85, 154, 172
    new racism 71, 153
    open 37
reactive ethnicity 12, 158
reactive transnationalism 12, 146
representation 47, 72, 114, 120, 121, 155, 157, 163
resistance 3, 47, 49, 72, 76, 132, 138, 145, 151, 165, 169, 171, 175

second generation 12, 13, 14
sexism 6, 30, 81, 115, 133, 162
social networks 8, 11, 14, 42, 43, 107, 144, 172
socio-political context 10, 23, 25, 32, 133, 138, 165, 166, 170
solidarity 12, 16, 20, 24, 69, 72, 78, 99, 101–105, 108, 111, 173, 174
Solomos, John 11, 89, 149
space of belonging 105–108, 123
super-diverse 16, 93

third space 143, 144, 169
transnational
    activities 6, 8, 10, 12, 41, 108, 114, 146, 158, 171
    context 5, 6, 7, 11, 16, 22, 25, 108, 138, 144, 162, 165, 169–174
    experiences 6, 12, 14, 16, 23, 32, 125

identities 107, 130, 158, 166, 170
links 14, 19, 20, 72, 73, 78, 108, 114, 115, 133, 145, 157, 171
migration 22, 120
social space 3, 22, 23, 98
Turkishness 61, 73, 82, 83, 137, 142, 144, 149, 150, 157–60, 163, 164, 166, 175

where are you from? 87, 88, 110, 132, 136, 155, 158, 175
whiteness 1, 2, 4, 6, 56, 81, 100, 101, 155, 175
hierarchies of whiteness 6
white saviourism 100
white space(s) 24, 69, 70, 98, 135
Windrush scandal 4, 30, 36, 139, 140
women struggle 129

youth crime 21

www.ingramcontent.com/pod-product-compliance
Lightning Source LLC
LaVergne TN
LVHW050008140426
836100LV00010B/61